THE CHIEF JUSTICES:
THE SEVENTEEN MEN OF THE CENTER
SEAT, THEIR COURTS, AND THEIR TIMES

THE CHIEF JUSTICES:
THE SEVENTEEN MEN OF THE CENTER
SEAT, THEIR COURTS, AND THEIR TIMES

by
Daniel A. Cotter

TWELVE TABLES PRESS
XII

www.twelvetablespress.com

P.O. Box 568
Northport, New York 11768

Library of Congress Cataloging-in-Publication Data

Name: Daniel A. Cotter
Title: The Chief Justices: The Seventeen Men of the Center Seat, Their Courts, and Their Times
Description: Northport, New York: Twelve Tables Press, 2019
ISBN 978-1-946074-25-6(print)/ISBN 978-1-946074-26-3(ebook)
Subjects: Law—United States/History
Classification: LCC## (Print)/LCC(ebook)
LC record available at https://lccn.loc.gov

Twelve Tables Press, LLC
P.O. Box 568
Northport, New York 11768
Telephone (631) 241-1148
Fax (631) 754-1913
www.twelvetablespress.com

Printed in the United States of America

Dedication
To Ann, the love of my life, and to my sons, John and Tim.
You make me better by being part of my daily life. Thank
you for your love and support.

Also to my mom and dad, who sacrificed much and
did without so their kids could do, and to my dad for
instilling in me an insatiable appetite to read often
and a wide variety.

Table of Contents

Part Two—The Supreme Court Emerges As Supreme

Acknowledgments

Countless people have contributed to this book. I am most grateful to my family, especially my wife, Ann, who has been with me the entire journey of my adult life and who gave invaluable insights and suggestions throughout the process. To the extent the book is of interest, her thoughtful input is to be credited. My sons, John and Tim, kept me focused on making progress on the end goal of finalizing this book, and John was extremely helpful in reviewing the manuscript and providing appropriate edits. Tim has asked me every chance he gets, "How is your book? Are you going to finish it?" I can respond that after many hours, fits and starts, the book is finished. How it is I will leave to the reader.

I must give special thanks to my former partners at Butler Rubin Saltarelli & Boyd LLP who were on the Publications Committee while I was there, submitting countless articles and writings that they reviewed and made better: Teresa Snider, Al Fowerbaugh, Jason Dubner, and Kevin O'Brien. I appreciate the many hours they devoted to reviewing my submissions. Special thanks also to my current firm, Latimer LeVayFyock LLC, for its support and encouragement, and a special thanks to my executive assistant Yan Goodwin, for her incredible assistance.

Special thanks to Professors Ann Lousin and Samuel Olken at my alma mater, The John Marshall Law School. Lousin has become a great friend over the years and has provided comments on many works I have written and reviewed the John Marshall chapter when I was at the beginning of the process. Olken worked with me to get a class, *SCOTUS Judicial Biographies*, approved at the law school. I remain eternally grateful to him for making sure this class was approved, and for allowing me to teach it.

Others who have made this book possible include Michael Gooding, Robin Johnson, Ross Richardson, Chris Rzany, and Byron Sondgeroth. I am grateful to the great folks at the *Chicago Daily Law Bulletin* who have given me a forum for my pieces over the years, as well as Constituting America for inviting me to participate in its annual 90 Day Study. I also thank both organizations for permitting me to use some of the work I have provided to them. Thank you to all of those who have read my articles over the years and let me know people were reading my materials and for providing constructive criticism. Finally, thank you to The John Marshall Law School for considering and approving my concept of teaching a law school class on the Supreme Court and its justices entitled, *SCOTUS Judicial Biographies*. I have had amazing students who have helped me explore in great detail a number of the justices who have sat on the Supreme Court from different times. I would be remiss if I failed to acknowlege and thank two other individuals who have made this book a reality- Stacy Cordery and Lew Gould.

Stacy was a professor at my alma mater, Monmouth College, when I was first considering a book on the SCOTUS. She informed me that her former professor, Lew Gould, was a Visiting Distinguished Professor at Monmouth College. I reached out to him and when I brought my son, Tim, down for sports camp in the summer, we visited and he read some of my materials and gave me strong encouragement, and inscribed a copy of his book: "For Dan, With hopes that his own writing will prosper." Thank you, Stacy and Lew.

Finally, for making this book a reality, I am forever indebted to Steve Errick and Twelve Tables Press.

Preface

While writing this book, and telling stories of the chief justices, I am often asked what has led me to this process. The subject of the Supreme Court and the people who have sat on the highest court in the nation has interested me from the weeks before I started law school. If anything, it has only grown since. I follow the Supreme Court closely, I tweet about it, I write about it. A number of factors have influenced my desire to write this book. When I attended law school, I worked full-time and went to law school at night. I had received a postgraduate scholarship from the National Football Foundation. Six months after my marriage to my wife, Ann, I received a letter from the foundation informing me that my scholarship was about to expire. I had successfully completed the Certified Public Accountant examination and tried to figure out what to do with the scholarship. I called every law school in Chicago and asked to audit their classes. The response was universal—we don't do that. Take the LSAT examination. I called the foundation—was it possible to obtain an extension? They granted me a six-month extension until January 1991. The game was afoot.

I signed up for the exam immediately and went to the bookstore. I bought all the study guides I could find and at night, did practice exams. I did well on the exam and then contacted the two schools in Chicago that had night programs starting in January: Chicago-Kent College of Law at Illinois Institute of Technology and The John Marshall Law School. I ended up accepting the offer from John Marshall, literally two blocks from my employer.

There, I discovered something right away—the law is in many ways a mystery and indecipherable, even for lawyers. Or at least not transparent. We received some pre-class materials that had numbering systems at the top like "549 N.E.2d 9." I had never been exposed to anything like this, and had not idea what I had gotten myself into.

Then classes started. I bought the few hundred dollars worth of books. I read the first fifty pages or so for my first night of class, Torts I. I underlined and highlighted and briefed them, including noting the court that rendered the opinion. And then quickly learned something—professors spent very little or no time on the jurisdiction where the case was decided, or the judges who wrote the opinions. No time was spent on the general societal factors that may have weighed in on the decision or explained the background for it, or the times and circumstances that may have influenced the jurisprudence.

I put that in the back of my head and saved it for later. I wanted to know more about the opinion writers, the times, and the decisions made. As a graduate from a liberal arts college, I was taught to be "intellectually curious" and a "lifelong learner" and to make connections between various points of information. I started to write about the founding of our nation and the Supreme Court, hoping to at least on a micro basis educate and promote a discussion. I also wanted to learn more about the third branch of our government.

I have been studying our nation's founding and history and the Supreme Court for many years. I have an extensive library on my personal library shelves (six shelves and growing) of SCOTUS books. In addition, I have taught *SCOTUS Judicial Biographies* since 2012. I originally designed the course as an exploration of the chief justice position (in a manner similar to how the 17 chief justices are portrayed in this book), but it was approved as a course designed to compare and contrast one chief justice and one associate justice from different eras. The proposal arose from my law school experience, one that was not atypical in that we never considered cultural context and did not pay much attention to the justices who issued the landmark cases being studied and analyzed by us. In addition, I write an almost weekly column for the *Chicago Daily Law Bulletin* and have written more than 150 columns on the Supreme Court and the nation's founding. In 2017, I wrote more than twenty columns for Constituting America on their Supreme Court series and in 2016, wrote many columns on the presidential elections, including SCOTUS involvement. As of publication of this book, I have penned more than forty essays for the Constituting America "90 Day Studies."[1] I often visit high schools and other settings to discuss our courts and the constitution. I am a merit badge counselor for the three Citizenship Merit Badges in Scouts and also present on the Constitution. I recently became a member (and currently co-chair) of the Chicago Lawyer Chapter of American Constitution Society.

I have been writing in the *Chicago Daily Law Bulletin,* a five-day-a-week legal publication that many lawyers in Chicago receive, for approximately six years. At first, I wrote monthly, then biweekly, then almost weekly. The topics ranged, but many of the columns explore the Supreme Court[2] and others have addressed various moments in our nation's history of note, such as the addition of the phrase, "under God," to the Pledge of Allegiance.

I have also taught the curriculum from the American Constitution Society, and several years ago, started the Twitter account, @scotusbios. At the Twitter handle, each

---

1. As with the *Chicago Daily Law Bulletin,* I have used some of the materials I wrote for Constituting America as starting points or additions for this book. Those too appear in the bibliography. The first two series I participated in were "The Intrigue of Presidential Elections" (2016) and "The Supreme Court" (2017). Essays can be found at http://constitutingamerica.org.

2. In many instances, the initial "skeleton" for a justice's chapter was a column or more that I had written at the *Chicago Daily Law Bulletin* for my column, "Cotter's Corner." The bibliography contains many of those original columns. Special thanks to my former colleagues at Butler Rubin Saltarelli & Boyd LLP, whose Publication Committee was kept busier than they might have liked because of the amount of stuff I sent their way on a not quite daily basis. At one point, the committee politely requested that from that time forward, I only submit one piece per week. That was no easy task for me.

morning I review the historical events that transpired on that date in history, including trying to find nuggets about the Supreme Court and its justices.

My writings have received a wide range of feedback and thoughts, mostly positive. My goal has at least been partially achieved—to educate about this co-equal branch of government. My goal with this book is to educate further, and permit some thoughtful discussions about the Supreme Court, its chief justices, and how each has shaped jurisprudence and the Court.

But there was more than just teaching. There was a goal to make the Supreme Court and its workings accessible. No, the previous sentence is not missing the word "more" before "accessible." The Court is not accessible to the average person; we know very little of the justices or the work that the Supreme Court does. Of the eighty or so opinions released each year, only the most controversial constitutional issues raise the public's interest. Yet, the Supreme Court to a very large extent even then is seen almost as nine black-robed Oracles at the Delphi.[3] There is an easy example of the inaccessibility of the Court. When the Supreme Court issued its opinion in *King v. Burwell*[4] on June 25, 2015, the initial reports were that the Patient Protection and Affordable Care Act aka ACA aka Obamacare had been struck down by the Supreme Court. Chief Justice

---

3. The Delphi Oracle was the high priestess of the Temple of Appollo at Delphi, someone who provided wise and insightful counsel or prophetic predictions.

4. *King v. Burwell*, 576 U.S. ____ (2015).

John Roberts' opinion began by concluding that the ACA
did not survive a Commerce Clause challenge. Reporters
who were handed the multi-paged majority opinion, with
a long dissent from then-Associate Justice Antonin Scalia,
immediately read the first paragraphs of Chief Justice Roberts' opinion and reported that the ACA was overturned.
However, the next page gave the real decision of the majority—that Congress had powers under its ability to tax
and the ACA was upheld.

Eric J. Segall wrote an excellent piece, "Invisible Justices:
How Our Highest Court Hides from the American People,"[5]
that describes this inaccessibility of the Supreme Court.
His law review article opens with:

> The Supreme Court of the United States is one of the
> least transparent governmental institutions in the
> United States. The Justices' reluctance to show them-
> selves on camera has been debated and criticized at
> length but is only one small part of a more disturbing
> and consistent pattern of secrecy. The Court acts in
> mysterious ways across a broad range of official duties.
> This Article examines how the Court uses that secrecy
> to hide important aspects of its work from the Ameri-
> can public.[6]

---

5. Segall, available at: http://readingroom.law.gsu.edu/gsulr/vol32/iss4/1.
6. *Id.* at 787.

In 2016, I developed a proposal to write this book. I did not want to write the traditional judicial biography. I have read more than one hundred of those, and they tend to be recitations of the cases that the courts decided during a particular term or under a series of justices. A great book in that method is a biography/autobiography written by one of my judicial idols, Justice John Paul Stevens. The book, *Five Chiefs: A Supreme Court Memoir,* covers the five chiefs Stevens worked for as a clerk or that were chiefs during his long career in Chicago, then his years on the Circuit Court of Appeals for the Seventh Circuit and finally during his long tenure on the SCOTUS. This book is not that kind of book—while for each "Court" I do write about a case or so for each justice, the main focus here is on who these seventeen individuals were, how they operate their Courts and what influences and legacies they left. My goal here is not to write another book about the details of how the Court came down on various issues, but to look at a broader level at the culture and context and experiences of that chief justice and address the continuum that way.

As we have seen repeatedly during election cycles and when the Supreme Court issues controversial decisions, the legal community and the general public do not fully understand the Supreme Court, how it functions, or the position of chief justice. The intent is that this book is designed to look at the chiefs not through case studies or through a more legalistic approach but to put the court, its decisions, and its role in our nation in a more cultural context. I believe that lawyers and non-lawyers alike are interested in the topic.

Most Americans do not know or understand civics or history. A major goal of this book is to provide an accessible, entertaining, interesting book that the general population will enjoy. But one also that the law student and law practitioner will find interesting and useful. I have been reading judicial biographies and the history of our Court and constitution for more than twenty-five years, and to my knowledge, this book is unique in its breadth of covering the entire Supreme Court through the center seat of chief justice and exploring some of the peaks and valleys of the Supreme Court from the beginning to present. We hope that the book will be used as a resource in that regard as well.

What connects the seventeen chief justices is a prominence in the legal community. For example, the first four chief justices were heavily engaged in our nation's founding, all having a role in the proposal that is the U.S. Constitution. However, prominence and legal successes are not sufficient. All of them also share a participation in politics at some level. The reality is that to sit on the highest court in the land, a job that currently only nine people at a time can have (and that only 114 have had the opportunity in the history of the Supreme Court), a lawyer must distinguish oneself from the pack of attorneys, and that involves political participation. But prior to the last thirty years or so, there were numerous appointees who after being seated did not always adhere to the nominating party's policies and procedures. For example, and most recently, David Souter and Sandra Day O'Connor come to mind. Seldom does that happen any longer.[7]

Beginning with the Reagan administration and continuing with the George W. Bush administration, the Republican Party has been very effective in screening federal judge nominees for being allegiant to the party line.[8] It is likely not a coincidence that the Reagan administration's counselor to the president, Edwin Meese III, has been involved in the Federalist Society for Law and Public Policy Studies from or near its inception, or that the Federalist Society was formed in 1982. The first Supreme Court Justice who sat on the Court and was a Federalist Society adviser and member was Antonin Scalia, confirmed in 1986 by a unanimous Senate vote, with the main focus being on Associate Justice William Rehnquist and his nomination to the chief justice position. As Jeffrey Toobin has explained:

> "For two generations, since the liberal heyday of Chief Justice Earl Warren, the Court was largely controlled by the moderate wing of the Republican Party. . . . The conservative ascendency at the Court owes much to

---

7. Several reasons can be pointed to. One is the invoking of the nuclear option for SCOTUS nominees by Senate Majority Leader Mitch McConnell. Another reason is the vetting process taking place of each nominee to ensure they are dedicated and committed to the positions of the party nominating the candidate.

8. President Trump and his team might be the most effective yet. For SCOTUS, as discussed in this book, President Trump compiled a list of potential nominees and for his first two vacancies, selected from the list as modified.

Republican victories in presidential elections and well-funded sponsors but also to the power of ideas."[9]

What has changed most recently is the extreme politicization of the nomination process and also of the Court, reflecting to a large degree the deeply divided partisanship that has become a major thread of our nation's fabric. The Court has become politicized. And the backing by dark money spent in the last three nominations, on the nominations of Merrick Garland, Neil Gorsuch, and Brett Kavanaugh, is staggering.[10]

---

9. Toobin, The Oath, p. 17.

10. The Judicial Crisis Network spent $7 million to block the nomination of Merrick Garland in 2017. Sessa-Hawkins & Perez, available at https://maplight.org/story/dark-money-group-received-massive-donation-in-fight-against-obamas-supreme-court-nominee. *See also* Eisman, available at https://www.commoncause.org/democracy-wire/anonymous-donor-footed-most-costs-in-gorsuch-fight/# (reporting that $10 million was spent backing the Gorsuch nomination); *see also* Kroll, available at https://www.rollingstone.com/politics/politics-news/brett-kavanaugh-supreme-court-dark-money-727706. One must ask the question of what such money means for the appearance of neutrality and how it creates substantial conflicts, especially when groups such as the Chamber of Commerce appear regularly before the Court and dark money groups are backing various challenges. In addition to Judicial Crisis Network, the Ethics and Public Policy Center and, in particular, its president, Ed Whelan, have been very involved in the process. During the Kavanaugh hearings, for example, Whelan engaged in a series of tweets naming a classmate of Kavanaugh's as a potential doppelganger for Kavanaugh in relation to alleged sexual assault. Whelan apparently worked with CRC Public Relations in developing the theory. Johnson, available at https://www.politico.com/story/2018/09/21/ed-whelan-kavanaugh-tweets-pr-firm-836405. Whelan and CRC are not new to the Supreme Court nomination process. When Roberts was going through his confirmation process, both names show up in news as well. For example, on August 16, 2005, *The New York Times* reported, "Mr. Whelan's statement of unqualified support was distributed by Creative Response Concepts, a public relations firm here with a prominent role in the confirmation effort." Greenhouse, available at

Anyone who disagrees about how politicized the Court and nomination process have become should carefully watch the opening statement of Supreme Court nominee Brett Kavanaugh on September 27, 2018, when the Senate Judiciary Committee held hearings regarding the sexual assault allegations of Christine Blasey Ford. Kavanaugh spoke of the Clintons and a left-wing conspiracy and smear campaign led by Democrats who were still angry about the election of President Donald J. Trump. The two parties were obvious in their views of how things were going to come out depending on the party. But the statements by Kavanaugh should raise concerns about someone who may sit on the Supreme Court for years, attacking a party and calling the prior hearings an embarrassment by the Democrats. When pushed on that by Senator Mazie Hirono, Kavanaugh did not answer.[11] On a partisan vote, Kavanaugh's

---

https://www.nytimes.com/2005/08/16/politics/politicsspecial1/robertss-files-from-80srecall-big-debates-of-era.html?mtrref=undefined&gwh=A87B29FB01B938B7FB7748FCB85340E8&gwt=pay. This is not to suggest that the nominees by Democratic presidents have not been supported financially by various outside groups.

11. Eric Segall, noted Supreme Court expert, tweeted on September 27, 2018, at 12:27 PM, during the referenced hearings, "My first tweets about Kavanuagh weeks ago were that he was the most partisan judge to be nominated in a long time. He is proving that with this speech. He hated Dems and loved W and Ken Starr. He is GOP all the way down and has been for decades." Segall has been self-described and otherwise "as extreme a critic of the Supreme Court as there is." Rosenberg (quoting Segall), available at https://www.salon.com/2018/09/30/can-the-supreme-court-be-saved-kavanaugh-hearings-could-be-a-turning-point. Segall has asserted that the Supreme Court is not a court but "their decisions resemble the work of a political veto council much more than a court of law." *Id.* Segall is especially critical of the judicial philosophy of originalism, referring to it as a "popular mask that for political decisions," albeit not the only jurisprudence

nomination was advanced to the Senate floor, 11-10, with
the caveat from Senator Jeff Flake that an FBI investigation
of up to one week take place before a vote by the entire
Senate. After an expedited, limited investigation was conducted, Kavanaugh was approved by the Senate, 50-48, the
second closest margin of votes in Senate history for a
Supreme Court nominee.[12]

Finally, we take to heart the words of Philip B. Kurland,
former professor extraordinaire at the University of Chicago Law School, who noted about judicial biographies:

> "A judicial biography requires of the biographer a thor-
> ough knowledge of the experiences of the subject's
> life; of the mores of the time, public as well as private;
> of judicial precedents and decisions; of relationships of
> the subject to other individuals, to groups, and to insti-
> tutions. If there were a checklist, it would be almost
> endless. But why write judicial biography at all?"[13]

The short answer is, civics is why we write judicial (or
any) biography. We must understand our nation's history, the good, the bad, and the ugly. Biography can help
us understand where we have been and the leaders who

---

trick justices use. *Id.* For an excellent analysis of why originalism is not a tenable
approach, *see* Segall's book, *Originalism as Faith.*

12. As discussed elsewhere, not all nominees to the Supreme Court have been
voted on with tallies. Many were done by voice vote or Senate acclamation, although
that is not likely in the future.

13. Kurland, at 489, 497.

guided and shaped the path. With that in mind, I have attempted to learn as much about the chiefs, reading primary and secondary sources, reading cases, reviewing contemporary accounts of the Courts during their times, and trying to be objective and non-judgmental in my portrayal of each chief justice and their contemporaries. We hope that you will come away from reading this book with a better understanding of who these seventeen men were (and in Roberts case, who he is) and how they helped shape the future of this great nation, the greatest place on earth. Not perfect, but great.

Chapter One

Introduction

Since the beginning of the Supreme Court of the United States in 1789, seventeen men have held the chief justice position. The first three chief justices held the position for a total of eleven years, and the next two (Marshall and Taney) held the chief justice position for sixty-three years (the two longest serving chiefs in our history). This book seeks to examine the position of chief justice more closely, to describe the position's origins and duties, and explore the court under each of the seventeen chiefs. Exploration includes the background and careers of the chiefs before becoming chief justice, discusses the cultural times, and places each Chief's rise and tenure in our nation's context, while discussing some of the key associate justices who sat with each of the seventeen. Each chapter also focuses on some key decisions of the chief justice's court.

All of the chief justices to date have been white men. Questions are often asked about the importance of this position, the chief justice, versus the other associate justices. There is no precise guideline for how the position is different from the others. The position was not in the U.S. Constitution, which simply provided:

> The judicial power of the United States, shall be vested in one Supreme Court, and in such inferior courts as the Congress may from time to time ordain and establish. The judges, both of the supreme and inferior courts, shall hold their offices during good behaviour, and shall, at stated times, receive for their services, a compensation, which shall not be diminished during their continuance in office.[1]

Congress addressed the lack of specificity when it passed the Judiciary Act of 1789,[2] which provided:

> "That the supreme court of the United States shall consist of a Chief Justice and five associate justices, any four of whom shall be a quorum . . ."[3]

For the first time, the term "justice"[4] was used to describe the federal judges who sit on the Supreme Court of the

---

1. U.S. Constitution, Article III, Section 1.

2. The Judiciary Act of 1789, Section 1, available at https://memory.loc.gov/cgi-bin/ampage?collId=llsl&fileName=001/llsl001.db&recNum=196. As we will see in the chapter on Oliver Ellsworth, the third chief justice, he was the principal drafter of the Judiciary Act of 1789.

3. Some argue that the term "justice" has no place in the vernacular. For example, Judge William Bauer, sitting on the U.S. Circuit Court for the Seventh Circuit, has had several conversations with the author and takes out his pocket copy of the U.S. Constitution each time he hears the term and, in his gravelly voice, says, "There is nothing in this or any constitution that applies the title justice on them."

4. The Judiciary Act of 1789, Section 1.

United States, and Congress established that one of the six justices would be the chief justice. No further definitions or duties were provided for in the Judiciary Act of 1789. Not much has been defined or added to the position's description since.

The seventeen chiefs (in order of when they were chief) are:

1. John Jay
2. John Rutledge[5]
3. Oliver Ellsworth
4. John Marshall
5. Roger B. Taney
6. Salmon P. Chase
7. Morrison Waite
8. Melville W. Fuller
9. Edward Douglass White
10. William Howard Taft
11. Charles Evans Hughes
12. Harlan F. Stone
13. Fred M. Vinson
14. Earl Warren
15. Warren E. Burger

---

5. There is some argument that because John Rutledge was a recess appointment of President George Washington and was then rejected by the U.S. Senate, he never officially served as chief justice. However, for completeness and because he was appointed to the role, we include him in this book. For more on John Rutledge, *see* Chapter 4.

16. William Rehnquist
17. John Roberts (presiding)

The Supreme Court of the United States has been in existence since the beginning of our nation in 1789, 230 years in 2019. Of that span, two justices, Marshall and Taney, held the position for a few days less than sixty-three years. Of the seventeen, the only other chief to serve more than twenty years was Fuller.[6]

Each Court has been labeled by the name of the chief, for example, the "Roberts Court." However, as we will see, in some cases there was an associate justice whose presence and legal work was so pervasive during his tenure as an associate that the court has been alternatively referred to as that associate's court. The best example of this is the "Brennan Court," named for Associate Justice William Brennan, who served under Chief Justices Warren, Burger, and Rehnquist. Brennan wrote a number of influential opinions during his long career and is second only to Associate Justice William O. Douglass in the number of opinions he authored. But his influence goes well beyond the number of opinions he wrote in his long career—he was influential in being able to cement majorities out of justices and to write the majority opinions in many important decisions during his tenure.

---

6. Roberts is on pace to be the fourth.

Justice John Paul Stevens (ret.), citing Byron White's comments that "the confirmation of any justice creates a new Court," proposes that each time a justice joins the court, it should be named after that justice—for example, in 1972, when Justices William Rehnquist and Lewis Powell joined the Court, it would be named "the Powell-Rehnquist Court [rather] than the Burger Court."[7] Stevens' argument is a valid one, but for this book, just as with his *Five Chiefs* memoir, we have divided the book into a chapter for each chief justice who has served. Using each time a justice joined the Supreme Court as a new Court might also include some courts or justices who had little to no impact on the Supreme Court.[8]

The most recent justice who some have referred to as his court is the "Kennedy Court" for Justice Anthony Kennedy's role as the swing vote in a number of cases during his long tenure, which ended on July 31, 2018. However, scholars debate over that attribution for a variety of reasons, including that he has not consistently led the majority votes on a variety of issues. Notwithstanding what his record is on various issues, he might be the last of the true "swing voters"[9] for some time.

---

7. Stevens, p. 7.

8. Not that every chief justice has had a major influence or impact on our nation's jurisprudence, as we shall see.

9. The term "swing voter" is used for a justice that will from time to time vote across party lines. Kennedy was in many 5-4 decisions as the deciding vote, and his vote in the 1992 decision, *Planned Parenthood v. Casey*, along with Justices Souter and O'Connor, upheld the core of *Roe v. Wade*, angering many, including

With that in mind, we will approach the subject in the following manner, and each of the chapters is briefly described.

1. **Introduction.** This chapter provides an overview of the position of chief justice and how it was created by legislative enactment. It discusses how the position is the same in many respects to the associate justice position, with some differences in conference and other arenas. It discusses the transitions and introduces readers to the SCOTUS.

2. **The Supreme Court Chief Justice: A Superior among Equals.** This chapter dives deeper into the chief justice position versus the associate justice position and discusses different leadership styles.

3. **John Jay: Governorship Calling.** John Jay was our first chief. In the early days, the SCOTUS did not hear many matters and Jay quit to run for New York governor. This chapter will discuss Jay's education and early career and will discuss his nomination, the cultural context at the time of his

---

purportedly a Justice Scalia clerk, Ed Whelan, who vowed at that time to replace any of these three justices with those opposed to *Roe*. For more on the Kennedy retirement, *see* "Kennedy retirement gives pause for reflection and some trepidation," *Chicago Daily Law Bulletin, Cotter's Corner,* July 2, 2018, available at https://www.chicagolawbulletin.com/potential-replacements-for-anthony-kennedy-2018 0702.

nomination, and some of the cases and associate justices he worked with. Also, we will discuss his post-judicial career.

4. **John Rutledge: Rejection and a Suicide Attempt.** Rutledge was a recess appointment and became the first nominee to the SCOTUS rejected by the Senate (in large part due to his vocal criticism of the Jay Treaty). Rutledge went home to South Carolina, where he attempted suicide.

5. **Oliver Ellsworth: The Forgotten Innovator and Founding Father.** Ellsworth was chief justice for just under five years, resigning due to poor health. While overshadowed by his successor, Ellsworth introduced the one opinion from the Court idea, replacing seriatim[10] opinions. John Marshall would continue and expand the practice.

6. **John Marshall: Establishment of Supreme Court's Supremacy.** Marshall was the fourth chief justice, but many mistakenly list him as first. His opinion in *Marbury v. Madison* established the Court as the final arbiter of laws among the three branches. He is the longest serving chief justice.

7. **Roger B. Taney: One Decision Makes a Legacy.** Taney succeeded Marshall and has been described

---

10. A seriatim opinion is one in which each judge reads his or her own opinion rather than there being one decision for the majority of the court.

as capable and overall a good judge, but one case, *Dred Scott v. Sandford*, made his legacy. Considered one of the worst decisions in the Court's history, the case defined the Taney Court.

8. **Salmon B. Chase: Reconstruction and Integrating the Court.** Lincoln nominated Chase when Taney died. One of Chase's first acts was to admit John Rock, the first African American admitted to the Supreme Court. Chase presided over the Court during Reconstruction.

9. **Morrison Waite: Narrow Interpreter of Thirteenth, Fourteenth, and Fifteenth Amendments.** Waite was a little-known nominee and derided by many when announced. He was a very good manager of the Court and the Court during his tenure was an extremely busy one. The Waite Court interpreted the Reconstruction Amendments very narrowly.

10. **Melville W. Fuller: Equal Justice under Law, Separate but Equal.** Fuller was a former Illinois State Bar Association president. The Fuller Court issued many important decisions and the two phrases (one for the good, one not) were from decisions Fuller issued. Waite served the third longest chief justice tenure.

11. **Edward Douglass White: An Elevation from Associate Justice.** White was the first associate

justice to be confirmed to chief justice (Rutledge was an associate justice, but never confirmed as chief and was also not a current member of the Court when nominated to the chief position). White originated the term, "Rule of Reason." White dissented 155 times, all in tax cases.

12. **William Howard Taft: A Former President Achieves His Goal.** Taft hated being president. He loved being a justice of the Supreme Court, the first and only time that a former president became a justice. The Taft Court was conservative on issues around the Commerce Clause.

13. **Charles Evans Hughes: White House Ambitions.** Hughes served as an associate justice of the Supreme Court but resigned to run as the Republican nominee for president in 1916. Hughes was the last sitting justice to resign to run for public office. Hughes sought to bring an end to the pro-business *Lochner* era.

14. **Harlan F. Stone: Playing All Positions.** Stone is the only justice to date to have served from most junior to most senior associate justice and then chief justice. Stone was the second justice to serve consecutively from associate justice to chief justice.

15. **Fred M. Vinson: The Last Democratically Appointed Chief.** Vinson was appointed by

President Harry S. Truman. Vinson also presided over the last Court to have been appointed by presidents of one party. Vinson died after hearing *Brown v. Board of Education.*

16. **Earl Warren:** ***Brown v. Board of Education,*** **Civil Rights, and Criminal Rights.** Warren became chief justice, *Brown* was reheard, and he was able to achieve a unanimous Court holding that separate was not equal. The Warren Court also issued a number of rulings for criminal defendants. Impeach Warren signs were seen throughout the South.[11]

17. **Warren E. Burger: A Minnesota Twin Goes to Bat, Expanding Warren Court Rulings.** Burger replaced Warren, and many conservatives expected a change in Court decisions. However, the Burger Court disappointed, expanding on some fronts the decisions of the Warren Court. Burger retired from the Court to Chair the Bicentennial Convention. The Burger Court also dealt with the Nixon administration issues.

18. **William Rehnquist: A Clerk, an Associate Justice, a "Great Chief Justice."** Rehnquist was a clerk for Justice Roberts and wrote a memo on

---

11. An example of one such sign can be found at http://www.historygallery .com/law/impeachwarren/impeachwarren.htm. *See also* Greene, available at http:// articles.chicagotribune.com/2000-07-12/features/0007120319_1_main-street-bill board-impeach-earl-warren.

Brown v. Board of Education asserting separate but equal was okay. The memo was a focus in his confirmation hearings. Justice Thurgood Marshall referred to Rehnquist as a "Great Chief Justice" and he generally is recognized as such. He became only the second chief to preside over a presidential impeachment hearing.

19. **John Roberts: A Legacy in Formation.** Roberts is the current chief justice. Some of his decisions have been questioned by the Right in recent years. His legacy and jurisprudence continue to be developed. At the age of 64 in 2019, and having served more than thirteen years, Roberts has the potential to preside over the Court for a record-breaking term, but time will tell.

20. **Conclusion.** This chapter will reflect on the history of the chief justice role and discuss the future of the Court.

The Court has been a body that has been more critical and more influential and the opposite at various times in its long history. The first three chief justices served when the nation was new and there were not many cases ready for adjudication at the highest court in the land. The first years of the Court are referred to as the Federal Court. Most of the time of the chief justices was administrative in nature, setting the process and budget and administering to what the Court's role was. Some administrative changes were started that would improve the overall administration of justice, but not be fully realized during their relatively short terms. Marshall would arrive on the scene around the time that issues of territories and Constitutional questions had percolated up to the highest court of the land, and the Marshall Court would contribute significantly to the prestige and legacy of the Supreme Court. The Marshall Court is often said to have had several "eras," times when the Court's makeup was different and the justices to a degree reflected those changes.

Taney followed and would preside over the Court as the nation struggled with the question of slavery, secession, and the Civil War. Taney preceded President Abraham Lincoln in death by less than one year.

When Taney died, Chase became chief justice and, during his short tenure, saw the end of the Civil War and the passage of the Reconstruction Amendments (Thirteenth, Fourteenth, and Fifteenth Amendments).

Waite replaced Chase. Waite was not the first, second, or even third choice of President Ulysses S. Grant but was the seventh pick. Waite is not considered a great chief justice. Waite led a court that very narrowly interpreted the Reconstruction Amendments. The Waite Court did expand the vested property rights, especially of corporations.

When Waite died, Fuller became chief justice. Waite was a Chicagoan and as of publication, was the third longest serving chief justice in our nation's history. Like Waite,

Fuller's time is mostly seen as a transition period for the Supreme Court. During Fuller's tenure, one of the most criticized decisions in the nation's history, *Plessy v. Ferguson*, was decided. Fuller is also known for a second phrase that has remained in the legal lexicon for more than 125 years—"equal justice under law."

White replaced Fuller as chief justice, becoming the first associate justice to directly become chief justice.[12] The White Court began what is often referred to as the Conservative Court.

Upon White's death, former President William Howard Taft achieved his dream of becoming chief justice, purportedly the only job he ever wanted. Taft's selection of White, rather than selecting Hughes while president, likely paid off in having an opportunity to serve on the Supreme Court. Taft's main contributions to the Supreme Court were the establishment of the Judicial Conference of the United States, passage of the Judiciary Act of 1925 (giving the Court more discretion on what cases it heard), and perhaps most importantly, overseeing the construction of the current U.S. Supreme Court Building.

Hughes, a friend of Taft who had been passed over for White several years prior, became chief justice upon Taft's retirement. Hughes would be in the center seat when President Franklin Delano Roosevelt implemented his New

---

12. Prior to White, Rutledge had been an associate justice, resigned, then was nominated and became a recess appointment chief justice.

Deal, and the Court was a heavily divided Court. Hughes is credited with working with Associate Justice Owen Roberts to make the "switch in time that saved nine" and saved the Court from potentially radical changes.[13]

Stone replaced Hughes and would preside over the Court from shortly before the attack on Pearl Harbor through the end of World War II and the beginning of the Red Scare/Cold War. The Stone Court addressed Japanese internment and the Rosenberg spy case.

Vinson replaced Stone. The period of Stone and Vinson is often assessed as a period of deep rifts on the Court among its members, triggered in large part by Felix Frankfurter and his strong personality. The Vinson Court began to address segregation in a series of cases and heard *Brown v. Board of Education,* but Vinson died suddenly and the case was carried over to the next term.

Warren replaced Vinson and, despite being appointed by a Republican president, Dwight D. Eisenhower, the Warren Court would actively address civil rights and criminal defendant rights.

Some have attributed the Warren Court and its activism as the major impetus for the way the nomination process is today and why Republicans have become so focused and

---

13. Currently, various discussions have been taking place about changing the makeup of the SCOTUS. Whether any are realistic to become law remains an open question.

energized and organized around judicial nominations, especially on the Supreme Court.[14]

Burger replaced Warren and was expected to lead a reversal of the precedents set by the Warren Court. The revolution did not happen as planned. The Burger Court would deal with Watergate and with the Vietnam War. Burger would retire to lead the Bicentennial Commission.

Rehnquist became chief justice, the third person elevated directly from associate justice. Rehnquist and the Rehnquist Court would begin to implement the revolution hoped for during the Burger Court, limiting some precedents and rolling back others, especially when it came to criminal defendants' rights.

When Rehnquist died, Roberts, who had been nominated to replace Associate Justice Sandra Day O'Connor, was nominated to become chief justice. Roberts has sat in that role for more than thirteen years at publication and, given his youth, could preside for many years to come. Roberts, with few exceptions, has continued the revolution and now presides over perhaps the most ideologically conservative court ever.[15]

Of the seventeen chief justices, nine were confirmed by Senate acclamation, the last being Earl Warren. One was rejected by the Senate (Rutledge). Of the seven who the

---

14. For an excellent work along those lines, *see* Kalman.

15. With the confirmation of Kavanaugh, the five conservative votes are Roberts, Thomas, Alito, Gorsuch, and Kavanaugh. Other Courts have included conservative blocs. *See* Four Horsemen discussion *infra*.

Senate actually voted on, two received more than 90% of the Senate approval (Waite (63-0) and Burger (74-3)). Of the remaining five, Roberts had the highest percentage (78% (78-22)). Rehnquist at 66.3% (65-33) is the second lowest margin percentage of the seven who have been confirmed by Senate vote (Taney had the lowest percentage (65.9%, 29-15)). The last SCOTUS[16] nominee to get more than eighty Senate votes for confirmation was Stephen Breyer, who was approved in 1994 by the Senate, 87-9. It is hard to imagine we will see any nominee come close to that in the foreseeable future- the politicization has become too engrained in the third branch.

---

16. The term SCOTUS as used at times in this book is the acronym that identifies the Supreme Court of the United States.

Chapter Two

The Supreme Court Chief Justice: A Superior among Equals[1]

Article II, Section 1, of the U.S. Constitution begins, "The judicial power of the United States, shall be vested in one Supreme Court . . ." The only reference in the Constitution to a chief justice is in Article I, Section 3, Clause 6, referring to impeachment trials of the president, and providing: "When the President of the United States is tried, the Chief Justice shall preside." The role of chief justice is not defined anywhere in the Constitution. Rather, other than the impeachment provision, the reference to the terms "justice" and "chief justice" were fleshed out in the Judiciary Act of 1789, providing in part:

"That the supreme court of the United States shall consist of a Chief Justice and five associate justices,

---

1. Much of this chapter originally appeared under my byline on March 21, 2016, in the *Chicago Daily Law Bulletin*.

any four of whom shall be a quorum, and shall hold annually at the seat of government two sessions, the one commencing the first Monday of February, and the other the first Monday of August."[2]

(Emphasis added.)

The Judiciary Act of 1789 has been amended several times over the years to change the number of justices who sit on the Supreme Court. Originally six justices sat on the Supreme Court, and the number has been as high as ten for a short period of time. The current number of justices (nine) and term (one beginning in October) is set forth at 28 U.S. Code Chapter 1, Section 1, which provides for a Supreme Court to consist of "a Chief Justice of the United States and eight associate justices."[3] Nowhere is the position of chief justice further defined and there is not a clear delineation of how the chief justice is different from the other eight justices. In many respects, the position is co-equal to that of the other eight associate justices.

However, through special functions designated to be performed only by the chief justice, the role does have the potential to be more powerful than the other eight positions. As George Orwell noted in "Animal Farm": "All

---

2. The Judiciary Act of 1789, 1 Stat. 73, available at http://legisworks.org/sal/1 /stats/STATUTE-1-Pg73.pdf.

3. 28 U.S. Code § 1.

animals are equal, but some animals are more equal than others."[4]

This chapter addresses ways in which the chief justice may exercise a different influence than the associate justices and exert a leadership position.

Chief Justice's Special Functions

Originally, the chief justice position was labeled Chief Justice of the Supreme Court. The position was created by Congress and not by the Constitution. Chief Justice Salmon Chase requested that the position be renamed Chief Justice of the United States. This was to reflect the Supreme Court as a co-equal branch of the U.S. government.

A vote of the chief justice on whether to issue certiorari or on a particular decision is equal to that of any other justice. The chief justice does not get extra time to ask questions from the bench. However, the chief justice has special functions that are not given to any other justice on the court, including: (1) moderating the conferences the justices hold to decide cases after oral arguments are completed and normally speaking first on each case to be decided; (2) acting as the presiding justice when the court is in session; and (3) assigning authorship of majority opinions when the chief is in that majority.

---

4. For an interesting view of the Chief Justice position and its importance, see future Chief Justices Hughes' thoughts as a lawyer, *infra* pgs. 250–51.

The first and third special functions give the chief justice an opportunity to mold the court's decisions. The chief justice also presides over presidential impeachment hearings, serves as the chief administrative officer for the federal courts, and is the head of the Judicial Conference of the United States. In addition to the administrative duties, the chief justice also has a number of honorary posts, including "Chancellor of the Smithsonian Institution, vice-president of the National Red Cross, and chairman of the National Art Gallery."[5] The chief justice is also a voting member of the Supreme Court and writer of numerous opinions.

Through exercise of these special functions, "a strong Chief Justice may dominate the court."[6]

Examples of Special Functions

Hughes was a strong chief justice by all accounts, using his position to seek additional support for a decision by moderating his own opinions. In addition, under Hughes' leadership, the Federal Rules of Civil Procedure became effective in 1938. Finally, he oversaw the Supreme Court during the New Deal and the court-packing plan, using his leadership and political skills to ensure that the Supreme Court remained independent.

---

5. Mason, p. 581.
6. Pusey, Vol. 2, p. 671.

Other chief justices have also exercised their special functions and other administrative duties to try to shape the court and its jurisprudence. For example, Chief Justice Warren E. Burger often used his position as chief justice to determine who would write an opinion. Reports in the Bob Woodward book, "The Brethren," and other sources discuss how Burger would at times change his vote in a crucial case to ensure that he was in the majority and could assign who would write the opinion. He did this in some of the most crucial cases decided while he was chief justice.

When John Marshall took over as chief justice, the practice of the court was to write seriatim opinions.[7] Through his leadership and oversight of the conferences and court administration, Marshall quickly changed that practice so that almost every court opinion was a unanimous one. (Of the 1,187 opinions issued by the Supreme Court between 1810 to 1835, only eighty-seven had dissenting or concurring opinions, less than 7%.)[8]

---

7. Seriatim opinions are ones in which each judge on the court issues his or her own opinion, so there is no opinion of the court.

8. Urofsky, Dissent, p. 47. The low rate of separate opinions was the "lowest rate of any period in the Court's history." *Id.*

At least one justice during the Marshall Court tenure, William Johnson, asserted that part of the reason for the vast majority of unanimous opinions was how justices were treated for disagreement. Johnson, writing to President Thomas Jefferson, indicated he disagreed with a decision and "I thought it a thing of course to deliver my opinion." Brookhiser, p. 108. He was mistaken, according to his letter to Jefferson:

"'But during the rest of the session I heard nothing but lectures on the indecency of judges cutting at each other, and the loss of reputation which [courts]

While this practice did not hold for an extended period of time, Marshall's ability to exercise his special functions and role led to increased prestige for the court in its early days.

One final example of the chief justice exercising the special functions of the position can be seen in the Warren Court. Chief Justice Earl Warren came to the Supreme Court after a life of public service culminating with his election as California governor. When Warren came to the court in 1953, the case of *Brown v. Board of Education* had already been briefed and argued. The justices were deeply divided on the case. Justice Felix Frankfurter asked for a rehearing on several questions, hoping to be able to convince other justices to join him in ending segregation.

The case was scheduled for rehearing and the summer before *Brown* was to be reheard, Chief Justice Fred M. Vinson died. Warren was nominated to replace Vinson. Warren, through his handling of the justices conferences and limiting discussion of *Brown*, was able to masterfully turn a divided court into a unanimous one. Warren assigned himself the task of writing the *Brown I* opinion. He produced a concise decision, keeping the draft locked in his chamber's vault as he edited it.

---

sustained by pursuing such a course. . . . I therefore bent to the current.'" (quoting Johnson letter to Jefferson). *Id.*

Conclusion

The chief justice's vote is equal to that of his colleagues. Notwithstanding that equal footing, through the chief justice's special functions and administrative role, he has the ability to be a superior among equals. Chief justices who are considered among the greatest of the seventeen chief justices have been able to use the different functions and role to advance the legacy and image of the Supreme Court.[9] As we will see in the chapters that follow, the chief justice has at times set the tone and the philosophy of the Court. Some have been more powerful forces of nature and able to effectively control the Court's outcomes on important matters (Marshall and Warren, for example) and others have not had that influence or leadership (Fuller and Waite, for example). What is clear is that while equal, the chief justice has an ability, along with the other justices that sit during his tenure, to shape jurisprudence and, in the balance, the nation's trajectory, for it is an honest assessment that:

> "To a degree not true of law in general, the law shaped by the Supreme Court bears the identifiable imprint of the experience, outlook, prejudices, and style of individuals who have been its members."[10]

---

9. For an attempt at ranking the chiefs (except for current Chief Justice Roberts), *see* **Appendix C**.

10. King, p. vii.

Part One

In the Beginning—A New Nation, Finding an Identity— The Federal Courts

Article III of the U.S. Constitution is brief in its wording and, despite being a major area of contention at the Virginia Ratifying Convention, sets forth very generally the duties of the Supreme Court.[1] Much is left to Congress to flesh out. One thing that was not done for many years after the beginning of our nation was setting aside special space for the Supreme Court of the United States. In addition, the first Supreme Court, nominated and confirmed in short time, failed to show up on time.[2] Travel was not easy, news did not travel fast, and the urgency was not there. John

---

1. The text of Article III "is just 376 words, half again as short as Article II." Toobin, The Oath, p. 2.

2. https://www.washingtonpost.com/podcasts/retropod/only-half-of-george-washingtons-supreme-court-nominees-showed-up-on-time/?utm_term=.346251c8927a.

Rutledge, one of the first associate justices,[3] never did much at all, including not fulfilling his riding circuit duties. In fact, Rutledge "did not decide a case as a federal judge at that time because before he could do so, he chose instead to accept the position of the chief justice of the South Carolina Supreme Court."[4]

Finally, with a new nation, few issues had been fleshed out yet at the lower courts and so there was not much substance to attend to that had made its way through the judicial system. The first three justices, all short-term holders of the center seat, would make their contributions to the Court and, while none had distinguished tenures as chiefs, add to the overall history and continuum of the Supreme Court, the highest court in the land.

But at the start, the Supreme Court truly was the weakest of the three branches and so lacking in prestige that John Jay rejected the second nomination of him to serve in that role.[5]

---

3. Rutledge also served as chief justice, a recess appointment, but would not be confirmed when the Senate reconvened. *See* chapter on Rutledge *infra*.

4. Stevens, p. 14.

5. For more information on John Jay's refusal, *see* chapter on John Jay *infra*.

Chapter Three

John Jay: Governorship Calling

Nominated by President George Washington
Confirmed September 26, 1789 by Acclamation
Tenure: October 19, 1789 to June 29, 1795 (resigned)
President During Tenure
George Washington

The First Chief Justice[1]

The first session of the Supreme Court sat on
February 2, 1790, in the new nation's capital, New
York City. Presiding over the first Supreme Court was
Chief Justice John Jay. John Jay was a Founding Father
of our country. A New Yorker, Jay became a member
of the Committee of Correspondence in 1774. He
drafted the Constitution of New York and was one of
the three delegates to the Treaty of Paris that ended the

---

1. Much of the introduction for this chapter and the next two was from an article in the *Chicago Daily Law Bulletin*, "Yes, there were chief justices before Marshall," *Chicago Daily Law Bulletin, Cotter's Corner*, December 17, 2014, available at *https://www.chicagolawbulletin.com/archives/2014/12/17/daniel-cotter-forum-12-17-2014*

Revolutionary War. He did not sign the Declaration of
Independence (his New York role prevented him from
voting on it) and he was not at the Constitutional
Convention but was one of the authors of the Federal-
ist Papers.

President Washington originally offered Jay the posi-
tion of secretary of state, which Jay rejected. Offered
the newly created position of chief justice (pursuant
to the Judiciary Act of 1789), he accepted. Jay's court
heard only three cases in his five-year tenure, the only
significant one being Chisholm v. Georgia. (That case
was the genesis of the Eleventh Amendment.) In 1795,
Jay resigned as chief justice to become the governor of
New York.

John Jay was the first chief justice. Selected by President
George Washington, he was not a surprise pick.[2] He was
serving as secretary of foreign affairs when Washington
was sworn in on April 30, 1789 in New York City.[3] Despite
his importance in our nation's history, Jay's status as a
Founding Father has not been celebrated or discussed as
extensively as some of his fellow Founders.

---

2. George Washington had the most Supreme Court nominations- eleven- of
any president and is the only president to nominate more than one chief justice,
having nominated three. For the number of confirmed justices by president, *see*
Appendix B.

3. Stahr, p. xi.

Early Career and Life

Jay was born in New York City on December 23, 1745 to Peter Jay, a wealthy merchant, and Mary Van Cortlandt, daughter of a twice mayor of New York City. Unlike most Founders, Jay was not British, but of Dutch and French Huguenot pedigree. Shortly after his birth, the Jay family moved to Rye, New York, where Jay grew up. At the age of 14, Jay attended King's College (now Columbia University). After graduating from King's College, Jay apprenticed in law under Benjamin Kissam, a well-respected and sought-after instructor.

After reading law, Jay was admitted to the New York bar and opened his own practice when finances permitted. In 1774, he became a member of the New York Committee of Correspondence.[4] The Committee of Fifty-One included Jay, who was appointed while he was on his honeymoon with Sarah Livingston, who was sixteen when they married. Jay became secretary of the Committee. The Committee would nominate Jay and four other individuals to represent New York City at the First Continental Congress.

Jay was at first a reluctant revolutionary. He believed the problems with Great Britain could be resolved and was hesitant about revolution. In a letter from 1774, he noted, "I sincerely wish it may terminate in a lasting union with Great

---

4. Committees of correspondence were formed in reaction to what was taking place in Boston with the Boston Tea Party and were a way for the colonies to communicate with each other about what to do with Great Britain.

Britain."[5] After the Declaration of Independence was signed, he became an ardent supporter of independence.

In 1775, after returning from the First Continental Congress, Jay became a member of the Committee of Fifty-One's successor, the Committee of Sixty. The Sixty was an inspection committee formed to make sure that the boycott of British goods, the Continental Association, was enforced. From 1775 until 1800, Jay would be front and center in the creation of this new nation, including working to ensure peace with Great Britain on more than one occasion.

Jay became a delegate to the New York Provincial Congress, where he helped the state draft its constitution. Because of those duties, Jay was not a signatory to the Declaration of Independence.

When New York ratified its constitution, Jay was appointed as the first chief justice of the Supreme Court of Judicature. Jay was hard on criminals, giving "stiff sentences."[6] Jay would not spend much time on the Supreme Court of Judicature, because another public duty arose—the Second Continental Congress. Jay, one of the youngest delegates at this Second Continental Congress, was elected president. He served in that position until September 28, 1779, when he left to be the Minister Plenipotentiary to Spain to seek peace with Spain. He also sought Spain's support of the colonies' fight for independence from Great

---

5. Stahr, p. 39.
6. Cushman, p. 2.

Britain. Despite Jay's best efforts, he was unable to secure a recognition of American independence, because Spain feared that such action might provoke revolution in its own colonies. However, Jay did receive financial aid from Spain. Jay would spend a good amount of time in Spain working to get Spain's support, finally leaving Spain on May 20, 1782. Despite his efforts, "Jay's mission to Spain is generally viewed as a complete failure."[7] Notwithstanding such characterization, his Spain efforts would come in handy when it came to his next mission—working on the peace treaty with Great Britain.

Commissioner to France

Jay and his wife left Spain and headed to Paris, France, where he joined John Adams and Benjamin Franklin to negotiate peace with England. Over the next year and a half these representatives would negotiate with Great Britain to end the Revolutionary War. France expected that the Americans would coordinate with the French, but Jay had "suspicions of French intentions" and so the Americans worked directly to achieve their nation's interests. The result was the Treaty of Paris, signed by the Great Britain and the American representatives on September 3, 1783. Great Britain recognized the United States' independence, a point strongly pressed by Jay, and established the boundaries of the new

---

7. Stahr, p. 144.

nation, extending to the Mississippi River. The Congress of the Confederation ratified the Treaty on January 14, 1784. Peace at last was had for the United States. John Adams credited Jay for having the most central role in the negotiations and his insistence on Great Britain recognizing our independence was a crucial element to the final treaty.

Secretary of Foreign Affairs

Even before Jay arrived back home, the Confederation Congress appointed him secretary of foreign affairs on May 7, 1784, a position Jay would retain for the next five years. The appointment was a recognition of the extensive efforts and abilities Jay demonstrated in international relations. On September 15, 1789, President George Washington made Jay acting secretary of state, the position that replaced the secretary of foreign affairs.

The Federalist Papers

Jay wrote five of the essays of *The Federalist Papers,* and also advocated for ratification of the Constitution in New York in an unsigned pamphlet, "Address to the People of the State of New York."[8] Jay may have written more of *The Federalist Papers* essays, but he fell ill and was limited in his ability to write.

---

8. Cushman, p. 3.

Chief Justice

George Washington signed the Judiciary Act of 1789 on September 24, 1789, and immediately submitted his selection of five associate justices and a chief justice. Washington "felt that the man to head this first Court must be not only a great lawyer, but a great statesman, a great executive and a great leader as well."[9] Several candidates emerged, but in the end Washington turned to Jay, who had become one of Washington's closest advisors, and sent Jay his commission along with a letter addressing Jay as "Chief Justice of the Supreme Court of the United States."[10] On September 26, 1789, the Senate approved Jay by acclamation and Jay took his judicial oath on October 19, 1789. He would serve for the next six years, implementing rules and procedures and ensuring the Supreme Court was functional.

The Court was not a busy one when it came to the hearing of disputes. A large part of this is the Supreme Court of the United States primarily acts as an appellate court, that is, it is not the original trier of fact. Given the newness of the Constitution, it is not surprising that the docket was not full at the beginning. The Court during Jay's tenure as chief justice would hear only four cases. Of those four, only one, *Chisholm v. Georgia*, was especially noteworthy.

---

9. Warren, Vol. 1, p. 33.
10. Warren, Vol. 1, p. 35.

Chisholm v. Georgia

Chisholm v. Georgia[11] was an important case and is credited with being the first significant case that the Supreme Court decided. The issue facing the Supreme Court in *Chisholm* was whether a state could be sued and subject to jurisdiction of the Supreme Court. The Supreme Court ruled, 4-1, that federal courts had the ability to hear disputes between private citizens and states. Congress and the states quickly rectified this decision, by passing a proposed amendment that was ratified, the Eleventh Amendment. The Eleventh Amendment provides:

> The Judicial power of the United States shall not be construed to extend to any suit in law or equity, commenced or prosecuted against one of the United States by Citizens of another State, or by Citizens or Subjects of any Foreign State.[12]

Congress passed the proposed amendment on March 4, 1794 and the states ratified it on February 7, 1795. It is the first amendment to the Constitution initiated because of a specific decision issued by the Supreme Court.

---

11. *Chisholm v. Georgia*, 2 U.S. 419 (1793).
12. U.S. Const. amend. XI.

The Jay Treaty

In February 1794, tensions were escalating between Great Britain and the United States. Senator Oliver Ellsworth approached President George Washington and urged the president to send an envoy to England to address the rising escalations that threatened another war between the two nations. President Washington nominated Chief Justice Jay as a special envoy. The Senate strongly debated the nomination on two main grounds—1) fears that Jay was pro-British and 2) concerns that a sitting justice of the Supreme Court should not also have a position reporting to the Executive Branch. Despite such concerns, Jay was approved, 18-8. Jay sailed for England.[13]

In March 1795, the Jay Treaty, as it came to be known, was submitted to the Senate, which approved the treaty on June 24, 1795, by a vote of 20-10. The Treaty took effect on February 29, 1796. While the Treaty achieved most of the United States' goals, it was derided as not obtaining sufficient concessions from Great Britain and also was attacked because it did not consider the views and intentions of the Jeffersonians.

---

13. While today such conduct would be frowned upon and not likely to occur, as we shall see it was not an uncommon practice in the early years of the nation.

No Advisory Opinions

The Jay Court established one very strong position that to this date has remained its policy—the Supreme Court of the United States can only address actual cases and controversies and will not issue advisory opinions. The issue arose in the context of neutrality toward Great Britain and France and activity that was taking place in the nation's capitol. President George Washington, after consulting with his cabinet, asked the Supreme Court to provide an opinion regarding the new nation's obligations. In England, this type of request was normal.

The Supreme Court rejected the request on August 8, 1793, responding to Secretary of State Thomas Jefferson:

> The Lines of Separation drawn by the Constitution between the three Departments of government—their being in certain Respects checks on each other—and our being Judges of a Court in the last Resort are Considerations which afford strong arguments against the Propriety of our extrajudicially deciding the question alluded to; especially as the Power given by the Constitution to the President of calling on the Heads of Departments for opinions, seems to have been *purposely* as well as expressly limited to the *executive* Departments.[14]

---

14. Casto, p. 79.

Jay's decision against advisory opinions has been "steadfastly followed throughout our history."[15]

Governor of New York

While overseas negotiating the Jay Treaty, Jay was elected the second governor of New York and, on June 29, 1795, he submitted his resignation as chief justice of the Supreme Court. Jay served as governor until 1801, when he retired from the governorship and would never serve in a public capacity again.

Reconfirmation

When Chief Justice Oliver Ellsworth resigned as chief justice in September 1800 due to poor health,[16] President John Adams nominated former Chief Justice Jay to the vacancy without Jay's knowledge. The Senate confirmed Jay's nomination, but Jay declined on the grounds of lack of power and prestige and because of the burdens of circuit riding. He replied to Adams in a letter:

> [T]he efforts repeatedly made to place the Judicial Department on a proper footing have proved fruitless. I left the Bench perfectly convinced that under a system so defective, it would not obtain the energy, weight,

---

15. Stevens, p. 12.
16. *See infra*, pgs. 69–70.

and dignity which are essential to its affording due support to the National Government, nor acquire the public confidence and respect which, as the last resort of the nation, it should possess. Hence, I am induced to doubt both the propriety and the expediency of my returning to the Bench under the present system.[17]

It was a stunning indictment, but likely was a valid assessment of the Supreme Court at the time. His words would become moot in the not too distant future when John Marshall became chief justice—"Jay would live to see" his views that the Court lacked authority or respect "proved wrong."[18]

Legacy

Jay's legacy on the Court is not a rich one, given the low volume of work the Court had on the docket. During the Court's first term, "it had no cases on appeal, no subpoenas to issue, and no clerk to issue them. In fact, the only business of the Court that first term consisted of securing a clerk, adopting a seal, and swearing in some two dozen lawyers for practice before it, of whom eleven were members of Congress."[19] It has been said the first decade of the Supreme Court was not memorable, with one historian

17. Warren, Vol. 1, p. 173.
18. Urofsky, Dissent and the Supreme Court, p. 44.
19. Urofsfky, Dissent and the Supreme Court, p. 37.

stating "the outstanding aspect of the Court's work during its first decade was its relative unimportance."[20]

The first Supreme Court, in its early years, was devoted to organization and not many constitutional issues had percolated up to it. However, that changed in 1793:

> "Foundational questions were inevitably the work of the Court's first years. In *Chisholm v. Georgia* (1793), the first constitutional case decided by the Court, [Justice James] Wilson wrote: 'The United States,' instead of the 'People of the United States,' is the toast given. This is not politically correct."[21]

Wilson desired becoming the chief justice, but for a variety of reasons, including his financial issues, he was never seriously considered, "In 1795 and 1796, Wilson was twice more passed over for chief justice."[22]

However, Jay's making it clear that the Court would not issue advisory opinions and his *Chisholm* decision showed his views that the new federal government was superior to that of the states.

Shortly after retirement from New York governor and public life, Jay's wife died. His long retirement ended on May 17, 1829, when he died after suffering palsy from an apparent stroke a few days prior.

---

20. *Id.* at 38 (quoting Bernard Schwartz).
21. Tartakovsky, p. 39.
22. *Id.* at 44.

Chapter Four

John Rutledge: Rejection and a Suicide Attempt

Nominated by President George Washington
Recess Appointment
Rejected, 14-10, by Senate on December 15, 1795
Tenure: August 12, 1795 to December 28, 1795
*   (Resigned, having been rejected)*
President During Tenure
*   Washington*

John Rutledge was a delegate to the Continental Congress and a delegate to the Constitutional Convention from South Carolina. Rutledge was a slave-owner and argued that any prohibition on slavery in the Constitution would prevent the Southern states from supporting the Constitution.

In 1789, he was nominated as the Supreme Court's first associate justice and was confirmed. He resigned in

1791 without having heard a single case to become the chief justice of the South Carolina Supreme Court.

Rutledge became a recess appointment when Jay resigned, and his term began immediately on June 30, 1795. Rutledge gave a speech roundly criticizing the Jay Treaty. That speech cost him support of the Washington administration and many senators, and eventually his nomination was rejected.

Rutledge resigned on December 28, 1795, and the rejection of his nomination ruined the man. He attempted suicide back in South Carolina and withdrew from public life.

Early Life and Career

John Rutledge was born in Charleston, South Carolina, on September 17, 1739, to John Rutledge Sr., a physician, and Sarah (nee Hext). At the age of 17, after being schooled by his father until his father's death and then by an Anglican priest, Rutledge began to study and read law under James Parsons. He went to London to continue his legal training, where he studied at Middle Temple.[1] Rutledge then returned to Charleston, setting up his legal practice. Rutledge thrived

---

1. Cotter, Daniel, "Although rebels, some Founding Fathers had ties to London legal community," *Chicago Daily Law Bulletin,* May 3, 2017. John Rutledge is one of thirteen Middle or Inner Temples members to be a signatory to the Declaration of Independence or the U.S. Constitution.

in his practice. He married Elizabeth Grimke on May 1, 1763 and was heartbroken when she died on July 6, 1792. They had ten children together, eight of whom lived to adulthood.

Rutledge was a South Carolina delegate to the Stamp Act Congress, the first Congress of the American Colonies, held between October 7 and 25, 1765, in New York City. Rutledge was the youngest delegate to attend. The Stamp Act Congress passed a Declaration of Rights and Grievances asserting that Parliament had no authority to issue and impose the tax because the colonies were not represented in Parliament. Great Britain rejected all such entreaties initially.

Returning to South Carolina from the Stamp Act Congress, Rutledge and other delegates found that all stamps had been destroyed, making it impossible to apply the stamp tax to anything. Legal processes were halted until South Carolina learned that the Stamp Act had been repealed.

Rutledge returned to private practice for the next several years and continued to be very successful.

In 1774, Rutledge and his brother, Ed, were both elected to the Continental Congress. Rutledge did not advocate complete independence but did argue that the colonies needed stronger rights. Rutledge's main contribution to this First Continental Congress was to successfully argue that each colony should have one vote.

Rutledge attended the Second Continental Congress in 1775, where he chaired the Committee on Government. Upon his return once again to South Carolina, he helped in the drafting of a state constitution that provided for the government to be independent and, when the new assembly convened, Rutledge was elected the first president of the Republic of South Carolina. Rutledge's main focus was on preparing South Carolina to defend against impending invasion by Great Britain. Rutledge ordered that Fort Sullivan be built. When ordered to evacuate because only half built, Rutledge refused, arguing he was in charge and only he could order such an evacuation. Rutledge soon earned the nickname, "Dictator John," for his refusal to obey anyone else's orders.

On June 28, 1776, the British attacked the fort made of palmetto logs packed with sand. Despite General Charles Lee's fears that the fort would fall immediately upon attack, the fort held up remarkably well, the palmetto logs absorbing the cannonballs without falling. Charleston was saved. To honor the fort and the battle that took place at it, South Carolina celebrates Carolina Day every year on June 28th. The South Carolina flag, adopted by the state in 1861, features the palmetto tree and the crescent seal from the soldiers' caps. A week later, Rutledge's brother, Ed, was one of the signatories to the Declaration of Independence in Philadelphia.

In 1778, the legislature drafted a new constitution that changed South Carolina from a republic to a state. The legislature overrode Rutledge's veto and, rather than fight it, Rutledge resigned, citing that the new constitution was too conclusive in terms of inability to reconcile with Great Britain. His retirement from public office would not last long.

In 1779, Rutledge was elected governor and possessed extraordinary emergency powers. This time, the British had greater success than in 1776, and Rutledge and the rest of the government fled Charleston to the part of South Carolina not controlled by the British. Because of term limits, Rutledge's term as governor ended on January 16, 1782. Rutledge returned to the Continental Congress, where he served a term.

Judge in South Carolina; South Carolina Delegate

In 1784, Rutledge was appointed to the South Carolina Court of Chancery, serving until 1791. In 1787, Rutledge was one of a handful of South Carolina delegates to the Constitutional Convention in Philadelphia. Rutledge served on the Committee of Detail and a number of other committees and also worked with Oliver Ellsworth on the compromise between large and small states. By the end of July 1787, the delegates to the Convention "had produced only refinements of the Virginia Plan's resolutions, now numbering nineteen statements of principle that did not make up a constitution."[2] The Committee of Detail was formed,

2. Stewart, p. 163.

with five members represented: Nathaniel Gorham, Oliver Ellsworth, James Wilson, Edmund Randolph, and John Rutledge.[3] (Three of the five would serve on the Supreme Court (Ellsworth, Wilson, and Rutledge)). Rutledge chaired the Committee of Detail, and the Committee over the next several days "hijacked the Constitution. Then they remade it."[4] At the Convention, Rutledge was a strong advocate for Southern states' rights, including slavery, and noted that without addressing the institution of slavery and permitting it, the South would not join. He stated slavery "was a matter of commerce, not morality, and of whether the southern states would remain in the Union."[5]

Despite his significant work on the Committee of Detail and contributions to the Convention, Rutledge had objections to the final product that was the U.S. Constitution; however, he endorsed it and was an advocate in South Carolina for its ratification. The South Carolina Ratifying Convention ratified the Constitution, 149-73, on May 23, 1788.[6]

Initial Supreme Court Nomination

When President George Washington signed the Judiciary Act of 1789 on September 24, 1789, he submitted a list of

---

3. *Id.* at 164.

4. *Id.* at 165.

5. Cushman, p. 9.

6. https://histcsac.wiscweb.wisc.edu/wp-content/uploads/sites/281/2017/07/sc-chronology.pdf.

justices to the Senate, including chief justice nominee Jay and five associate justices, including Rutledge. Rutledge was disappointed in not being named chief justice by President Washington. Rutledge would never attend any session of the Supreme Court, either in this short tenure or when he was a recess appointment as chief justice.[7] Rutledge suffered from gout and he never attended the New York session. He did briefly and partially perform his duties of riding circuits, along with fellow Supreme Court Justice James Iredell, the two traveling the Southern Circuit.

On March 4, 1791, Rutledge became the first Supreme Court justice to resign his position. He became the chief justice of the South Carolina Court of Common Pleas and General Sessions, a position he held until June 30, 1795, when he was made a recess appointment as chief justice of the Supreme Court.

Tragedies Hit

Shortly after resigning his post as associate justice and returning to South Carolina, Rutledge's wife, Elizabeth Grimke Rutledge, died on April 22, 1792, at the age of 50. It was a devastating blow to Rutledge and he would never fully recover mentally from his loss.

---

7. His contribution to the Supreme Court was negligible as "his output as a judge consisted of less than five pages of opinions and his impact on the Court was negligible." Lankevich, p. 238.

Rutledge also suffered severe financial losses from his investment in merchant ships. Finally, his mother died on the same day as his wife in 1792.

Supreme Court Appointment

When Rutledge learned that Jay had been elected Governor of New York, he wrote to President Washington, indicating his interest and availability in the chief justice position.[8] On June 12, 1795, Rutledge wrote Washington:

> "[W]hen the office of the Chief Justice of the United States becomes vacant, I feel that the duty which I owe to my children should impel me to accept it, if offered, tho' more arduous and troublesome than my present station, because more respectable and honorable."[9]

Washington saw Rutledge's letter "as a proverbial godsend"[10] and accepted the offer, advising Rutledge it would be a recess appointment because the Senate was not back in session until December. Rutledge would not attend a formal session of the Supreme Court as chief justice, although he did preside over two privateer cases. Rutledge attended the Supreme Court term in August; however, a major blunder

---

8. Harrington, p. 43.
9. Cushman, p. 10.
10. Lankevich, p. 63.

before arriving in Philadelphia made his nomination problematic and cause the Senate to reject his nomination.

Issues Created by Rutledge Speaking Out on the Jay Treaty

Rutledge was not enamored with the Jay Treaty. He made a mistake on July 16, 1795, when at a meeting at St. Michael's Church in Charleston, he gave an impassioned speech against the Jay Treaty. He was not alone in condemning the treaty, but partisans reported his comments to Washington and when his nomination was before the Senate, Rutledge became the first Supreme Court justice nominee (and only chief justice nominee) that the Senate rejected, by a vote of 14-10. The exact statements that Rutledge was alleged to have made at St. Michael's Church are not definitive, but some reports described Rutledge as being "mounted upon the head of a hogshead" and rallying the mob in attendance to "reprobate the treaty and insult the Executive of the Union" and other reports suggested he "had rather the President should die (dearly as he loved him) than he should sign the treaty."[11]

Whatever the exact words Rutledge spoke, his nomination was dead on arrival. Federalists were uniform in making sure that someone who rejected the treaty would not be confirmed. Rutledge arrived in Philadelphia on August 12,

---

11. Warren, Vol. 1, p. 130.

1795 and took his judicial oath. Two privateer cases were decided that term. Rutledge then went to his circuit riding duties, never to return to the Supreme Court.

It is important to reflect on the consequences of Rutledge's negative comments about the treaty with Great Britain. But for that comment, all indications are that Rutledge would have been confirmed. As has been stated about this event:

> The rejection of Rutledge was an event of great importance in American legal history, which has hitherto received cursory attention. But for his unfortunate Charleston speech he would undoubtedly have been confirmed, despite the rumor as to his mental condition. As his death did not occur until the year 1800, the Chief Justiceship, if held by him, would have become vacant at a time when it is extremely unlikely that President Adams would have appointed John Marshall as his successor. Thus upon the event of one chance speech regarding a British treaty hinged the future course of American constitutional law.[12]

A Suicide Attempt and Rejection

On December 26, Rutledge attempted to kill himself by jumping fully clothed off a wharf in Charleston. Two slaves

---

12. Warren, Vol. 1, p. 139.

saw him and rescued him.[13] While there have been biographies and writings about Rutledge claiming that the story of his attempted suicide was exaggerated and political gamesmanship, but the better contemporary evidence is that is what happened. A contemporary account captured what Rutledge had done on that fateful day:

> "A Negro child was near, and struck with the uncommonness of the sight she called to some Negroes on the deck of a vessel. . . . The fellows had the presence of mind to run with a boat hook and catch hold of [Rutledge's] arm—he made violent opposition to them but they dragged him out and detained him by force, they calling out for assistance, while he cursed and abused them, and would drive them away."[14]

Two days later, Rutledge formally resigned from the Supreme Court, resulting in the shortest chief justice tenure (Rutledge also served the shortest associate justice tenure in the Supreme Court's history).[15]

---

13. Fisher, available at https://www.senate.gov/reference/resources/pdf/RL31112.pdf.

14. William Read to Jacob Read, December 29, 1795, South Caroliniana Library, University of South Caroina, quoted by Stewart, p. 253.

15. Cotter, Daniel A., "The three shortest Supreme Court tenures," *Chicago Daily Law Bulletin*, January 4, 2016.

Legacy

Rutledge died on June 21, 1800 at the age of 60. His legacy with the Supreme Court is negligible but is an important part of the chief justice tapestry. However, his involvement in the drafting of the document that became the U.S. Constitution should not be overlooked (as it mostly has been). As David O. Stewart wrote:

> "History's tendency to overlook Rutledge's role at the Convention may be traced in part to his devotion to the interests of the South; also, unlike the posterity-conscious Virginians, he left behind little correspondence that grants an intimate view of his strategies, his hopes, and his judgments."[16]

16. Stewart, p. 254.

Chapter Five

Oliver Ellsworth: The Forgotten Innovator and Founding Father

Nominated by President George Washington
Senate Vote, 21-1, on March 4, 1796
Tenure: March 8, 1796 to December 15, 1800
(Resigned)
Presidents During Tenure
Washington
Adams

Upon the resignation of Rutledge, President Washington nominated Associate Justice William Cushing, but Cushing rejected the nomination in February 1796.[1] (The position obviously did not have the prestige and honor or responsibilities it eventually would post-Marshall.) Cushing presided over the Supreme Court's

---

1. Cushing based his refusal on his age. In 1796, Cushing was fifty-seven years old. Despite his believing he was too old, Cushing would remain on the bench until his death on September 13, 1810.

*February Term. Washington turned to Oliver Ells-
worth, nominating him on March 3, 1796. The Senate
unanimously approved Ellsworth the next day.*

*Ellsworth was a delegate to the Constitutional
Convention from Connecticut and one of many lawyers at the Convention. He was one of the drafters of
the Constitution. He was one of the main proponents
of the bicameral legislative setup. He left the Convention before signing and eventually became a big advocate of judicial review as a drafter of the Judiciary Act
of 1789.*

*Ellsworth served until September 30, 1800, when he
resigned for poor health reasons. His tenure was short,
although two of his court's decisions—Hylton v. United
States and New York v. Connecticut—established the
court's power of judicial review (fleshed out by Marshall
a few years later) and witnessed the first exercise of the
Court's original jurisdiction in state disputes. Ellsworth
also established the precedent of unified court opinions,
which Marshall would adopt and enforce.*

When Rutledge's nomination was rejected, and Rutledge
resigned, President George Washington needed a solid
nominee to fill the role of chief justice. As noted in the
introductory notes, Washington initially asked Cushing
to serve, but Cushing rejected his request. While we may
have forgotten this Founder, during his time Ellsworth

was an influential leader. Ellsworth was Washington's last Supreme Court nomination, but an important one.[2]

Early Career and Life

Ellsworth was born on April 29, 1745, in Windsor, Connecticut, to Captain David and Jemima (nee Leavitt). Windsor was Connecticut's first English settlement. Ellsworth attended Yale University for a brief time, but then transferred to the College of New Jersey (later renamed Princeton).[3] He received his A.B. from Princeton and returned to Connecticut, where he for a short period of time began studies to become a Congregationalist minister. Ellsworth quickly abandoned that plan and turned to the study of law, initially apprenticing for Matthew Griswold.[4] Ellsworth then moved his apprenticeship to Jesse Root.[5] In 1771, after serving four years as an apprentice, which put him in debt,[6] Ellsworth was admitted to the Connecticut bar. As is the

---

2. As outlined in **Appendix B**, Washington is the only president to nominate more than one chief justice, and two of the three were confirmed by the Senate.

3. While at Yale, Ellsworth ran into trouble both years, the first for "cleaning the yard," an activity often associated with protesting, and in his second year, he was disciplined for drinking wine.

4. Matthew Griswold served as King's Attorney for New London County for many years and eventually served as governor of Connecticut.

5. Jesse Root was a prominent lawyer in Connecticut and was a member of the Connecticut Council of Safety during the American Revolution. Root also joined the Connecticut militia. He served as a delegate to the Continental Congress from 1778 until 1782. Root served as chief justice of the Connecticut Supreme Court from 1796 to 1807.

6. Toth, p. 23.

case now with lawyers freshly admitted, gaining a thriving practice was difficult in Ellsworth's time, and in his first year as a lawyer, he made only a single pound.[7]

A year later, Ellsworth married sixteen-year-old Abigail Wolcott. They had a happy marriage, and had nine children together, seven of whom survived infancy. The marriage to Wolcott turned out to be a boost to his career, as Wolcott's family was a prominent one in Connecticut. However, Ellsworth struggled to gain business for many years.

In 1773, Ellsworth entered politics when he won a seat in the Connecticut General Assembly to represent Windsor. The next year, Ellsworth became justice of the peace for Hartford County. After moving to Hartford, he became state's attorney for Hartford County. By 1779, Ellsworth's fortunes had changed substantially—he had more than 1,500 cases on his docket.[8]

In 1777, Ellsworth became involved in national politics when he was selected by Connecticut to represent the state at the Continental Congress, a position he would serve in for the next four years. Two committees he served on especially benefited him when he became chief justice of the Supreme Court of the United States—the Committee on International Treaties and the Committee of Appeals.[9] The

---

7. *Id.*

8. *Id.* at 29 ("No other litigator in Connecticut was busier.").

9. The Committee of Appeals was a five-member tribunal within Congress that reviewed admiralty appeals. The ratified Articles of Confederation incorporated this concept. "As the first court established by America's national

latter would inform his drafting when it came to the Judiciary Act of 1789. The Committee of Appeals was a precursor of sorts to the Supreme Court, but with limited scope and authority. The Committee of Appeals was part of the Continental Congress.

An early case that Ellsworth sat on while serving on the Committee of Appeals would drag on for a period of more than thirty years. In September 1778, a British sloop, *Active*, was captured when Captain Gideon Olmstead and several other American prisoners aboard the ship overpowered the crew and planned to sail to a friendlier port. An American privateer and a Pennsylvania state brigantine brought *Active* into Philadelphia, the captains of the two ships making the capture claimed *Active* as a prize. A state admiralty court divided the prize money into four parts, including to Olmstead and his fellow shipmates. Olmstead appealed to the Continental Congress, which gave Olmstead the entire amount of prize money. Pennsylvania refused to honor the decision and the first instance of a state and federal clash was born. The case dragged on for thirty years.[10] Ellsworth would use his experience on this committee and improve upon it when he returned to Congress in 1789.

---

government with the authority to review cases that had been tried in state courts, the Committee of Appeals was a precursor to the United States Supreme Court." *Id.* at 38.

10. In *United States v. Peters*, 9 U.S. 115, 136 (1809), Chief Justice John Marshall would uphold the Committee of Appeals decision.

Another major issue that Ellsworth worked on during his time in the Continental Congress was the currency crisis. Working with fellow Connecticut representative, Roger Sherman, they proposed a resolution to retire the continentals and exchange them for new paper currency that Congress would pay states two new dollars for every forty devalued continentals returned. The resolution passed by one vote. Despite passage, the currency plan failed to solve the currency crisis facing the colonies.

Return to Connecticut Service

While Ellsworth represented Connecticut in the Continental Congress, he also served as a member of the Connecticut legislature's upper house. When the Revolutionary War ended in 1783, Ellsworth returned full-time to Connecticut. Ellsworth "aspired to a seat on the Superior Court"[11] and in 1784, he became a judge on the Connecticut Supreme Court of Errors, but quickly moved to the Connecticut Superior Court. When Ellsworth joined the Connecticut Superior Court, it followed the practice of William Murray, Lord Mansfield, who was lord chief justice of the King's Court, of issuing "an anonymous and unanimous 'opinion of the court.'"[12] However, the legislature passed a law that required each judge to give a seriatim opinion in

---

11. Casto, p. 29.
12. Urofsky, Dissent, p. 40.

questions of interpretation of law. The judges "ignored the mandate and adopted the practice of majority opinions for the court with an occasional dissent."[13] The Supreme Court of the United States early in its history also issued seriatim opinions. That would change before too long.[14]

Constitutional Convention

In 1787, Ellsworth and two other delegates from Connecticut were selected to attend the Constitutional Convention in Philadelphia. Along with Ellsworth, Samuel Johnson and Roger Sherman represented Connecticut.[15] Congress had authorized "a Convention of delegates who shall have been appointed by the several states be held at Philadelphia for the sole and express purpose of revising the Articles of Confederation and reporting to Congress and the several legislatures such alterations and provisions therein as shall when agreed to in Congress and confirmed by the states render the federal constitution adequate to the exigencies of Government & the preservation of the Union."[16] As we know, that is not what happened when the fifty-five men opened the convention in May 1787.

---

13. *Id.* at 41.

14. *Id.* at 41–42.

15. Besides New York, Connecticut was the only state that had delegates to the Constitutional Convention that also represented the state at the ratifying convention. Jensen, p. 406.

16. "Report of Proceedings in Congress," February 21, 1787, available at http://avalon.law.yale.edu/18th_century/const04.asp.

Ellsworth proposed the words *United States* be used to describe the nation, a term that had been used in the Declaration of Independence as well as the Articles of Confederation.

Ellsworth may well have saved the Constitutional Convention from breaking up. Big states and small states fought over representation in the Congress. His Connecticut colleague, Roger Sherman, is credited with proposing or initiating the "Connecticut Compromise," but Ellsworth was its spokesman and main advocate. He "would be largely responsible for articulating the rationale for the Connecticut Compromise."[17] The Connecticut Compromise[18] was a method of a bicameral Congress, with the House being apportioned based on population and two representatives each in the Senate, or upper house.

Ellsworth expressed his views for a strong national government during the Constitutional Convention and after it. He never wavered from those views.

Ellsworth was selected to be a member of the Committee on Detail.[19] The five-member committee[20] spent from July 24 to August 6, 1787, drafting the report. The Convention adjourned for most of that time waiting for the

---

17. Toth, p. 61.

18. The compromise is also referred to as the "Great Compromise."

19. The Committee of Detail was formed to draft a document reflecting the agreements made to date by the Constitutional Convention.

20. In addition to Ellsworth, the members of the Committee of Detail were John Rutledge (Chair), Edmund Randolph, James Wilson, and Nathaniel Gorham.

Committee to issue its report. During the Committee's work, Ellsworth advocated a view known as electoral federalism, which focused on local communities having wide latitude in how its representatives were selected.[21] Ellsworth made it clear that the people must have participation: "The people will not readily subscribe to the National Constitution if it should subject them to be disenfranchised."[22]

In the Committee on Detail, Ellsworth supported a number of provisions in the drafting that benefited the South, which appears to reflect his realization that the chances of ratification of the U.S. Constitution by all the states were dependent upon striking a delicate balance in the document's provisions.

Ellsworth departed the convention in late August and so, despite his valuable contributions to the end product and his work on the Committee on Detail, his signature does not appear on the final version of the Constitution. Ellsworth had duties to attend to back in Connecticut.

Ratification Advocacy

Ellsworth strongly advocated for the ratification of the Constitution when he returned to Connecticut, writing a series of thirteen letters as "A Landholder."[23] The letters were

---

21. Toth, p. 71.
22. Farrand, p. 201.
23. The letters are available at https://www.infoplease.com/history-and -government/other-federalists/part-iv-landholder.

effective in gaining support for ratification in Connecticut. Before the Landholder Letters, though, Ellsworth and Sherman wrote a letter dated September 26, 1787, to Governor Samuel Huntington that enclosed a copy of the proposed Constitution and urged it be adopted and ratified. The letter closed:

> The Convention endeavored to provide for the energy of government on the one hand and suitable checks on the other hand to secure the rights of the particular states, and the liberties and properties of the citizens. We wish it may meet the approbation of the several states and be a mean of securing their rights and lengthening out their tranquility.[24]

The Landholder Letters at the time were considered as important in some cases as *The Federalist Papers* but did not have the same lasting impact or recognition over time. One theory posited is that the writings of Ellsworth have not "been so memorable [due to] his emphasis on *ad hominem* attacks."[25]

Ellsworth was selected to serve as a delegate in the Connecticut Ratifying Convention, where he served as "the Constitution's leading advocate."[26] Many of the arguments he made as "A Landholder" would be stated on the floor

---

24. Letter to Governor Huntington, available at http://teachingamericanhistory.org/library/document/roger-sherman-and-oliver-ellsworth-to-governor.
25. Casto, p. 55.
26. *Id.* at 56.

during debates. Ratification by Connecticut was by no means a sure thing—like many of the colonies, the issue divided more urbane merchants on one side with the rural farmers on the opposite side. Ellsworth opened the Connecticut Ratifying Convention by asserting why the Constitution was needed:

> It is observable that there is no preface to the proposed Constitution; but it evidently presupposes two things: one is the necessity of a federal government; the other is the inefficiency of the old Articles of Confederation. A union is necessary for the purposes of national defense. United, we are strong; divided, we are weak. . . . A union, sir, is likewise necessary considered with relation to economy. Small states have enemies as well as great ones. They must provide for their defense. The expense of it, which would be moderate for a large kingdom, would be intolerable to a petty state. . . . We must unite in order to preserve peace among ourselves. If we are divided, what is to hinder wars from breaking out among the states? States, as well as individuals, are subject to ambition, to avarice, to those jarring passions which disturb the peace of society. What is to check these? If there is a parental hand over the whole, this, and nothing else, can restrain the unruly conduct of the members.
>
> Union is necessary to preserve commutative justice between the states. If divided, what is to hinder the

large states from oppressing the small? . . . A more energetic system is necessary. The present is merely advisory. It has no coercive power. Without this, government is ineffectual or, rather, is no government at all. But it is said, such a power is not necessary. States will not do wrong.[27]

His strong views of the judiciary's role were also expressed in very clear language, on January 7, 1788, when he stated:

This Constitution defines the extent of the powers of the general government. If the general legislature should at any time overleap their limits, the judicial department is a constitutional check. If the United States go beyond their powers, if they make a law which the Constitution does not authorize, it is void; and the judicial power, the national judges, who to secure their impartiality, are to be made independent, will declare it to be void. On the other hand, if the states go beyond their limits, if they make a law which is a usurpation upon the federal government the law is void; and upright, independent judges will declare it to be so. Still, however, if the United States and the individual states will quarrel, if they want to fight, they may do it, and no frame of government can possibly prevent it.[28]

---

27. Oliver Ellsworth's speech at the Connecticut Ratifying Convention, January 4, 1788, available at http://consource.org/document/oliver-ellsworths-speech-at-the-connecticut-ratification-convention-1788-1-4.

28. Elliot, Vol. 2, p. 196.

Ellsworth would breathe life into these words a year later, when a Senator, drafting the Judiciary Act of 1789. Two days later, by a vote of 128-40, the Connecticut Ratifying Convention ratified the U.S. Constitution, becoming the fifth state to do so.[29]

Senator Ellsworth

With the new capitol in New York and the First Congress ready to begin its important work in the new nation, Ellsworth was elected to represent Connecticut as a Senator. After the work of the electoral college was complete in electing George Washington as first president of the United States and John Adams as first vice president, the Senate selected a committee tasked with addressing the workings of the judiciary.[30]

The Senate appointed Ellsworth committee chair, and he would go to work drafting what remains the basic structure of our federal court system. While other members of the committee contributed, Ellsworth was the main drafter along with William Paterson from New Jersey,[31] using his experience in the Continental Congress and as a state court judge to draft a framework for a workable federal judicial system. This bill, the Judiciary Act of 1789, was the biggest

---

29. The first four states to ratify were Delaware, Pennsylvania, New Jersey, and Georgia.

30. Casto, p. 59.

31. Warren, Vol. 1, p. 8.

accomplishment for Ellsworth during his seven years of Senate service. The Act has been called "the most important and the most satisfactory Act ever passed by Congress" by retired Supreme Court Associate Justice Henry Billings Brown in 1911.[32] The Judiciary Act of 1789 established the framework that survives to this day, with some tweaks.[33] Adopted on September 25, 1789 when President George Washington signed the bill into law, the Act provided for a chief justice and five associate justices.[34] Ellsworth would fill the chief justice position in less than seven years. The Act did not identify how the position of chief justice was different from that of associate justice, or what tasks and responsibilities might belong to the chief.[35]

In addition, the Act fleshed out the requirements of the U.S. Constitution, Article III, Section 1, which provides that "the judicial Power of the United States, shall be vested in one supreme Court, and in such inferior Courts as the Congress may from time to time ordain and establish."[36] The Act provided for thirteen judicial districts. It also provided for the justices to "ride circuit" by having appellate courts with a district court judge and two justices sitting on panels.

---

32. *Id.* at 12.

33. A copy of the Judiciary Act of 1789 can be found at https://memory.loc .gov/cgi-bin/ampage?collId=llac&fileName=002/llac002.db&recNum=481.

34. This was the first time the term "justice" had been used in a law to describe the judges who would sit on the Supreme Court of the United States.

35. *See* Chapter 2 *supra*.

36. U.S. Constitution, Article III, Section 1.

In addition to the Judiciary Act, Ellsworth was influential in sponsoring the Senate's acceptance of the Bill of Rights.

Supreme Court Nomination

After John Rutledge's nomination was defeated by the Senate and Associate Justice William Cushing turned down the nomination presented to him by President George Washington, Washington turned to Ellsworth and, on March 3, 1796, made the formal nomination of Ellsworth. The Senate confirmed Ellsworth the next day. Associate Justice James Wilson, who had wished the position, was said to be disappointed, but the confirmation of Ellsworth by the Senate was generally well received.

Supreme Court Legacy

The Supreme Court early in its history did not address many issues of notable import. However, despite that, the Ellsworth Court achieved two items that the next chief justice, John Marshall, would enhance and make his name for- unified court opinions rather than seriatim opinions[37] and his court issued several opinions that helped to define

---

37. Seriatim in Latin means "in series," that is, each justice would write his own opinion and there was no "opinion of the court." As we will see, John Marshall took this change seriously and many of the early Marshall Court opinions were unanimous ones.

the scope and power of judicial review.[38] One of the first cases decided by his Court, although he did not participate, was *Ware, Adm'r v. Hylton*, a case addressing "whether State laws confiscating and sequestering debts due to a British enemy or allowing their payment in depreciated currency were valid against the provisions of the treaty with Great Britain."[39] John Marshall, future chief justice, represented the debtors before the Supreme Court. The Court, despite being impressed with the advocacy of Marshall, decided that the treaty prevailed over any state law.

The day after issuing that first important decision, the Supreme Court issued its decision in *Hylton v. United States*, a case involving a carriage tax passed by Congress and whether such tax was a direct tax requiring apportionment among the states. Most importantly, the *Hylton* case was the first Supreme Court decision in which judicial review was utilized to determine whether an act of Congress was constitutional. While Justice Marshall a few years later would get credit for giving the Supreme Court such authority in *Marbury v. Madison*, it was in fact this earlier case decided

---

38. As will see in the next chapter, it is John Marshall and the Marshall Court often credited with the ability of the Supreme Court of the United States to have the power of judicial review. It is important to note that Ellsworth and the Ellsworth Court had the same view. As noted, Ellsworth first served on the Committee of Appeals, drafted the Judiciary Act of 1789, and otherwise was extremely influential in the resultant federal court system, including the Supreme Court.

39. Warren, Vol. 1, p. 144.

by the Ellsworth Court that implicitly acknowledged such judicial powers were vested in the Supreme Court.

Special Envoy to France

In early 1799, President John Adams believed that peace could be achieved with France and nominated William Vans Murray to be minister plenipotentiary to France to negotiate such peace. The Senate recommended that two additional envoys be appointed along with Murray. Adams named Ellsworth and also named Patrick Henry, who declined. Governor William R. Davie of North Carolina would accompany Ellsworth.[40] While today the dual roles would potentially be prohibited,[41] in the early days of the Republic it was not deemed problematic.

After several months of negotiation over the quasi-war, the Treaty of Mortefontaine was agreed upon and signed and would be approved by the Senate and ratified by President Adams. Ellsworth, who had developed a kidney ailment while in France, wrote President Adams his resignation letter:

> "Constantly afflicted with the gravel, and the gout in my kidnies . . . I must therefore pray you, Sir, to accept

---

40. Casto, pgs. 118–19.

41. But see chapter on Earl Warren and the Warren Commission that he sat on while chief justice, or Robert Jackson's participation in the Nuremberg Trials.

this my resignation of the office of Chief Justice of the United States."[42]

Adams offered the chief justiceship to Jay, but Jay refused the position, citing riding circuits as well as the lack of prestige. Adams turned to his secretary of state, John Marshall, who accepted and earned the prestige of the Supreme Court.

Conclusion

John Marshall may be the "Father of the Supreme Court." He might also be considered first when it comes to legacy and assessment of accomplishment. However, he was not the first chief justice. Three esteemed contemporaries set the tone and Marshall expanded and strengthened what his predecessors had established. Ellsworth's use of the majority opinion in place of seriatim and his Court's review of Congressional acts became two of the cornerstones of the Marshall Court.

---

42. Casto, p. 124.

Part Two

The Supreme Court Emerges As Supreme

The first three chief justices did not tackle many constitutional issues; the main focus was on the Court's organization and operations and on developing the Court and sorting through the challenges presented by riding circuit. When John Marshall became the chief justice, the issues were beginning to be presented at the Supreme Court, having wound their way through the lower courts in most instances. Over the next thirty-four years, Marshall would lead the Court through the challenges and the Supreme Court would emerge as a much stronger institution.

Chapter Six

John Marshall: Establishment of Supreme Court's Supremacy

Nominated by President John Adams
Confirmed by Senate Acclamation on
  January 27, 1801
Tenure: February 4, 1801 to July 8, 1835 (Died)
Presidents During Tenure
  Adams
  Jefferson
  Madison
  Monroe
  Quincy Adams
  Jackson

John Marshall: The Greatest Chief Justice

Many people regard John Marshall as the first chief justice, but he was in fact the fourth. He was the chief justice who established the Court's position in the organization of the American government, that of a co-equal branch of government and final arbiter of the rights of Americans. The longest serving chief justice, he is almost universally regarded as the "great" chief justice. His greatest opinion, Marbury v. Madison, established a key feature of American jurisprudence, that the judiciary can hold that a statute violates the constitution.

Introduction

Before John Marshall became the chief justice in 1801, the Supreme Court was almost unknown and carried little, if any, prestige. The first three chief justices presided over courts that frankly had very little to do. The first, John Jay of New York, presided over four cases in his five years on the court. The court spent much of its time establishing procedures and swearing in attorneys. In fact, Jay spent much of his time assisting President George Washington in the new administration. In 1795 he resigned from the court to become the Governor of New York.

To be the second chief justice, Washington selected an associate justice, John Rutledge, as a recess appointment made on June 29, 1795. When the U.S. Senate returned, it rejected the nomination by a vote of 14-20, on December 15, 1795. On March 3, 1796, Washington nominated his third and final chief justice, Oliver Ellsworth. The Senate confirmed Ellsworth the next day. On December 15, 1800, Ellsworth resigned due to poor health.

In fact, during the eleven years before Marshall, the court had so little on its docket that it disposed of just seventy-nine cases, only sixty-one of which it fully adjudicated. It fell to President John Adams to select the next chief justice. He chose his secretary of state, John Marshall of Virginia. To use an analogy to baseball, Marshall became the clean-up hitter who put the court on the scoreboard.

The Times

When John Marshall was born in 1755, the Declaration of Independence was almost twenty-one years away and the French and Indian War was a year old. That war saw Marshall's friend and our nation's first president, George Washington, in combat for the first time. The dominant claims of the present United States belonged to France and Spain, with the east coast thirteen colonies representing the British claims.

In 1775, the colonies of Great Britain began a war that would last for the next eight years. The Revolutionary War followed a period in which growing hostilities between the colonies and Great Britain occurred. On March 1, 1781, the first written constitution of the United States, the Articles of Confederation, was ratified, with states remaining sovereign and independent. With the British surrender in 1783, the new nation was independent.

After a few years of existence under the Articles of Confederation, the states convened in Philadelphia in 1787, ostensibly to review and consider amendments to the Articles of Confederation, but what emerged was a new charter, a new constitution, the U.S. Constitution. It would be a relatively brief document, consisting of 4,543 words in its original, unamended form, including signatures, that would be reviewed and decided upon by the Supreme Court in the coming years.

When the Constitution was ratified in Virginia, "the roads were execrable and scarcely deserved the name. The few bridges usually were broken."[1] The reality was that "coaches were rarely seen. There were thousands of respectable men in the Commonwealth who had never seen any other four-wheeled vehicle than a wagon and there were thousands who had never seen a wagon at the time when the Constitution was ratified."[2] The United States, including some of the settled areas in Kentucky, Illinois, and Ohio, had a density of "fewer than five persons to the square mile" and there was "[s]carcely any communication" that was happening among them.[3]

---

1. Beveridge, Vol. 1, p. 260.
2. *Id.*
3. *Id.* at 264.

When John Marshall became chief justice in 1801, the identity of the next president of the United States had not been determined. The original Constitution authorized each member of the Electoral College to vote for two names for president. When the votes were tallied, Thomas Jefferson and Aaron Burr each had received seventy-three votes, meaning the U.S. House of Representatives would for the first time in the nation's young history decide a presidential election. (Georgia had incorrectly completed its ballot and, if it had been rejected, no single candidate would have received a majority of seventy votes required and there would have been a runoff election among the top five finishers.) The outgoing House of Representatives included several states that remained Federalist and voted on the first thirty-five ballots for Burr. Sixteen states (Vermont, Kentucky, and Tennessee joined the original thirteen colonies) had one vote each, and on the thirty-sixth ballot, Jefferson received ten states' votes, Burr received four, and two had no result. With that long process, Jefferson was sworn in by Marshall.

A major issue that the new nation faced from its founding through all of John Marshall's life and until the Civil War was the "peculiar institution"[4] of slavery. The original Constitution included the infamous three-fifths clause, and politics and presidential elections for the next seventy-five years

---

4. The term "peculiar institution" was believed to be first used by Southern politician, John Calhoun, to refer to slavery, when he defended the practice.

would involve the question of slavery. The Marshall Court would rule only once on the question, and that case dealt with the international slave trade and not domestic slavery.

James Fenimore Cooper "identified five distinctive features of early-nineteenth-century American culture" that portray life during Marshall's tenure on the Supreme Court as chief justice.[5]

The Early Years of John Marshall

John Marshall was born on September 24, 1755, in Germantown, Virginia, to Thomas Marshall and Mary Randolph Keith, the granddaughter of William Randolph. (Randolph was a prominent politician in Virginia.) Marshall was a cousin of Thomas Jefferson (Jefferson was a grandson of William Randolph), whom he despised, and the feelings were mutual. Marshall served in the Continental Army and he and his dad were friends with General George Washington. Marshall experienced the miserable winter at Valley Forge and this experience combined with his war experience deeply influenced his strong views on nationalism over states' rights. His war experience also strengthened his admiration for Washington as a man and leader. Marshall was also admired by the soldiers according to the journals and diaries left by the soldiers who experienced

---

5. *See* White, pgs. 12–40, describing the five areas and the credibility to be afforded to Cooper in his book, *Notions of the Americans: Picked up by a Traveling Bachelor* (2 vols., 1828).

the horrible winter at Valley Forge—"the name of John Marshall is singled out as conspicuously for these comforting qualities."[6] Marshall admired General Washington, who conducted himself with an "iron military rule."[7] Perhaps Marshall recognized, as did others, that had Washington "died, or had he been seriously disabled, the Revolution would have ended."[8] The lessons and experience during the war that Marshall obtained were "the roots of the greatest of his constitutional opinions."[9]

Upon his return to Virginia with the rank of captain[10] in the Eleventh Virginia Continental Regiment in 1780 after four years of service, he entered private practice and grew an impressive book of business. Marshall's experiences in the Continental Army, witnessing close up and personal the challenges and difficulties and death and the problems of a weak national government not permitting raising of revenues or soldiers under the Articles of Confederation were the "fountainhead of John Marshall's National thinking."[11] In 1782, he became a member of the Virginia House of Delegates, serving on and off from 1782 to 1796.

---

6. Beveridge, Vol. 1, p. 117.

7. *Id.* at 120. The Beveridge accounts of a stern general in Washington are not often talked about. We think of George Washington only in a calm manner.

8. *Id.* at 121.

9. *Id.* at 126.

10. This promotion to captain came three days after the Battle of Monmouth. Beveridge, Vol. 1, p. 138.

11. Beveridge, Vol. 1, p. 147.

John Marshall married Mary Willis Ambler "Polly" Marshall on January 3, 1783. He met Polly while making visits to the Ambler household and family tradition suggests that he fell in love with the sixteen-year-old rather than one of her older sisters and, after spending time at dances with her, asked her to marry. Thomas Jefferson had courted Polly's mother, and that may have been part of the reason the two cousins bitterly hated each other. Polly refused Marshall's marriage invitation, but legend has it that she sent a cousin after Marshall with a lock of her hair, which he sent back entwined with his own in a locket. The Marshalls were married for forty-eight years, until Polly's death in 1831. Just before her death, she gave the locket back to Marshall, who in turn wore it until his death. When Polly died, Marshall wrote a year later:

> "I have lost her! And with her I have lost the solace of my life! Yet she remains still the companion of my retired hours—still occupies my inmost bosom. When I am alone and unemployed, my mind unceasingly turns to her."[12]

All accounts are that the two enjoyed a happy marriage. Polly had ten children, only six of whom lived to adulthood. Marshall was a good father, attentive to his home, according to reports from the time. Polly suffered from various

---

12. Bevridge, Vol. 4, p. 527.

medical conditions and was often a recluse and unable to accompany Marshall on his travels.

Marshall and the Virginia
Ratifying Convention

On the third day of the fall session of the Virginia legislature in 1787, the Virginia House approved a convention to consider ratification of the proposed U.S. Constitution. The Virginia legislature strongly debated whether to adopt or reject the document as it was submitted, or to condition any approval upon certain amendments and revisions. Marshall proposed a resolution that won the day, "that a Convention should be called and that the new Constitution should be laid before them for their free and ample discussion." The Senate followed slowly, and on January 8, 1788, a law passed calling for a state convention.

Information back in the 1780s was not as instant as it is today. If one included the territories where many settlers were populating, the density of people living in the United States was less than five people to the square mile. A letter from Virginia to Boston could take as long as a month to reach the recipient. With this slowness of information a fact, the Virginia Convention of 1788 commenced on June 2, 1788. The delegates arriving in Richmond believed that the fate of the Constitution hung in the balance with how Virginia decided. Even so, upon arrival at the Convention, "some members of the Virginia State Convention had never seen a copy of the Constitution until they arrived in Richmond to deliberate upon it and decide its fate."[13] While the Virginia Convention ensued, New Hampshire became the ninth state to ratify the Constitution and it became effective. However, had Virginia rejected ratification, the future of the United States would be in question. As noted, many of the 168 delegates had not seen a copy of the Constitution until they arrived in Richmond, Virginia. A healthy majority of Virginians were opposed to the concept of a strong national government contemplated by the Constitution and the Virginia Convention began with that view prevalent among the delegates. As the Virginia Convention began on June 2, 1788, "the Nation's proposed fundamental law had not received deliberate consideration in any quarter; nor had it encountered weighty debate from those opposed to it."[14] The Nation was watching closely how the important Commonwealth of Virginia decided, for "she also was the most important State in the Confederation in population and, at that time, in resources."[15]

Delegates had been elected by their counties, and John Marshall, along with Governor Edmund Randolph, was elected to represent Henrico County. Marshall was a nationalist whose experience in the Revolutionary War and with the ineffective Articles of Confederation convinced him of

---

13. *Id.* at 320.
14. *Id.* at 355.
15. *Id.* at 359.

the need for a strong national government. In his nationalist thoughts he was not alone:

> "More than one fourth of the Virginia Convention of
> one hundred and seventy members had been soldiers
> in the Revolutionary War; and nearly all of them fol-
> lowed Washington in his desire for a strong National
> Government."[16]

Marshall did not speak as much as James Madison and
Randolph for the Federalists,[17] but he proved to be a very
effective and instrumental delegate at the Virginia Convention, countering his formidable opposition, including
George Mason.[18] After the convention concluded, James
Madison wrote Jefferson (who was in Paris) about the
convention. Marshall delivered three speeches at the Virginia Convention, with his "oration on the judicial powers
of the federal government" being the best known of the
three speeches.[19] He gave two other speeches "on the general distribution of powers under the new form of government and the other on the control and training of the

---

16. *Id.* at 360.

17. According to Herbert A. Johnson, Marshall's "role in the floor debates
was relatively minor when compared with the efforts of his colleagues Edmund
Pendleton, James Madison, Edmund Randolph, and George Nicholas." Johnson,
Vol. 1, p. 252.

18. Beveridge, Vol. 1, p. 369. George Mason "was the author of Virginia's
Constitution and Bill of Rights. . . . He had been a delegate to the Federal Convention and, with Randolph, had refused to sign the Constitution." *Id.*

19. Johnson, Vol. 1, p. 252.

militia,"[20] both of which advanced the Federalist positions effectively and also "represent the first clear enunciation of Marshall's political and constitutional philosophy."[21] Madison listed Marshall fifth in importance of all delegates elected for the nationalist/Constitutionalist position.

In Marshall's first speech on the convention floor, he asked the question of "whether democracy or despotism be most eligible"[22] and concluded the Constitution was the "best means of protecting liberty."[23] Marshall went toe to toe with Patrick Henry and other Anti-Federalists. The Anti-Federalist contingent was a strong one, led by Henry and George Mason, as well as James Monroe. Marshall's speeches on the convention floor, especially advocating for Article III, were instrumental in the Virginia Convention ratifying the U.S. Constitution by the slim margin of 89-79. The "debate on the Judiciary was the climax of the fight,"[24] and Marshall handled the arguments advocating the nationalist's side. In a precursor of his famous enunciation in

---

20. For an interesting discussion of what the word "militia" may have meant at the time of the Constitution ratification and at the beginning, one should read John Marshall's speech on June 16, 1788, at the Virginia Ratifying Convention. *See* Johnson, Vol. 1, pgs. 272–74, for a copy of Marshall's complete speech on the topic. In it, he discusses the national militia and arming militia for defense. This book is not the place to reopen that discussion, but it is interesting historical data coming from the state where the Bill of Rights derived.

21. Johnson, Vol. 1, pgs. 252-53.

22. Beverdige, Vol. 1, p. 409.

23. *Id.* at 410.

24. *Id.* at 444.

Marbury v. Madison, Marshall on June 20, 1788, spoke about Article III of the Constitution:

> "This part of the plan before us is a great improvement on that system from which we are now departing. . . . If [Congress] were to make a law not warranted by any of the powers enumerated, it would be considered by the judges as an infringement of the Constitution which they are to guard. They would not consider such a law as coming under their jurisdiction. They would declare it void. . . . To what quarter will you look for protection from an infringement on the Constitution, if you will not give the power to the Judiciary? There is no other body that can afford such a protection."[25]

Marshall rebutted each criticism of the judiciary lobbed by George Mason. The Federalists having won on Article III, the final area of fight by the Anti-Federalists was focused on resolutions to amend the Constitution. On June 24, 1788, Delegate George Wythe moved the Virginia Convention to ratify the Constitution. Henry arose for a final great speech of his life, arguing against ratification without amendments. The proposal to add amendments, many of which became the Bill of Rights, failed to be a condition of ratification, but

---

25. The Founder's Constitution, John Marshall speech, available at http://press-pubs.uchicago.edu/founders/documents/a3_2_1s26.html. Reading the entire speech on the floor by Marshall is worthwhile. Marshall brings great passion and also sense to his arguments, and on this topic, Marshall's views won the day. His general views on the judicial branch that he applied several years later are on full display in this speech.

proved to be valuable guidance when Congress met in 1789. After further debate, on June 26, 1788, the Virginia Convention voted to ratify the Constitution by the slim margin of 89-79. This slim margin would not have been possible had eight members of the Convention not voted against their constituents' directives, and two ignored the instructions given them.[26] Marshall contributed to the end result with his persuasive oratory and logic, and "left the convention as he entered it, an uncompromising advocate for increased federal power and a strong supporter of an independent federal taxing authority."[27]

Marshall Groomed by His Former General

After the Convention, Marshall returned to the private practice of law in Fauquier County and Richmond, Virginia. His practice thrived, and he argued before the Virginia Supreme Court and before the U.S. Supreme Court.[28] Marshall turned down offers from President Washington to serve as attorney general or as minister to France. However, in 1797, he agreed to serve on a three-man contingent to represent the United States in France, in what became

---

26. Beveridge, Vol. 1, p. 475.

27. Johnson, Vol. 1, p. 255.

28. His sole argument before the Supreme Court of the United States was in *Ware v. Hylton*, a case involving British debt. Marshall lost the case but his argument was hailed as great lawyering by those who witnessed it.

known as the "XYZ Affair" or "Mission."[29] Marshall rejected extortion efforts by French Foreign Minister Talleyrand and other French leaders, leading to his and Charles Pinckney's expulsion from France. Talleyrand demanded a bribe to receive the U.S. contingent, and the team rejected Talleyrand's demands. Marshall returned to the states a hero for his stand in France and his name first became nationally recognized because of it.

In 1798, President John Adams offered Marshall a Supreme Court seat but Marshall declined it, recommending his friend and George Washington's nephew, Bushrod Washington. Marshall ran for and won a seat in the U.S. House of Representatives instead. He served in that capacity for one year, then Marshall became secretary of state in May 1799, taking office in June 1800. Marshall had turned down the secretary of war position President Adams offered Marshall in May 1800.[30] After debating the position of secretary of state for several weeks, Marshall accepted and remained in that position until 1801.

Rejection of the Chief Justiceship by a Former Chief Justice

When Ellsworth resigned in late 1800, Adams named former Chief Justice Jay, who was completing his term as New

---

29. Beveridge, Vol. 2, p. 256.
30. *Id.* at 485.

York Governor, to the position without consulting with Jay. On January 2, 1801, Jay sent Adams a letter rejecting the nomination. Jay wrote:

> I left the bench perfectly convinced that under a system so defective it would not obtain the energy, weight, and dignity which are essential to its affording due support to the national government, nor acquire the public confidence and respect which, as the last resort of the justice of the nation, it should possess ... [my return] would give some countenance to the neglect and indifference with which the opinions and remonstrances of the judges on this important subject have been treated.[31]

Having been rejected by Jay, and having considered a number of other potential nominees, President Adams turned to his loyal secretary of state, John Marshall, and "with no herald announcing the event, no trumpet sounding, suddenly, and without previous notice even to himself,"[32] Adams nominated Marshall for chief justice of the Supreme Court on January 20, 1801, and after some delay, the Senate confirmed Marshall on January 27, 1801. Like Jay before him, Marshall would serve in the dual role of chief justice and secretary of state for a period of time.[33]

---

31. National Archives, Founders Online, available at https://founders.archives .gov/documents/Adams/99-02-02-4745.

32. Beveridge, Vol. 2, p. 553.

33. *Id.* at 558–59.

Chief Justice Marshall

When Adams offered Marshall the chief justice position, which he accepted, the Senate confirmed Marshall and he became chief justice in 1801. However, little would be done his first year on the bench, as a result of passage of the Judiciary Act of 1802 which repealed the changes in the 1801 act, and resulted in a hiatus of the Court from December 1801 until February 1803.

When court resumed in February 1803, the first order of business the Court decided was *Marbury v. Madison*. The case addressed the issue of the appointments of a number of "midnight judges," including Marbury, by lame duck President Adams.

Marbury v. Madison (1803): A Landmark Decision Establishing the Court's Role[34]

The Senate confirmed Marshall on January 27, 1801, and he became chief justice. However, a Democratic-Republican Party-led Congress repealed the Judiciary Act of 1801 (aka the "Midnight Judges Act") and subsequently replaced it with the Judiciary Act of 1802, causing the

---

34. Much of the narrative in this section originally appeared in Constituting America's 90 Day Study: A History of Our Country's Judicial System. Cotter, *Marbury v. Madison (1803)*, available at https://consitutingamerica.org/marbury -v-madison-1803-a-landmark-decision-establishing-the-supreme-courts-role-gues -essayist-daniel-a-cotter/.

Supreme Court to be on hiatus from December 1801 until February 1803.

When the Court resumed hearing cases in February 1803, one of the first orders of business was deciding *Marbury v. Madison*, which presented the question of whether Adams had the power to issue the appointments to a number of "midnight judges," including Marbury. On February 24, 1803, the Court issued its opinion in *Marbury, setting* a precedent that would make the Supreme Court "supreme" when it came to deciding Constitutional questions. While the Supreme Court previously had suggested the principle, the Marshall Court made clear in *Marbury* that, when it came to judicial review, "It is emphatically the province and duty of the Judicial Department to say what the law is."[35]

The story of the election of 1800 and the events leading to the *Marbury* decision are worth telling. Marshall was the secretary of state and was involved in the commissions of judges ordered by President John Adams.

The Election of 1800 and the Changing of Parties

The Election of 1800 was a hard-fought presidential contest in which Vice President Jefferson defeated President Adams. The election saw the passing of the Presidency from Adams' Federalist Party to Jefferson's Democratic-Republicans, and Congressional control changed in the same

---

35. *Marbury v. Madison*, 5 U.S. 137 (1803).

manner. Such a political change was a first in the United States' brief history.

The Judiciary Acts of 1801 and 1802 and the Midnight Judges

Adams and the lame-duck Federalist Congress passed the Judiciary Act of 1801, which expanded the circuits and jurisdiction of the Federal courts, added a number of justices of the peace (including the justice of the peace seat that Marbury was offered), and reduced the number of Supreme Court Justices from six to five effective upon the next retirement. One of the Act's goals was to eliminate Jefferson's ability to nominate a justice.

On March 3, 1801, the night before his term as president ended, Adams named his judicial appointees (the "midnight judges"). The Senate approved the appointees, and the next day Secretary of State John Marshall, who had just become the chief justice of the Supreme Court but still remained secretary of state, was to deliver the commissions to the midnight judges. Marshall delivered some of them, but given the number, and because he believed the appointments were routine, he did not deliver all of them. Rather, Marshall thought that the next secretary of state would deliver the remaining commissions, including that of William Marbury.

Jefferson believed the commissions for Adams' appointees were void and instructed his acting secretary of state,

Levi Lincoln, to immediately stop delivery of the remaining commissions. The new Congress quickly repealed the Judiciary Act of 1801 and replaced it with the Judiciary Act of 1802, which was enacted on April 29, 1802. The Act of 1802 provided for six federal judicial circuits, with one Supreme Court Justice from each circuit. The Act of 1802 also eliminated the Supreme Court's summer session, providing instead for a single Court session commencing on the first Monday in February of each year. As a result of the Act of 1802, no session of the Supreme Court officially took place in 1802 and the Court did not sit from December 1801 until February 1803, when the first Court session pursuant to the Act of 1802 commenced.

Marbury and the Petition for His Commission

Marbury filed a petition directly with the Supreme Court, seeking to have the new secretary of state, James Madison, ordered to deliver the papers for Marbury's commission as Justice of the Peace in the District of Columbia. In December 1801, Marbury applied for a writ of mandamus. The Supreme Court agreed to hear the case, despite pressures that the Justices might be impeached for doing so. Because of the repeal of the Act of 1801 and the subsequent enactment of the Act of 1802, the Supreme Court did not sit in session from the end of 1801 until February 1803. When the Supreme Court returned in February 1803, the second case it heard was *Marbury v. Madison*, on February 11, 1803.

The Decision

On February 24, 1803, John Marshall announced the unanimous 4-0 decision of the Supreme Court (Justices William Cushing and Alfred Moore missed oral arguments and did not participate in the decision due to illness). Marshall, despite his direct involvement in the failure to deliver the midnight judges' commissions, did not recuse himself from participating in the case. In his opinion, Marshall stated that Marbury was entitled to his commission and that the Judiciary Act of 1789 gave the Court the authority to issue a writ of mandamus that would enforce Marbury's right. However, Marshall found that the Constitution defined the Court's original jurisdiction and that Congress could not expand such jurisdiction by statute. As a result, that portion of the Judiciary Act of 1789 authorizing the Court to enter writs of mandamus was found unconstitutional. *Marbury* is the only decision during Marshall's tenure as chief justice in which the Court ruled an act of Congress was unconstitutional. In supporting the decision, Marshall stated for the Court:

It is emphatically the province and duty of the Judicial Department to say what the law is. Those who apply the rule to particular cases must, of necessity, expound and interpret that rule. If two laws conflict with each other, the Courts must decide on the operation of each.[36]

With that statement, Marshall definitively established the Court's role as interpreter of the U.S. Constitution. The Constitution provided no guidance for which branch of government had the final word on such questions. While many legal scholars have noted that the interpretive power had been exercised by the Supreme Court prior to *Marbury*, and that the Founding Fathers had discussed judicial authority at the Constitutional Convention, Marshall's definitive assertion of Supreme Court power remains controlling precedent 216 years later. It is one of his many powerful decisions that makes Marshall perhaps the greatest chief justice in our nation's history.[37]

A Chief and His Court

When John Marshall took his seat as chief justice on January 31, 1801, he joined a Supreme Court consisting of all Federalist justices. Over the next thirty-four years, Marshall would preside over a Supreme Court whose members changed from time to time, but that established an incredible number of judicial precedents and interpretations that

---

36. *Marbury v. Madison*, 5 U.S. 137 (1803).
37. For a very rough ranking of the chiefs, *see* **Appendix C**.

have stood the test of time and remain the law of the land. When Marshall joined the court in 1801, the Supreme Court consisted of five associate justices:

- William Cushing—September 27, 1789 (the only one of the original justices remaining on the bench);
- William Paterson—March 4, 1793;
- Samuel Chase—January 27, 1796;
- Bushrod Washington—December 20, 1798; and
- Alfred Moore—December 10, 1799.

One practice that Marshall continued upon and consistently instituted, part by leadership and part by his personality, was unified majority opinions. (Ellsworth had begun the practice during his short tenure as chief justice, but as noted, the Supreme Court did not have much work in its first eleven years, and Ellsworth issued few opinions.) Previously, each justice had issued a seriatim opinion. For many years, the unified opinion would continue on the Marshall Court, but eventually eroded as the initial justices on the Supreme Court when Marshall joined it were replaced. The unanimity and cohesiveness eventually were replaced by a divided court that was not as close during Marshall's long tenure as chief justice.

The Court during Marshall's time was in "session for as little as six weeks,"[38] but during that period, justices spent much time "riding circuit." The justices were:

---

38. White, Marshall Court, p. 157.

"living and working together in a boardinghouse; sitting during arguments not behind a long single bench but at individual desks; announcing the decisions of cases sometimes within days, and nearly always within two to three weeks, after they were argued; often not knowing when the official reports of their decisions would appear."[39]

The Marshall Court issued an average of forty decisions per term. But to anyone thinking that the Court did not work as hard as the current courts, "[t]he life of a Marshall Court Justice was clearly a strenuous one."[40] One major advantage of riding circuit[41] was that the Marshall Court justices "devoted a portion of their energies to channeling lower court cases up to the Supreme Court."[42] One procedure by which many cases came before the Supreme Court was the writ of error, which typically came from state courts.[43] Another procedure was the certificate of division, which permitted appeal where circuit court judges certified difference of opinion on a question of law.[44] With the Supreme Court justices having double duty as circuit court judges, the ability to control the Court's docket was assured

---

39. *Id.*

40. *Id.* at 163.

41. There does not appear to be many advantages to the old practice.

42. White, Marshall Court, p. 164.

43. *Id.* at 165. According to White, numerous major cases came to the Supreme Court by writ of error, including: *Fletcher v. Peck, Martin v. Hunter's Lessee, Cohens v. Virginia,* and *Gibbons v. Ogden. Id.*

44. *Id.*, p. 173.

to a large extent. The case, *Trustees of Dartmouth College v. Woodward*,[45] is an example of the parties seeking a *pro forma* certificate of division to get the matter before the Supreme Court.[46]

When Moore resigned, he was replaced by William Johnson, a President Jefferson nominee. When Paterson died in 1806, he was replaced by Henry Brockholst Livingston, a President Jefferson nominee, and when a new seat was established in 1807 by the U.S. Congress, President Jefferson nominated Thomas Todd. The Court was changing from a Federalist one to a Republican one. However, despite the makeup of the party appointing the justices, the rulings did not substantially change.

Another seven justices would join the Marshall Court during his long tenure:

- Gabriel Duvall—November 23, 1811;
- Joseph Story—February 3, 1812;[47]
- Smith Thompson—September 1, 1823;
- Robert Trimble—May 9, 1826;

---

45. 4 Wheat. 518 (1819).

46. The certificate of division was a method of appellate jurisdiction created by the Judiciary Act of 1802 that was available when the SCOTUS justices were riding circuit. When the resident district judge and the circuit-riding SCOTUS justice sat, and allowed the sitting panel to certify there was a division of the case. It was a precursor in many ways to present certiorari practices, but it permitted the Supreme Court to control its docket and get cases to the Supreme Court it wanted to hear.

47. The more than eleven year gap between Story and Thompson was the longest period in the Court's history where the Supreme Court members did not change.

- John McLean—March 7, 1829;
- Henry Baldwin—January 6, 1830; and
- James Moore Wayne—January 14, 1835.

Marshall is the longest serving chief justice of the Supreme Court in its long history, but many others who were members of the Marshall Court also served long tenures. Of the fifteen longest serving justices in Supreme Court history, the following six were part of the Marshall Court:

- John Marshall—fourth;
- Joseph Story—ninth;
- James Moore Wayne—tenth;
- John McLean—eleventh;
- Bushrod Washington—thirteenth; and
- William Johnson—fourteenth.

Current advocates of term limits for Supreme Court justices because we are living longer should review that list and see if their arguments hold water. Because of Marshall's long tenure on the Supreme Court, and even with these long tenures, fifteen of the ninety-seven associate justices in our Supreme Court's history sat on the Marshall Court.[48]

---

48. The following chart lists the justices who were on the Marshall Court and their tenures as Supreme Court justices.

Justice	Nominating President	Begin of Tenure	End of Tenure	Reason for End
Cushing	Washington	9/27/1789	9/13/1810	Death
Paterson	Washington	3/4/1793	9/8/1806	Death

Of all the justices who sat with Marshall during his long tenure, no one was closer than Joseph Story, Marshall's biographer and greatest admirer, who served along with Marshall for twenty-three years.

Marshall's personality and leadership helped bring a great level of comity to the Court. Back in the early days of the Supreme Court, the justices roomed together and spent much time together. For the first dozen years of the Marshall Court, the justices of the Supreme Court all worked together seamlessly and generally spoke with one voice. The Oyez Project refers to this period as the first phase of the Marshall Court.[49]

According to the Oyez Project, the Marshall Court during the second phase (from 1813 to 1819) produced very little of

Justice	Nominating President	Begin of Tenure	End of Tenure	Reason for End
Chase	Washington	1/27/1796	6/19/1811	Death
Washington	Adams	12/20/1798	11/26/1829	Death
Moore	Adams	12/10/1799	1/26/1804	Resignation
Johnson	Jefferson	5/7/1804	8/4/1834	Death
Livingston	Jefferson	1/20/1807	3/18/1823	Death
Todd	Jefferson	3/3/1807	2/27/1806	Death
Duvall	Madison	11/23/1811	1/12/1835	Resignation
Story	Madison	2/3/1812	9/10/1845	Death
Thompson	Monroe	9/1/1823	12/18/1843	Death
Trimble	Quincy Adams	5/9/1826	8/25/1828	Death
McLean	Jackson	3/7/1829	4/4/1861	Death
Baldwin	Jackson	1/6/1830	4/21/1844	Death
Wayne	Jackson	1/14/1835	7/5/1867	Death

49. *See* https://www.oyez.org/justices/john_marshall.

note.[50] For the next three years, what the Oyez Project refers to as the "golden period," a number of cases of lasting importance were issued.[51] The final phase saw Marshall's power waning and more states' rights justices sitting on the Court.[52]

During the time frame from 1816 to 1823, whether any lasting cases were issued, "the Court had a remarkable percentage of unanimous or near unanimous decisions."[53] However, one practice of the Marshall Court that may have skewed percentages somewhat is the practice of not recording opinions when not in the majority. As a result, "the perception of a united Court speaking in one voice that represented all its members is illusory."[54]

Justice Joseph Story: The Youngest Justice Appointed to the Court[55]

Joseph Story was Marshall's strongest ally and biggest admirer. In his *Commentaries on the Constitution of the United States*, Story lavished great praise on Chief Justice Marshall. Story begins with a dedication of the *Commentaries* to Chief Justice Marshall:

---

50. *Id.*
51. *Id.*
52. *Id.*
53. White, Marshall Court, p. 184.
54. *Id.* at 189.
55. Much of the narrative in this section originally appeared in Constituting America's 90 Day Study: A History of Our Country's Judicial System. Cotter, *Justice Joseph Story (1779-1845))*, available at https://constitutingamerica.org/ justice-joseph-story-1779-1845-guest-essayist-daniel-a-cotter/

When, indeed, I look back upon your judicial labors during a period of thirty-two years, it is difficult to suppress astonishment at their extent and variety, and at the exact learning, the profound reasoning, and the solid principles which they everywhere display. Other judges have attained an elevated reputation by similar labors, in a single department of jurisprudence. But in one department (it need scarcely be said that I allude to that of constitutional law), the common consent of your countrymen has admitted you to stand without a rival.[56]

He then profusely praised Marshall as one of his greatest sources:

From two great sources, however, I have drawn by far the greatest part of my most valuable materials. These are, _The Federalist_, an incomparable commentary of three of the greatest statesmen of their age, and the extraordinary Judgments of Mr. Chief Justice Marshall upon constitutional law. The former have discussed the structure and organization of the national government, in all its departments, with admirable fulness and force. The latter has expounded the application and limits of its powers and functions with unrivalled profoundness and felicity. The Federalist could do little more than state the objects and general bearing of

---

56. Story, p. xvii, Dedication to the Honorable John Marshall, LL.D.

these powers and functions. The masterly reasoning of the Chief Justice has followed them out to their ultimate results and boundaries with a precision and clearness approaching, as near as may be, to mathematical demonstration.[57]

While most lawyers in private practice at the age of 32 are preparing for potential consideration for, and transition to, partnership, Story at that same age, after a distinguished government and law firm career in Boston, took his seat on the U.S. Supreme Court in 1811, becoming the eighteenth Justice of the Supreme Court and the youngest justice appointed to the Supreme Court. For the first two-thirds of his judicial career, Story served alongside Marshall, and as noted, they became best friends and mutual admirers. Story served on the Court for almost thirty-four years, writing a large number of opinions and dissents. His tenure coincided with those of two of the longest serving chief justices in the Supreme Court's history, John Marshall and Roger B. Taney. He served twenty-three years under Marshall and the final eleven under Taney.

Early Life and Career

Story was born in Marblehead, Massachusetts on September 18, 1779, to Dr. Elisha Story, a participant in the Boston Tea Party, and Elisha's second wife, Mehitable

---

57. *Id.*, Preface.

Pedrick. Story was the first of eleven children of the second marriage, and the eighth child of Elisha. He attended Marblehead Academy, which he left after the schoolmaster beat him in front of his classmates and later enrolled at Harvard University at the age of 16. Story graduated from Harvard in 1798, finishing second in his class.

Story then read law under U.S. Representative Samuel Sewall, who later became chief justice of the Massachusetts Supreme Judicial Court. Story also read law under Samuel Putnam. In 1801, Story was admitted to the bar at Salem, Massachusetts, and went on to work for a prominent shipping firm, George Crowninshield & Sons. In 1805, Story was elected to the Massachusetts House of Representatives, serving approximately two years, until he successfully ran for the U.S. House of Representatives from Massachusetts' second district, to fill the vacancy created by the death of a Crowninshield son. Story served less than one year and was not up for reelection in 1808. Story returned to private practice but then returned to politics, winning election as a state representative again and becoming Speaker of the Massachusetts House in 1811.

Supreme Court

When an opening on the Supreme Court became available during James Madison's presidency as a result of William Cushing's death, Madison nominated Story (Story was the fourth choice of Madison for this vacancy). Story was nominated on November 15, 1811 and was confirmed by the U.S. Senate a mere three days later by Senate voice vote. Madison hoped that Story would serve as a counter to the positions and views of Chief Justice John Marshall, but Madison's hopes were not fulfilled. Story quickly became a strong ally of Marshall and sided with him on many of the Court's most important decisions over the next twenty plus years. Story issued a large number of opinions for the Marshall Court, second only to the chief justice. After Marshall's death, Story served another dozen years under Chief Justice Roger B. Taney. Story did not like the fragmentation on the Taney Court and believed that the Taney Court favored states' rights over nationalism too strongly.

Story brought his expertise in commercial law to the Supreme Court and, riding circuit in the New England region, brought national jurisprudence to the North. The process of circuit riding enabled both Story and Marshall to influence which cases reached the Supreme Court. Story's judicial philosophy was based on "legal science," believing that proper and uniform application of law would make the United States stronger.

Story's scientific judicial philosophy at times led to unintended consequences, such as his opinion in *Prigg v. Pennsylvania* (1842),[58] which held that any state law that interfered with enforcement of the Fugitive Slave Act of 1793 was unconstitutional. The *Prigg* case gave slavery national constitutional

---

58. *Prigg v. Pennsylvania*, 41 U.S. 539 (1842).

standing. Story claimed that the decision was an antislavery opinion, but the opinion also led to a number of "personal liberty laws" being enacted in the Northern States. Eventually, in 1850, the Fugitive Slave Act of 1793 was replaced with a harsher one. Around the same time as *Prigg*, Story authored the decision in *The Amistad* (1841),[59] holding that the Africans who had been sold into slavery were free. *The Amistad* was the first time that the Supreme Court decided a domestic slavery case, and *Prigg* was the second instance. (Story was portrayed in the movie version of *Amistad* by Justice Harry Blackmun—the only known time one Justice has played another Justice in a movie.) Story also was very much opposed to slavery but believed the language of the Constitution expressly authorized the institution.

Story strongly advocated federal jurisdiction and nationalism, causing Andrew Jackson to call him "the most dangerous man in America." Early in his judicial career, Story authored the opinions in *Fairfax Devisee v. Hunter's Lessee*[60] and *Martin v. Hunter's Lessee*,[61] finding in the latter that Section 25 of the Judiciary Act of 1789, which gave the Supreme Court the jurisdiction to review state judicial decisions that interpreted the Constitution and federal laws, was constitutional. (In both cases, Marshall did not participate as the cases involved his family's investments

---

59. *United States v. The Amistad*, 40 U.S. 518 (1841).
60. *Fairfax's Devisee v. Hunter's Lessee*, 11 U.S. 603 (1813).
61. *Martin v. Hunter's Lessee*, 14 U.S. 304 (1816).

in properties, although some historians have asserted the language of the decisions has a Marshall-esque flavor.) Virginia initiated an anti-Court movement after the *Martin* decision, but the supremacy of the Supreme Court was further cemented by Story's opinion.

During his long judicial tenure, Story was also a prodigious author, with numerous treaties on law and commentaries to his credit, including his three-volume *Commentaries*, a source that is still consulted for understanding the Founders' language. Story's nine commentaries consistently advocated nationalism and economic liberty.

In 1819, Story was elected to the Harvard Board of Overseers. Beginning in 1829, Story also taught for many years at Harvard University as the Dane Professor of Law. Story planned to retire from the Court to further pursue his interests in writing and teaching, but died unexpectedly of an illness on September 10, 1845, having served more than thirty-three years on the Supreme Court.

Legacy of Story

Story had a long and distinguished career on the Supreme Court. His judicial philosophy and his interest in preserving the union led to decisions that were not always consistent. Story is the ninth longest serving justice in the Court's history and also has the longest tenure as the junior justice on the Supreme Court—he served in that role for eleven years until Smith Thompson became the nineteenth Justice in 1823. Story is also considered the second most influential justice on the Marshall Court after Marshall himself.

The Lasting Legacy of the Marshall Court

The Marshall Court issued more than 1,000 decisions during Marshall's tenure, with the chief justice writing 519 of those opinions. (In addition, as noted in several cases where Marshall recused himself, the language and style of the decisions are very Marshall-esque.) In addition to *Marbury*, the Marshall Court issued a large number of other landmark and important decisions, including:

- *Strawbridge v. Curtiss* (1806) (federal diversity jurisdiction);
- *Fletcher v. Peck* (1810) (first time Supreme Court ruled a state law unconstitutional);
- *Martin v. Hunter's Lessee* (1816) (Supreme Court's authority to review state court judgments);
- *Trustees of Dartmouth College v. Woodward* (1819) (The Constitution protects charter of a private corporation);
- *McCulloch v. Maryland* (1819) (upholding Second Bank of United States);
- *Cohens v. Virginia* (1821) (supremacy of federal over state law);
- *Gibbons v. Ogden* (1824) (Federal control over interstate commerce pursuant to the Commerce Clause of the Constitution);

- *The Antelope* (1825) (Supreme Court reviews legitimacy of international slave trade for the first time);
- *Ogden v. Saunders* (1827) (State bankruptcy law); and
- *Wheaton v. Peters* (1834) (copyrights and common law copyright).

Only once during his thirty-four-year judicial career did Marshall dissent from a Constitutional decision. In *Ogden v. Saunders* (1827), he argued that Congress held exclusive power over bankruptcy laws, pursuant to the Contract Clause, but was alone in dissent.

In the *Dartmouth* case, the Marshall Court addressed the Contracts Clause of the U.S. Constitution and weakened the ability of states to interfere in contractual relationships. The *Dartmouth* case also addressed corporate bodies and their protections under the U.S. Constitution.

Landmark Decisions of the Supreme Court: *Trustees of Dartmouth College v. Woodward* (1819)[62]

Dartmouth College was chartered in 1769 by King George III. In 1816, over thirty years after the conclusion

---

62. Much of the narrative in this section originally appeared in Constituting America's 90 Day Study: A History of Our Country's Judicial System. Cotter, *Trustees of Dartmouth College v. Woodward (1819)*, available at https://constitut ingamerica.org/trustees-of-dartmouth-college-v-woodward-1819-guest-essayist -daniel-a-cotter/.

of the American Revolution, New Hampshire's legislature attempted to alter Dartmouth College's charter by giving the Governor of New Hampshire authority to appoint trustees to the board and creating a state board with veto power over trustee decisions—in effect, converting the school from a private to a public institution. The existing trustees filed suit against William Woodward, the newly appointed secretary under the new charter, claiming that the acts of the legislature violated the Constitution. The main issues presented by the trustees' suit were whether the Contract Clause of the U.S. Constitution applied to private corporations and whether the corporate charter of Dartmouth College could be changed by the New Hampshire legislature.

Background of the Case

Dartmouth College is one of the nine colonial colleges chartered by Great Britain before the Revolutionary War. The original 1769 charter set forth the purpose and mission of the college and also granted land to the college, with the primary purpose and mission of the college to educate Native Americans. In 1816, in response to the college's trustees deposing the school's president, the New Hampshire legislature amended the college's charter. The amended charter placed control of appointing officers and trustees with the governor, appointed new trustees, and changed the name of "Dartmouth College" to "Dartmouth University."

The Controversy

Trustees of Dartmouth, who were largely Federalists, sued in New Hampshire state court challenging the actions of the Republican-dominated legislature and Republican governor to change Dartmouth College's charter. The New Hampshire Courts ruled in favor of the governor and legislature.

The Supreme Court Decision

Daniel Webster, an alumnus of Dartmouth College, was selected by the trustees to argue their position before the Supreme Court of the United States. Webster was one of the greatest constitutional scholars of his time, arguing 223 cases before the Supreme Court, earning the nickname the "Great Expounder of the Constitution."[63]

Webster argued that the New Hampshire legislature had violated the Contract Clause of the Constitution by passing a law "impairing the Obligation of Contracts." Article I, Section 10 of the Constitution provides in pertinent part:

"No State shall . . . pass any Bill of Attainder, ex post facto Law, or Law impairing the Obligation of Contracts, or grant any Title of Nobility."[64]

---

63. For an article about those appearing frequently before the Supreme Court, see *Meet the lawyers who argued more than 100 cases before high court, available at https://www.chicagolawbulletin.com/archives/2017/07/31/lawyers-100-cases-7-31-17*

64. U.S. Constitution, Article I., Section 10.

Webster and his team asserted that the state legislature through its action had taken property rights from one group and given them to another group, in violation of the Contract Clause. Webster purportedly ended his oral argument with the statement:

> "It is, Sir, as I have said, a small college. And yet there are those who love it!"[65]

The Supreme Court ruled in favor of the Trustees by a 5-1 vote. In the decision written by Chief Justice John Marshall, the Court found that the college charter was a contract and that the charter made it clear Dartmouth College was a private entity and not a public one. Marshall's opinion held that the Contract Clause was drafted to prevent states from taking actions directed at private property, and that the charter of Dartmouth College was a contract between New Hampshire (the successor to the King) and the college, which was protected from legislative interference. Marshall went on to describe the details of how a corporation functions:

> A corporation is an artificial being, invisible, intangible, and existing only in contemplation of law. Being the mere creature of law, it possesses only those properties which the charter of its creation confers upon it

---

65. "Peroration, The Dartmouth College Case," March 10, 1818, Source: Stewmaker, 168–69, available at https://www.dartmouth.edu/~dwebster/speeches/dartmouth-peroration.html.

either expressly or as incidental to its very existence. These are such as are supposed best calculated to effect the object for which it was created. Among the most important are immortality, and, if the expression may be allowed, individuality—properties by which a perpetual succession of many persons are considered as the same, and may act as a single individual. They enable a corporation to manage its own affairs and to hold property without the perplexing intricacies, the hazardous and endless necessity, of perpetual conveyances for the purpose of transmitting it from hand to hand. It is chiefly for the purpose of clothing bodies of men, in succession, with these qualities and capacities that corporations were invented, and are in use. By these means, a perpetual succession of individuals are capable of acting for the promotion of the particular object like one immortal being. But this being does not share in the civil government of the country, unless that be the purpose for which it was created.[66]

Almost two hundred years later, Justice John Paul Stevens cited some of this language in his dissent in *Citizens United v. Federal Election Commission,* in arguing that corporations, as artificial entities, did not have the right to invoke First Amendment protections.

---

66. *Trustees of Dartmouth Coll. v. Woodward,* 17 U.S. 518, 623–37 (1819).

Associate Justice Joseph Story in his concurring opinion asserted that a state legislature could insert reservation clauses into corporate charters that would permit the state to amend a particular charter.

The *Dartmouth College* decision was a landmark one because it imposed a significant constitutional limitation on states' authority to intervene in and change state charters and contracts. The case significantly strengthened the Contract Clause and encouraged economic growth.

Marshall and Slavery and the Future of the Union

Marshall was born and raised in Virginia and was a slaveholder; yet, he was also in favor of abolition. Marshall grew more concerned about the fate of the United States with the issue of slavery dividing the nation. In 1823, he became the first president of the Richmond branch of the American Colonization Society. The society's goal and purpose were to relocate the freed American slaves to Liberia. Toward the end of his tenure as chief justice, a combination of slavery and President Andrew Jackson's defiance of Supreme Court orders caused Marshall a great deal of despair. On September 22, 1832, he wrote friend and colleague Joseph Story:

> I yield slowly and reluctantly to the conviction that our constitution cannot last. I had supposed that north of the Potowmack a firm and solid government competent to the security of rational liberty might be preserved.

Even that now seems doubtful. The case of the south seems to me to be desperate. Our opinions are incompatible with a united government even among ourselves. The union has been prolonged thus far by miracles. I fear they cannot continue.[67]

On October 6, 1834, the last year of Marshall's life, he sent another letter to Story, lamenting the weakening union and presidents openly ignoring the federal government and law.

Marshall's Tenure

Marshall served longer than any other chief justice in the history of the Supreme Court of the United States, at thirty-four years, 152 days. In that time, Marshall served under six U.S. Presidents:

- John Adams;
- Thomas Jefferson;
- James Madison;
- James Monroe;
- John Quincy Adams; and
- Andrew Jackson.

Marshall administered the presidential oath at nine inaugurations, more than any other chief justice. (Roger Taney,

---

67. Beveridge, Vol. 4, p. 559 (quoting letter from Marshall to Story).

who succeeded Marshall as chief justice and is the second longest serving chief justice in the Supreme Court's history, presided over seven. On several other occasions, someone else administered the oath.)

Marshall referred to the Constitution as a living one. In his decisions, he reflected that approach, establishing the rule of law and the jurisdiction of not only the Supreme Court, but the entire Article III judiciary.

Death and Legacy

On July 6, 1835, John Marshall died in Philadelphia, Pennsylvania, while there for medical treatment. Legend has it that the Liberty Bell rang during his funeral procession and that is when it cracked, but the story likely is false, as no contemporary newspaper column reported this. In his will, Marshall offered his elderly manservant, Robin, the choice of freedom and moving to Liberia or his continued enslavement. The elderly Robin chose to remain a slave to Marshall's daughter.[68]

Alexis de Tocqueville recognized the incredible work that the Marshall Court had done and its lasting impact on the United States, writing:

> The peace, the prosperity, and the very existence of the Union are vested in the hands of the seven judges. Without their active co-operation the Constitution

---

68. Brookhser, p. 258.

would be a dead letter; the Executive appeals to them against the encroachments of the legislative powers; the Legislature demands their protection from the designs of the Executive; they defend the Union from the disobedience from the States, the States from the exaggerated claims of the Union, the public interest against the interests of private citizens, and the conservative spirit of order against fleeting innovations of democracy. Their power is enormous, but it is clothed in the authority of public opinion. They are the all-powerful guardians of a people which respects law, but they would be impotent against popular neglect or popular contempt. The force of public opinion is the most intractable of agents, because its exact limits cannot be defined; and it is not less dangerous to exceed than to remain below the boundary prescribed. The Federal judges must not only be good citizens, and men possessed of that information and integrity which are indispensable to magistrates, but they must be statesmen—politicians, not unread in the signs of the times, not afraid to brave the obstacles which can be subdued, nor slow to turn aside such encroaching elements as may threaten the supremacy of the Union and the obedience which is due to the laws.[69]

---

69. De Tocqueville, available at https://www.marxists.org/reference/archive /de-tocqueville/democracy-america/ch08.htm.

In the last year of his life, President John Adams, who had appointed John Marshall, stated, "My gift of John Marshall to the people of the United States was the proudest act of my life."[70] Heady words from someone who had done much and accomplished much in his lifetime. His good friend, Joseph Story, wrote a poem a few months after Marshall passed, beginning with the lines:

> To Marshall reared—the great, the good, the wise,
>   Born for all ages, honored in all skies;
> His was the fame to mortals rarely given,
>   Begun on earth but fixed in aim on Heaven.
> Genius and learning and consummate skill,
>   Moulding each thought, obedient to will . . .[71]

Some minor difference of opinion existed about Marshall. For example, the Democratic editor of the *New York Evening Post* took the occasion of Marshall's passing to reflect on what he saw as Marshall's overly granting of powers to the government:

> [A]t the same time we cannot so far lose sight of those great principles of government which we consider essential to the permanent prosperity of man, as to neglect the occasion offered by the death of Judge Marshall to express our satisfaction that the enormous

---

70. Supreme Court Historical Society, available at http://supremecourthistory.org/timeline_court_marshall.html.
71. Beveridge, Vol. 4, p. 592.

powers of the Supreme tribunal of the country will no longer be exercised by one whose cardinal maxim in politics inculcated distrust of popular intelligence and virtue, and whose constant object, in the decision of all constitutional questions, was to strengthen government at the expense of the people. . . .[72]

That critique was and remains a small minority view of Marshall. When a bronze statue of Marshall was unveiled by Chief Justice Morrison Waite in 1884, Waite paid tribute to Marshall:

Comparatively nothing had been done judicially to define the powers or develop the resources of the Constitution. . . .

As year after year went by and new occasion required, with his irresistible logic, enforced by his cogent English, he developed the hidden treasures of the Constitution, demonstrated its capacities, and showed beyond all possibility of doubt, that a government rightfully administered under its authority could protect itself and against the world.

Hardly a day now passes in the court he so dignified and adored, without reference to some decision of its

---

72. Warren, Vol. 1, pgs. 809–10.

time, as establishing a principle which, from that day to this, has been accepted as undoubted law. . . .[73]

John Marshall is considered the "Father of the Supreme Court." While not the first chief justice, his rulings in various matters made the Court supreme. I have asked my students in SCOTUS Judicial Biography if you took away his top three or four decisions, would Marshall still be considered great? The response has been that, like a rock band or actor, it is impossible to not consider these huge constitutional hits in the consideration of his legacy. Many of the matters facing the Marshall Court were ones of first impression, with various provisions and issues tested for the first time. The Marshall Court tackled such matters and delivered decisions that gave guidance and affirmation to our Constitution. Many Supreme Court scholars point to his opinion in *Marbury v. Madison* as his greatest, but others refer to *McCulloch v. Maryland*. According to one of Marshall's biographers, Alfred Beveridge, the *McCulloch* case "was the first in importance and in the place it holds in the development of the American Constitution."[74]

In the last case that John Marshall participated in, *Mitchell v. United States,*[75] he reiterated the role of the judiciary and how they must go about their business of deciding cases. Chief Justice Marshall stated:

---

73. Waite et al., pgs. 16–18.
74. Beveridge, Vol. 4, p. 282.
75. *Mitchell v. United States,* 34 U.S. 711 (1835).

"Though the hope of deciding causes to the mutual satisfaction of parties would be chimerical, that of convincing them that the case has been fully and fairly considered, that due attention has been given to the arguments of counsel, and that the best judgment of the court has been exercised on the case, may be sometimes indulged. Even this is not always attainable. In the excitement produced by ardent controversy, gentlemen view the same object through such different media, that minds not unfrequently receive therefrom precisely opposite impressions. The court however must see with its own eyes, and exercise its own judgment guided, by its own reason."[76]

The great chief would not speak again from the bench.

Part of Marshall's legacy may be that in the years before Marshall sat in the chair as chief justice, little of substance was submitted to, or decided by, the Supreme Court of the United States. Perhaps too the timing of his appointment early in our nation's history and his early experiences in the Revolutionary War, at the Virginia ratifying convention and as a diplomat, also influence the esteem that he continues to receive. Finally, potentially his decisions and legacy are bolstered by the court that followed, the Taney Court, which whatever else it may have done has

---

76. *Mitchell*, 34 U.S. 711, 723.

the legacy of the *Dred Scott v. Sandford* decision marring it. But he is considered the greatest chief justice for a reason. Because he was. According to www.historynet.com, John Marshall is one of the nine greatest justices who have served on the Supreme Court; the site groups Marshall with Chief Justices Charles Evans Hughes and Earl Warren as the "Three Game Changers."[77] The Oyez Project begins its biography of the fourth chief justice:

> John Marshall is one of the most influential justices to have served on the Supreme Court of the United States, if not the most influential.[78]

It is hard to argue with that categorization. Marshall set the tone and gave the Supreme Court the final word on questions involving our government and the U.S. Constitution. Without his tenure, the Supreme Court would just be the "Court." As has been stated: "When Marshall was appointed Chief Justice of the United States in 1801 the office was of dubious prominence and uncertain duration. . . . By the time of Marshall's death in 1835, however, the office of Supreme Court Justice had become a major source of power in American government."[79]

---

77. *See* chapters on Hughes and Warren, *infra*.
78. https://www.oyez.org/justices/john_marshall.
79. White, Marshall Court, p. 292.

The current chief justice, John Roberts, answered a question about "who were the most important [Chief Justices] in shaping the Courts over the years" by answering:

> "Well, of course, there's one that stands out above all the rest. We call him the 'Great Chief,' and that's John Marshall. He really was the first person to take the job seriously. . . . He served in it for three decades, and he's responsible for establishing the principle that the Court has the authority and the responsibility to review acts of Congress for constitutionality. So he really established the Court in a prominent position as one of the three co-equal branches of government."[80]

As The John Marshall Law School professor Samuel R. Olken, an expert on John Marshall among other Supreme Court matters and a great historian of the nation and Supreme Court, has stated about Marshall:

> "Through the confluence of institutional change, the opportunity for the Court to decide numerous constitutional issues of seminal importance and his own extraordinary ability to draw upon the intellectual talents of his colleagues, John Marshall transformed the Supreme Court into a powerful and respected bastion of judicial review. For these reasons, his is the Chief Justiceship by which all others are measured;

---

80. Lamb et al., p. 4.

therein lies the special significance of his name and its close association with the majesty of the Supreme Court."[81]

John Quincy Adams perhaps summed it up best in his diary, discussing the concern raised when John Marshall passed:

He has held this appointment thirty five years. It was the last act of my father's administration, and one of the most important services rendered by him to his country. All constitutional governments are flexible things; and as the Supreme Judicial court is the tribunal of last resort for the construction of the Constitution and the laws, the office of Chief Justice of that Court is a station of the highest trust, of the deepest responsibility, and of influence far more extensive than that of the President of the United States. The Associate Judges from the time of his appointment have generally been taken from the Democratic or Jeffersonian party. Not one of them, excepting Story, has been a man of great ability. Several of them have been men of strong prejudices, warm passions, and contracted minds; one of them, occasionally insane. Marshall, by the ascendancy of his genius, by the amenity of his deportment, and by the imperturbable command of his temper, has given a permanent and systematic

---

81. Olken, pgs. 743, 745.

character to the decisions of the Court, and settled many great constitutional questions favorably to the continuance of the Union. Marshall has cemented the Union which the crafty and quixotic democracy of Jefferson had a perpetual tendency to dissolve. Jefferson hated and dreaded him. . . . It is much to be feared that a successor will be appointed of a very different character. The President of the United States now in office, has already appointed three Judges of the Supreme Court; with the next appointment, he will have constituted the Chief Justice and a majority of the Court. He has not yet made one good appointment. His Chief Justice will be no better than the rest.[82]

Adams would not have long to wait to see who Jefferson picked.

---

82. Warren, Vol. 2, pgs. 2–3.

Part Three

A Peculiar Institution, a Nation Divided, a Civil War

Up until the Taney Court, only one major case concerning slavery, *The Antelope*, had been heard by the Supreme Court of the United States. Yet, the nation had addressed the issue through its elections, through its laws, and through the growing tensions between slaveholding states and free states. Congress entered into a number of compromises as the nation expanded and states and territories were added. Taney's tenure as chief justice would see the Court contribute to the divide. Taney, who believed he and the other members of the Court were addressing the issue and calming the tensions when it issued its *Dred Scott* decision, got it wrong. The nation would almost sever, and a brutally bloody Civil War erupted.

Chapter Seven

Roger B. Taney: One Decision Makes a Legacy

Nominated by President Andrew Jackson
Confirmed by Senate, 29-15, on March 15, 1836
Tenure: March 28, 1836 to October 12, 1864 (Died)
Presidents During Tenure
  Jackson
  Van Buren
  Harrison
  Tyler
  Polk
  Taylor
  Fillmore
  Pierce
  Buchanan
  Lincoln

Chief Justice John Marshall, the nation's fourth, served thirty-four and a half years in that role. Roger B. Taney, who succeeded Marshall, served for twenty-eight and a half years. The two are the first and second longest serving chief justices.[1] *Taney's tenure would be marked by continued national struggles over the institute of slavery, and his Court's decision in Dred Scott has not only been assailed as wrongly decided but also an event that helped contribute to the South's secession from the Union and Civil War. During his last years on the court, he was a nemesis of President Abraham Lincoln. Contemporaries and future judges and legal scholars consider Taney to be a decent judge, but his legacy is tarnished and reduced significantly because of Dred Scott.*

Early Life and Career

Roger Brooke Taney was born in Calvert County in southern Maryland on March 17, 1777.[2] He was raised Catholic by his parents, Michael and Monica.[3] Michael was a tobacco plantation owner[4] who was the fifth Michael in the Taney line, a family that had come to Calvert County around 1660.[5] Michael also served as a first lieutenant in the Maryland state militia.[6] At the time of Taney's birth,

---

1. Cotter, "Taney: The first Catholic U.S. Supreme Court justice." Some narrative of this chapter is also based on the same article.
2. Cushman, p. 116.
3. *Id.*
4. *Id.*
5. Swisher, p. 3.
6. *Id.* at 4.

Catholics in America represented a distinct religious minority. Until Taney was 15 years old, his education consisted of private schools and tutors, and then he entered Dickinson College, obtaining his bachelor's degree in 1795 as his class valedictorian.[7]

Taney chose a career in law, reading law at the law office of Jeremiah Townley Chase, a chief justice of the General Court of Maryland.[8] At the time Taney read law at Chase's office, the General Court "was an institution of great importance."[9] In 1799, Taney was admitted to the bar and set up shop in Annapolis, "trying to find enough work to justify his remaining there, but with little success."[10]

Taney was elected to the Maryland House of Representatives the same year he became a member of the bar and served one term before returning to private practice after losing reelection. The seat he held in the state house was one his dad held just before him.[11]

Around the time of his loss for reelection, his predecessor as chief justice, John Marshall, was beginning his long tenure as chief justice and "was building the Supreme Court into one of the most powerful institutions in the country."[12]

---

7. Cushman, p. 116.
8. *Id.*
9. Swisher, p. 25.
10. *Id.* at 30.
11. *Id.* at 31.
12. *Id.* at 39.

Taney originally was a Federalist, but because of the War of 1812 controversy in Maryland, the Federalists splintered and Taney became aligned with the "Coodies" and became the "King Coody."[13] He supported Federalist positions "such as a national bank" but "also believed in states' rights, particularly on the issue of slavery."[14] Taney had emancipated slaves he inherited from his father, but his states' rights views were clear on slavery—Taney "believed the federal government had no right to limit the institution of slavery and that questions involving slavery should be resolved by individual states."[15]

He married Anne Key—a sister of "The Star-Spangled Banner" author and lawyer Francis Scott Key—in 1806, and the couple had seven children. Of the seven children, the only boy died when he was three years old and would have been the only child of the Taneys to be raised Catholic like his father.[16]

Considered one of the promising young lawyers in Maryland, Taney fluctuated between governmental service and private practice over the course of his career. Despite originally being a Federalist, Taney strongly supported Andrew Jackson and left the Federalists to become

---

13. Cushman, p. 117. The Coodies derived their name from an individual, Abimelech Coody. Swisher, p. 61.

14. Cushman, p. 117.

15. Id.

16. Swisher, pgs. 101–02.

a Democrat.[17] From 1816 to 1821, Taney served in the Maryland Senate.[18]

After a very successful law practice, Taney was elected Maryland attorney general in 1827.[19] In 1831, he resigned from his state position to become acting secretary of war for a short period before taking another Cabinet post as attorney general of the United States. The appointment was well received by the local Virginia and Maryland press, with one paper excitedly stating:

> "A lawyer surpassed by none in the country, a gentleman whose name is identified where it has been heard, with everything that is pure and elevated in character, a ripe scholar. . . ."[20]

Views on Slavery

Despite providing manumission to his slaves and also defending slaves in a case during his career, Taney was an anti-abolitionist, and as attorney general, he expressed his views in two opinions that were consistent with subsequent decisions he wrote as chief justice of the Supreme Court, including the *Dred Scott* decision. In a case involving a South Carolina law that required that free negroes

17. Cushman, p. 117.
18. Swisher, p. 120.
19. Cushman, p. 117.
20. Swisher, p. 141.

on foreign ships coming into port be seized, Taney asserted slave states had the right to protect themselves against laws that would result in the importation of free negroes, stating in his opinion:[21]

> The African race in the United States even when free, are everywhere a degraded class, and exercise no political influence. The privileges they are allowed to enjoy are accorded to them as a matter of kindness and benevolence rather than of right. . . . They were not looked upon as citizens by the contracting parties who formed the Constitution. They were evidently not supposed to be included by the term citizens. And were not intended to be embraced in any provisions of the Constitution but those which point to them in terms not to be mistaken.[22]

"In this fashion Taney stated his doctrine as to the social and legal position of negroes in the United States, the doctrine which was to be hotly condemned twenty-five years later when announced in his opinion in the *Dred Scott* case."[23] His argument in the South Carolina matter was that

---

21. For an excellent analysis of the May 28, 1832 opinion from Taney to Livingston, *see* Powell, pgs. 83–90, and then a supplemental memo from Taney, available at http://www.greenbag.org/v5n1/v5n1_from_the_bag_powell.pdf.

22. Taheny,p. 55, available at http://ecommons.luc.edu/luc_theses/390.

23. Swisher, p. 154.

"a legislature was the sole judge as to the proper exercise of the powers which belonged to it."[24]

Failed Nomination to Treasury Secretary

In 1833, President Andrew Jackson nominated Taney for Treasury Secretary, but the Senate eventually rejected his nomination, at least in part due to the divisive nature of his views on slavery. In addition, Taney had "been employed at the Union Bank as an attorney"[25] and also had views that were at odds with the banking industry, who worked diligently to make sure Taney's nomination was rejected.[26] President Jackson had delayed formally submitting Taney to the Senate for confirmation for nine months, during which time Taney held the position and was instrumental in the demise of the National Bank of the United States, demanding all funds be withdrawn from the bank and "sealing the bank's fate."[27] Following his defeat for Secretary of the Treasury, Taney returned to private practice in Maryland. Things were tough for Taney as he had given up his private practice when he was working as Secretary of the

---

24. *Id*. at 155.
25. Cushman, p. 118.
26. Swisher, pgs. 286–87.
27. Cushman, p. 118.

Treasury[28] and his work with trying to close the Bank of the United States made him no friends.

Supreme Court Nomination

A defiant President Jackson next nominated Taney in January 1835 for the position of associate justice to replace the retiring Associate Justice Gabriel Duvall.[29] On January 15, 1835, Jackson submitted Taney's nomination to the Senate.[30] Taney was respected and "had friends among the respectable conservatives of the country, including Chief Justice Marshall," who sent Senator Benjamin Watkins Leigh a note informing the senator Marshall had positive information regarding Taney.[31] The Senate rejected the nomination by "postponing its decision indefinitely after a close vote"[32] of 24 to 21.[33]

When John Marshall died after a stagecoach accident in early July 1835, President Jackson did not disclose whom he would nominate to fill the vacancy of chief justice, but many believed that it would be Taney.[34] On December 28, 1835,

---

28. But apparently not while he was attorney general. That would not be tolerated in current times.

29. When Taney read law at Chase's office, Duvall was a judge on the same General Court and Taney became friends with Duvall. Swisher, p. 27.

30. Swisher, p. 312.

31. *Id.* at 313.

32. Cushman, p. 118.

33. Swisher, p. 314.

34. Warren, Vol. 2, p. 10.

Jackson submitted Taney's name for chief justice.[35] Taney was confirmed after a long and heated opposition by a close Senate vote- 29-15, on March 15, 1836.[36] Many senators were not present, as other matters occupied the Senators, and "the *National Intelligencer* lamented the fact that the lateness of the hour had prevented fuller attendance."[37] Taney

---

35. Swisher, p. 317.

36. Cushman, p. 118. Of the seventeen chiefs, several have been confirmed by acclamation (Jay, Marshall, Chase, White, Taft, Stone, Vinson, and Warren). Of the remainder, one was outright rejected by the Senate (Rutledge). Of the eight who were confirmed by the Senate, Taney's small margin of votes in favor of his nomination is the closest vote for chief justice. Of the Supreme Court justices whose Senate confirmation votes are recorded, Taney's margin of fourteen votes ranked eighth all-time in closest Senate votes. The closest margin in history was one vote (24-23) for Stanley Matthews, President James Garfield's lone Supreme Court nomination. In what is a huge anomaly or telling statement about the politics involved in the process in the late twentieth and early twenty-first centuries, four of the top ten closest margins of victory are for justices who sit on the Court presently:

- Second place—Brett Kavanaugh—50-48
- Fourth place (tied) all-time—Clarence Thomas—52-48
- Sixth place—Neil Gorsuch—54-45
- Ninth place—Samuel Alito—58-42

The list of the ten closest margins where Senate recorded votes and nominees confirmed were (current bolded):

1. Stanley Matthews- 1
2. **Brett Kavanaugh- 2**
3. Nathan Clifford- 3
4. Lucius Quintus Cincinnatus Lamar II- 4
5. **Clarence Thomas- 4 (tied for 4th)**
6. **Neil Gorsuch- 9**
7. John Catron- 13
8. Roger B. Taney- 14
9. **Samuel Alito- 16**
10. Philip Pendleton Barbour- 19

37. Swisher, p. 322.

was very partisan and President Jackson rewarded his "partisan warrior who helped [him] kill the Bank of the United States."[38]

The fact that after the 1834 elections, Jacksonian Democrats controlled the Senate represents a key distinction between this final nomination and Taney's previous failed nominations for public office and likely led to his long-awaited successful confirmation. Taney was officially sworn in on March 28, 1836,[39] and presided until his death on October 12, 1864. Taney's initial work as chief justice had him on circuit in the Fourth Circuit, hearing cases there. On January 9, 1837, "Taney sat with his brethren of the Supreme Court for the first time."[40]

Jackson thought very highly of Taney and looked often to him for advice and guidance, all the way through the end of his Presidency. Jackson asked for Taney's help in drafting Jackson's farewell speech, which Taney did. The speech revealed much of Taney's thinking, which was released on March 4, 1837.[41] Among other things, the farewell speech "urged that citizens of every state studiously avoid everything calculated to wound the sensibility or offend the just pride of the people of other states."[42]

---

38. Schermerhorn, available at https://www.cnbc.com/2018/09/28/supreme -court-difficult-nominations-have-led-to-historical-injustices.html?__source =sharebar%7Cemail&par=sharebar.

39. Swisher, p. 325.

40. *Id*. at 358.

41. *Id*. at 335.

42. *Id*. at 336.

The Taney Court

When Taney began his tenure as chief justice of the Supreme Court of the United States, the Court was held in "relatively high prestige" that had been "acquired for the most part during the years when John Marshall was Chief Justice."[43] The Taney Court issued a series of decisions that substantially narrowed the role of federal government in economic regulation. Unlike Marshall, he and other Jackson Supreme Court appointees favored the powers of the states over the powers of the federal government.

The Taney Court also issued opinions in a number of noteworthy cases, such as the *Charles River Bridge* and *Amistad* cases. The *Charles River Bridge* case[44] was decided during Taney's first term as chief justice but had come before the Court six years earlier so still had to be decided.[45] The Taney Court decided cases in a variety of areas, with three major groups dominating his Court: (1) rights of corporations, (2) the Commerce Clause of the U.S. Constitution, and (3) questions of property and slavery.[46]

Despite the longevity of Taney as chief justice and the various developments in law the Taney Court made, the Taney Court is remembered most for the 1857 decision in *Dred Scott v. Sandford*,[47] holding by a 7-2 margin that

---

43. Swisher, p. 347.
44. *Charles River Bridge v. Warren Bridge*, 11 Peters 420 (1837).
45. Swisher, p. 361.
46. *Id.* at 351–52.
47. *Dred Scott v. Sandford*, 60 U.S. 393 (1857).

Congress had no authority or power to prevent the spread of slavery into federal territories and that, at the time of the country's founding, African Americans were not U.S. citizens nor was such citizenship contemplated.

One justice, Benjamin Robbins Curtis, was so upset by the decision that he left the bench, the first and only justice known to have resigned on principle.

Roger Taney's legacy was made by the *Dred Scott* decision. When the U.S. House of Representatives passed a bill in 1865 to commission funds for a bust of Taney to be placed in the Supreme Court along with his predecessors, Senator Charles Sumner argued against it, calling the *Dred Scott* decision "more thoroughly abominable than anything of the kind in the history of the courts."

Taney, the twenty-fourth justice and fifth chief, was the first of thirteen Catholic justices. Currently, five of nine justices are Catholic.

Dred Scott Decision[48]

Dred Scott was born into slavery in Virginia around 1799 but was moved to Missouri where he was sold to Dr. John Emerson, an army surgeon. Given Dr. Emerson's military career, he moved frequently and took Scott with him.

---

48. Much of the narrative in this section originally appeared in Constituting America's 90 Day Study: A History of Our Country's Judicial System. Cotter, *Dred Scott v. Sandford (1857)*, available at http://constitutingamerica.org/dred -scott-v-sandford-1857-guest-essayist-daniel-a-cotter.

Eventually, Dr. Emerson moved with Scott to the State of Illinois and the Territory of Wisconsin, both free territories. While in the Wisconsin Territory, Scott married Harriett Robinson, another slave who was also sold to Dr. Emerson. In 1838, Dr. Emerson married Eliza Irene Sandford from St. Louis. In 1843, Dr. Emerson died shortly after returning to his family from the Seminole War in Florida. His slaves continued to work for Mrs. Emerson and were, as was common at the time, occasionally hired out to others. In 1846, Dred and Harriet Scott each filed suit in St. Louis to obtain their freedom, on the basis that they had lived in a free state and territory, and the rule in Missouri and some other jurisdictions at the time was "once free, always free." When the suit reached the Supreme Court of the United States, the main issue presented was whether slaves had standing to sue in federal courts.

Background of the Case

Numerous precedents in Missouri case law, including *Rachael v. Walker* (1837) established the legal principle of "once free, always free." The judge declared a mistrial when the case was heard in 1847, and when it was retried in 1850, the St. Louis court ordered Dred Scott free—the Scotts agreed that only Dred's case would proceed in order to save money and avoid duplicate efforts and all parties agreed that the outcome of Dred's case would also apply to Harriet. In *Scott v. Emerson* (1852), the Missouri Supreme Court decided against Scott, reversing the lower court decision, and noting that Missouri law would not be subject to outside antislavery arguments. By its decision, the Missouri Supreme Court overturned the long-held principle of "once free, always free." The Missouri Supreme Court explained its decision in stark terms and why it was overruling precedents:

> Times are not now as they were when the former decisions on this subject were made. Since then not only individuals but States have been possessed with a dark and fell spirit in relation to slavery, whose gratification is sought in the pursuit of measures, whose inevitable consequences must be the overthrow and destruction of our government.

The Controversy

Seeking to have the Supreme Court of the United States opine on the legality of Missouri's invalidation of the "once free, always free" principle, Scott's attorneys filed a new suit in federal court, *Dred Scott v. John F. A. Sandford* (Sanford's name was misspelled due to a clerical error).

The U.S. District Court for the District of Missouri directed the jury to consider the question of whether Scott was free, or a slave based on Missouri law. Based on the *Emerson* decision, the jury found that Scott was a slave.

The Supreme Court Decision

Scott appealed to the Supreme Court. Initially, the Supreme Court was inclined to affirm the Missouri Supreme Court decision based on *Strader v. Graham (1851)*, a decision of the Supreme Court allowing the Court to affirm a state supreme court decision without hearing it on the merits. However, some of the justices suggested that the Supreme Court address issues that until then remained unresolved, including those that Sanford's attorneys raised during the federal lawsuit, such as Scott's ability to sue in federal court and whether a black person could be a citizen of the United States. The main issue before the Supreme Court was whether Scott had ever been free.

The case originally was argued on February 11–14, 1856, but the justices were divided on their views and with the presidential election of 1856 coming, Taney "was doubtless relieved, when [Associate Justice] Samuel Nelson, declaring himself in doubt on certain points, requested that the case be reargued."[49] Taney granted Nelson's request, and the rehearing took place on December 15–18, 1856, after the election was over.

After the oral arguments, and when President-elect Buchanan visited Washington prior to his inauguration, Buchanan wrote Justice John Catron, "asking him whether the Dred Scott case would be decided before the date of

49. Swisher, p. 489.

inauguration."[50] Catron inquired and informed Buchanan the case was to be decided at the next conference.[51] Buchanan also wrote to Justice Robert Cooper Grier, attempting to influence his position and have him vote as a Northerner with the majority.[52]

Delivered on March 6, 1857, the Court, by a 7-2 decision, held that blacks were not and could not be citizens of the United States and, as a result, Scott lacked standing to sue in federal courts. The Court also found that Scott had never been free, finding that Congress exceeded its authority when it forbade or abolished slavery in the territories, invalidating the Missouri Compromise. Having found a lack of standing, this second issue should not have been addressed by the Court. Chief Justice Roger Taney wrote for the majority:

> In discussing this question, we must not confound the rights of citizenship which a State may confer within its own limits and the rights of citizenship as a member of the Union. It does not by any means follow, because he has all the rights and privileges of a citizen of a State, that he must be a citizen of the United States. He may have all of the rights and privileges of the citizen of a State and yet not be entitled to the rights and

---

50. *Id.* at 495.
51. *Id.* at 496.
52. *Id.* at 501–02.

privileges of a citizen in any other State. For, previous to the adoption of the Constitution of the United States, every State had the undoubted right to confer on whomsoever it pleased the character of citizen, and to endow him with all its rights. But this character, of course, was confined to the boundaries of the State, and gave him no rights or privileges in other States beyond those secured to him by the laws of nations and the comity of States.[53]

The *Dred Scott* decision is a landmark decision because it answered questions regarding slavery that the Court had not previously addressed. It is also one of the most infamous decisions, furthering the great divide facing the nation regarding the question of slavery and moving the country further down the path toward the Civil War. The *Dred Scott* decision undermined the prestige of the Supreme Court and virtually all legal scholars consider it to be the worst decision ever issued by the Supreme Court. The *Dred Scott* decision was overturned when the Civil War ended, and the Civil War Amendments were ratified. However, the *Dred Scott* decision began a long period of time where the Supreme Court "declined in popular esteem."[54] The decision should not have surprised much, given the "Taney

---

53. *Dred Scott v. Sandford*, 60 U.S. 393, 405 (1857).
54. Magrath, p. 4.

Court was staunchly pro-slavery, rejecting states' rights when Northerners asserted them to oppose slavery."[55]

Legacy

The *Dred Scott* decision, rather than eliminating slavery as a national issue of debate, angered Northeners and strengthened the Republican Party, which was anti-slavery. In 1860, Abraham Lincoln won the presidency, and secession ensued by the southern states. Taney remained on the Court, taking the position that the states had a right to secede and also blaming the Republicans and especially Lincoln for starting the war. Taney and Lincoln would butt heads for the remaining time that Taney was on the Supreme Court and, in *Ex parte Merryman*,[56] Taney held that power to suspend habeas corpus resided in Congress and a president had no power to do so. The *Merryman* decision was one that Taney filed with a federal circuit court and not as a Supreme Court justice. Toward the end of the Civil War, in 1863, the Supreme Court held in the *Prize Cases*[57] that President Lincoln had the power to order a blockade and seize ships, with Chief Justice Taney dissenting.

---

55. Schermerhorn, https://www.cnbc.com/2018/09/28/supreme-court-difficult-nominations-have-led-to-historical-injustices.html?_source=sharebar%7Cemail&par=sharebar.

56. *Ex parte Merryman*, 17 F. Cas. 144 (1861).

57. *Prize Cases*, 67 U.S. 635 (1863).

Taney died on October 12, 1864, aged 87.

As noted, the decision issued by the Taney Court in *Dred Scott* has (fairly) cast a large shadow on the legacy and lasting reputation of Taney. His tenure as chief justice of the Supreme Court "started and ended" with "sharp and lingering controversy."[58] According to Stevens, the only good to come from the decision was Abraham Lincoln criticizing it and "helped get him elected president of the United States."[59] But contemporaries were divided on the decision, and despite his dissent in *Dred Scott,* Curtis referred to Taney as a "man of singular purity of life and character." More recently, Justice Antonin Scalia, in his dissent in *Planned Parenthood v. Casey,* referring to Taney's "great Chief Justiceship," apparently agreed with Curtis.

Chief Justice Charles Evans Hughes once wrote an essay for the *ABA Journal* entitled *"Roger Brooke Taney: A Great Chief Justice."*[60] Jackson wrote:

> It is unfortunate that the estimate of Chief Justice Taney's judicial labors should have been so largely influenced by the opinion which he delivered in the case of *Dred Scott.* ... [T]he *Dred Scott* cased passed into history as an event pregnant with political consequences of the highest importance, and having a most serious effect upon the prestige of the Court. . . .

58. Siegel, Vol. 3, p. 241.
59. Stevens, p. 20.
60. Choper, article reprinted at pages 53–63 from 1931.

Nothing could be more unjust than to estimate the judicial work of the days of Taney by a disproportionate emphasis upon the decisions which were called forth by the vexed questions growing out of the institution of slavery and the prospect of its extension. Rather I should like to take this opportunity to recognize the importance services of Chief Justice Taney in setting forth principles that are guiding stars in constitutional interpretation. . . .[61]

Notwithstanding those comments and praise, Taney will forever be remembered for the *Dred Scott* decision. The assessment that "few Chief Justices have dominated the Court as completely as Taney. His tenure served to consolidate and refine Marshall's Federalist jurisprudence rather than dismantle it in favor of states' rights"[62] cannot overcome *Dredd Scott* and its aftermath.

---

61. *Id.* at 57–58.
62. Siegel, p. 241.

Part Four

End of a Civil War, Reconstruction of a Nation

By the time Taney died in 1864, the Civil War was near an end.[1] Days after the end of the Civil War, President Abraham Lincoln would be assassinated by John Wilkes Booth. Reconstruction was in its infancy and would last until the late 1870s.[2] The Court was about to enter into a different phase, after sixty-three years with two chief justices at the helm. As former Chief Justice William Rehnquist stated:

> "With the passing of Chief Justice Taney, the Supreme Court of the United States evolved into a significantly different institution. The dominance of Marshall and Taney during most of their sixty-three-year hegemony largely eclipsed the numerous associate justices with

---

1. The Civil War officially ended on April 9, 1865, upon surrender by General Robert E. Lee.

2. Reconstruction derived its name from President Abraham Lincoln's "Proclamation of Amnesty and Reconstruction," issued on December 3, 1863, which established a process for postwar reconstruction of the South.

whom they served. But for more than half a century following the Civil War, the four Chief Justices fell sufficiently short of the stature of Marshall and Taney as to permit, if not require, the emergence of associate justices in leadership roles."[3]

With Chase as chief justice, the president now had a majority made up of his appointees. But like presidents before (and after) Lincoln who had an ability to change the makeup of the court with his appointments, the decisions issued by the Chase Court would not always be consistent with the president who made the appointments.

During this period, the size of the Court changed. Originally made up of a chief justice and five associate justices, Congress had increased the number of justices to a total of seven in 1807 and in 1837, that number was bumped again to nine. In 1863, the total increased to ten pursuant to the Tenth Circuit Act of 1863,[4] which recognized the circuit courts of the federal judiciary. In 1866, after President Lincoln died and was replaced by President Andrew Johnson, Congress acted to shrink the size of the Supreme Court significantly, when it enacted the Judicial Circuits Act of 1866, which provided:

Be it enacted by the Senate and House of Representatives of the United States of America in Congress

3. Rehnquist, p. 70.
4. 12 Stat. 794.

assembled. That no vacancy in the office of associate justice of the supreme court shall be filled by appointment until the number of associate justices shall be reduced to six; and thereafter the said supreme court shall consist of a Chief Justice of the United States and six associate justices, any four of whom shall be a quorum; and the said court shall hold one term annually at the seat of government, and such adjourned or special terms as it may find necessary for the despatch of business.[5]

Finally, in 1869, Congress reset the size of the Supreme Court back to nine justices, where it remains to this day.[6] While President Franklin Delano Roosevelt attempted a plan to expand the size of the Supreme Court to up to fifteen justices, that effort was rejected.

5. Judicial Circuits Act of 1866, 14 Stat. 209.
6. Judiciary Act of 1869, also Circuit Judges Act of 1869, 16 Stat. 44.

Chapter Eight

Salmon P. Chase: Reconstruction and Integrating the Court

Nominated by President Abraham Lincoln
Confirmed by Senate Acclamation on
   December 6, 1864
Tenure: December 15, 1864 to May 7, 1873 (Died)
Presidents During Tenure
   Lincoln
   Johnson
   Grant

When Chief Justice Taney died in October 1864, President Lincoln followed through on his mentioning of Salmon Chase as a potential Supreme Court justice. Chase became a member of the bar in 1829, practicing in Cincinnati, Ohio, with a varied practice, including as an abolitionist attorney. Early in his career, he compiled the Statutes of Ohio and became a member of the Cincinnati City Council in 1840. In 1848, he drafted the platform of the Free Soilers Party, and was elected on its ticket to the U.S. Senate. Devoted to the cause of abolition, he was a co-founder of the Republican Party. After serving one term as senator, he became the governor of Ohio and then returned to the Senate in 1861 but resigned to become U.S. Secretary of the Treasury. He resigned that position in June 1864.

Chase became the sixth chief justice on December 6, 1864. His tenure as chief justice may be best remembered for having presided over the impeachment trial of President Andrew Johnson in 1868. In Texas v. White, 74 U.S. 700, 724 (1868), a significant case initiated by the Reconstruction government of Texas alleging illegal sale of U.S. bonds, he noted in his opinion, "The Constitution, in all its provisions, looks to an indestructible Union composed of indestructible states." Chase served as chief justice from 1864 until his death on May 7, 1873.[1]

---

1. Much of the introduction for this chapter and the next three were from an article in the *Chicago Daily Law Bulletin*, "Four chief justices spanned nearly six decades on court," *Chicago Daily Law Bulletin, Cotter's Corner,* January 27, 2015, available at https://www.chicagolawbulletin.com/archives/2015/01/27/daniel-cotter -forum-01-27-2015.

Early Life and Career

Salmon P. Chase was born on January 13, 1808,[2] to Janette Ralston and Ithamar Chase in Cornish, New Hampshire. Ithamar operated a local tavern and also a glass factory. Chase was nine when his father passed away. Chase is the great grandson of Samuel Chase, the ninth Justice of the Supreme Court of the United States, who was impeached by Congress. In perhaps a coincidence that would not be repeated, Chase presided over the impeachment hearings of President Andrew Johnson, the first president to be impeached in our nation's history.[3] Chase was the first chief justice of the Supreme Court born in the nineteenth century.

Chase's mother had ten children and so, not long after Ithamar died, Chase was sent to live with Uncle Philander Chase, a member of the Protestant Episcopal Church. After studying under his uncle, who became president of Cincinnati College, and completing Cincinnati College's two-year curriculum, Chase entered the junior class of Dartmouth College, where he graduated with distinction in 1826. Chase taught at Royalton Academy while attending Dartmouth.

Upon graduation from Dartmouth College, Chase moved to the District of Columbia, where he opened a classical

---

2. Warden, p. 18.
3. *See* pages 161–165 for details on the impeachment hearing.

school. Chase also began to study law under then-U.S. Attorney General William Wirt.[4] Chase met Wirt through his work at the school, where he taught Wirt's son.

Admitted to the bar in 1829, Chase moved to Loveland, Ohio. As a lawyer in Ohio, Chase focused on commercial law in Cincinnati. Chase married three times, each time marrying society belles, but each died early.

Chase was a strong advocate for abolition, taking a stance against the institution of slavery as early as the 1830s. Chase was "morally outraged by the treatment of slaves."[5] The actions of Chase in representing abolitionists earned him the nickname, "Attorney General for Runaway Negroes."[6] Chase's views on slavery caused him to join the Liberty Party.[7] By the late 1840s, Chase joined the Free-Soil Party.[8] Chase drafted the Free-Soil Party's platform.

---

4. William Wirt was the longest serving attorney general in U.S. history, serving in that position from November 1817 to March 1829. Wirt argued a number of important cases before the Supreme Court of the United States, including *Gibbons v. Ogden* and *McCulloch v. Maryland*.

5. Cushman, p. 192.

6. *Id.*

7. The Liberty Party was formed in 1840 and had a platform for abolition and took a position that the U.S. Constitution was an antislavery document. The Liberty Party never gained any significant traction.

8. The Free-Soil Party solely was focused on preventing the expansion of slavery into Western territories.

Argument before the Supreme Court

Chase's abolitionist work led him to argue a case before the Supreme Court of the United States, *Jones v. Van Zandt*,[9] in 1847. In *Jones*, Chase advocated the position that the federal government had no power to create slavery and that slavery could only exist by nature of local law. If a slave left a slave state and went to a state where slavery was not legal, his slavery ended, and the slave became a freeman. In *Jones* and other cases on the issue, Chase was not successful in his arguments.

Senate Service

Chase was elected as a Senator in 1848 on the Free-Soil ticket, and for the rest of his life would be involved in public service. During his first time in the U.S. Senate, Chase was an antislavery champion, along with fellow Senator Charles Sumner. Sumner and Chase were good friends. Chase strongly argued against the Compromise of 1850 and the 1854 Kansas-Nebraska Bill.

Governor of Ohio

Chase's antislavery efforts led to the creation and establishment of the Republican Party. In January 1854, he and

---

9. *Jones v. Van Zandt*, 46 U.S. 215 (1847).

Joshua Giddings drafted a manifesto, "Appeal of the Independent Democrats in Congress to the People of the United States," which *The New York Times* published on January 24, 1854. The manifesto raised the specific question of whether slavery should be permitted in Nebraska. The manifesto, signed by six members of Congress, was published in response to a bill introduced in the Senate, the Kansas-Nebraska Bill, which Giddings and Chase feared revoked the Missouri Compromise. The manifesto pleaded for redress of their concerns, stating in part:

> At the present session a new Nebraska bill has been reported by the Senate Committee on Territories, which, should it unhappily receive the sanction of Congress, will open all the unorganized Territories of the Union to the ingress of slavery.

> We arraign this bill as a gross violation of a sacred pledge; as a criminal betrayal of precious rights; as part and parcel of an atrocious plot to exclude from a vast unoccupied region immigrants from the Old World and free laborers from our own States, and convert it into a dreary region of despotism, inhabited by masters and slaves.

> Take your maps, fellow citizens, we entreat you, and see what country it is which this bill gratuitously and recklessly proposes to open to slavery. . . . This immense region, occupying the very heart of the North

American Continent, and larger, by thirty-three thou-
sand square miles, than all the existing free States
including California . . . this immense region the bill
now before the Senate, without reason and without
excuse, but in flagrant disregard of sound policy and
sacred faith, purposes to open to slavery.[10]

His concerns would continue to flesh out over the next
several years, ending in Civil War.

In 1855, Chase successfully ran for Governor of Ohio,
becoming the first Republican governor of the state. Chase
was a champion of women's rights as governor. He served
four years in that role, then ran for president as a Republican, but lost the nomination to Abraham Lincoln, who
would go on to win the election later in 1860.

Chase was reelected to the U.S. Senate in 1860, and was
sworn in, but only served two days, then resigned. President
Lincoln had tapped Chase to serve as his Secretary of the
Treasury, and the Senate confirmed his role.

Secretary of the Treasury

Lincoln realized that Chase was a well-known Republican from his term in the Senate and recognized that
prominence by naming Chase Treasury Secretary. Chase
was tasked with financing the Civil War and set up methods

---

10. Appeal of the Independent Democrats in Congress to the People of the
United States, copy available at http://www.ushistory.org/gop/appeal.htm.

to do so, including obtaining short-term loans to finance the war. In addition to his Treasury duties, Chase also was involved with helping to organize the North's war efforts, "due partly to the ineffectiveness of Edwin M. Stanton, the secretary of war."[11]

Chase was not a supporter initially of issuing paper as legal tender to help pay debts, but rather supported hard money—gold or silver coin. The result was the greenback note, first issued in 1861–1862. The paper currency often had Chase's picture on it.

In addition to the "greenbacks," Chase also advocated for a national banking system, allowing for a common currency and to strengthen the Union. In Lincoln's 1864 State of the Union, President Lincoln noted, "The national system will create a reliable and permanent influence in support of the national credit and protect the people against losses in the use of paper money."[12]

Chase repeatedly offered his resignation to Lincoln, who finally agreed on June 30, 1864, taking Chase by surprise, according to his diary. Lincoln's message read:

> "Your resignation of the office of Secretary of the Treasury, sent me yesterday, is accepted. Of all I have said in commendation of your ability and fidelity, I have

---

11. Cushman, p. 193.

12. Office of the Comptroller of the Currency, *Lincoln and the Founding of the National Banking System,* available at https://www.occ.gov/about/what-we-do /history/lincoln-founding-national-banking-system.html.

nothing to unsay; and yet you and I have reached a point of mutual embarrassment in our official relation which it seems can not be overcome, or longer sustained, consistently with public service."[13]

His retirement from public service would not last long.

Nomination to Supreme Court

On October 12, 1864, Chief Justice Taney died. Taney had been ill the entire prior term and was eighty-seven years old. Lincoln now had a vacancy to fill for a position that had been occupied by only two men the past sixty-three years. Upon Taney's death, the public and press figured Lincoln would turn to his former Treasury Secretary. The *Independent* wrote, "The country expects the President to fulfill the wishes of the people by the appointment of Chase."[14] But not everyone was excited about Chase, citing his ambition for the presidency as well as his not having performed any legal work in many years. Even President Lincoln, years before Chief Justice Taney's death, noted:

> "I have only one doubt about his appointment. He is a man of unbounded ambition and has been working all his life to become President. That he can never be; and

---

13. https://abrahamlincolnandthecivilwar.wordpress.com/2014/06/30/resig nation-of-treasury-secretary-salmon-p-chase-is-accepted-washington-shocked.
14. *Independent*, October 30, 1864, quote and cite available at Warren, Vol. 2, p. 399.

I fear that if I make him Chief Justice, he will simply become more restless and uneasy, and neglect the place, in his strife and intrigue to make himself President. If I were sure that he would go on the Bench and give up his aspirations and do nothing but make himself a great Judge, I would not hesitate a moment."[15]

On December 6, 1874, President Lincoln formally nominated Chase, and the Senate confirmed Chase's nomination on the same day by acclamation. Reaction to the nomination was mostly positive, but some newspapers expressed disappointment at what was seen as another political appointee. For example, the *Boston Advertiser* noted:

"It was urged by many, and with some force, while this appointment was still in doubt, that in filling such a place, the President's choice should properly fall upon some man of legal eminence, rather than anybody whose name had long been connected with politics, and that by such a course, Mr. Lincoln might do something towards raising the Supreme Judicial tribunal of the Nation above the embittered discussion of the past few years. . . ."[16]

Chase would not use politics on the bench as some feared, but like prior administrations that had been able to reshape the makeup of the Supreme Court by the nominees,

---

15. Warren, Vol. 2, p. 400.
16. *Id*. at 407.

did not change the Court positions or outcomes in any significan way. President Lincoln would have been disappointed in the lack of "radical changes" that came from the Chase Court. Despite a five-man majority of Lincoln appointees, the Chase Court in many respects followed what had been set out by the Taney Court.

Impeachment of a President

Chase did make history during his tenure as chief justice, presiding over the first impeachment trial of a president. The impeachment was triggered by a continued struggle between the executive and legislative branches that had been going on for many years, dating at least back to President Lincoln and some of his wartime actions. In 1867, Congress passed an act, the Tenure of Office Act, over the veto of President Johnson.[17] The Tenure of Office Act, passed via veto override on March 2, 1867, accompanied two other bills that Congress enacted to curtail the power of President Johnson: (1) the (First) Reconstruction Act and (2) the Command of the Army Act. The Reconstruction Act divided the ten unreconstructed states into five military districts that were subject to martial law.[18] The second, the Command of

---

17. For a copy of the act passed by Congress, *see* https://www.senate.gov /artandhistory/history/resources/pdf/Johnson_TenureofOfficeAct.pdf; for a discussion of the Tenure of Office Act, *see, e.g.,* https://www.history.com/topics/ten ure-of-office-act.

18. Fridlington, p. 14.

the Army Act, restricted the powers of the president and his secretary of war by requiring that every army order had to be submitted through General of the Army Ulysses S. Grant and provided he could not be fired without Senate approval.[19]

The Tenure of Office Act provided that the president could not "remove subordinate officials without the consent of the Senate."[20] The Act protected certain cabinet appointments in particular, providing:

> "Provided, That the Secretaries of State, of the Treasury, of War, of the Navy, and of the Interior, the Postmaster-General, and the Attorney general, shall hold their offices respectively for and during the term of the President by whom they may have been appointed and for one month thereafter, subject to removal by and with the advice and consent of the Senate"[21]

The Act also provided that when the Senate was not in session, the president had the ability to suspend the cabinet officers. President Johnson attempted to obtain the resignation of Secretary of War Edwin Stanton, who refused to resign. On August 5, 1867, Johnson sent Stanton a note informing him that Stanton's resignation was accepted, with one problem—Stanton had not done so. When Stanton

---

19. *Id.* at 15.
20. *Id.*
21. http://teachingamericanhistory.org/library/document/tenure-of-office -act.

continued to refuse, Johnson sent him a second note, and appointed as interim Secretary of War General Grant.

On January 3, 1868, when the new Congress convened, the Senate rejected the president's action by a vote of 35-16. President Johnson rejected the Senate's decision, asserting the Act was unconstitutional.

On February 21, 1868, attempting to get the Supreme Court to rule the Act unconstitutional, Johnson appointed General Lorenzo Thomas to replace Stanton. Rather than address Johnson's actions directly, the House of Representatives took quick action to impeach Johnson. By a vote of 126-47,[22] the House voted to impeach on February 24, and a week later, the House voted eleven articles of impeachment against the president, on allegations that he had violated both the Tenure of Office Act and the Command of the Army Act.[23]

Chief Justice Chase presided over the Senate impeachment trial, pursuant to the mandate of the Constitution when the president of the United States is the one impeached, providing:

> "The Senate shall have the sole Power to try all Impeachments. When sitting for that Purpose, they shall be on Oath or Affirmation. When the President of the United States is tried, the Chief Justice shall preside:

---

22. *See* Glass, available at https://www.politico.com/story/2015/02/this-day -in-politics-115420.

23. Fridlington, p. 17.

And no Person shall be convicted without the Concurrence of two thirds of the Members present."[24]

The impeachment trial began on March 30, 1868, with
Benjamin Butler making an opening statement on behalf
of the House Managers. History shows that Butler did not
do a great job, labeling the president as accidental and only
in position because of an assassination. When the House
Managers rested, former Associate Justice Benjamin Robbins Curtis rose to give his opening statement in defense of
President Johnson, arguing that Johnson had not violated
the Tenure of Office Act and that it was unconstitutional.
Curtis, who had resigned from the Supreme Court as a matter of principle after dissenting in the *Dred Scott* case,[25]
represented the president in the hearings.

Closing arguments lasted eleven days, with the House
lawyers arguing for six days and the president's team for
five. House Manager John Bingham gave a moving final
summation, arguing:

> "May God forbid that the future historian shall record
> of this day's proceedings, that by reason of the failure
> of the legislative power of the people to triumph over
> the usurpations of an apostate President, the fabric of
> American empire fell and perished from the earth! . . .
> I ask you to consider that we stand this day pleading

---

24. U.S. Constitution, Article I, Section 3.
25. *See* Cotter, available at http://constitutingamerica.org/chief-justice-roger
-taney-1777-1864-guest-essayist-daniel-a-cotter.

for the violated majesty of the law, by the graves of half a million of martyred hero-patriots who made death beautiful by the sacrifice of themselves for their country, the Constitution and the laws, and who, by their sublime example, have taught us all to obey the law; that none are above the law; . . . and that position, however high, patronage, however powerful, cannot be permitted to shelter crime to the peril of the republic."[26]

On May 16, the Senate took a vote on the eleventh article of impeachment against Johnson, falling one vote short of the required supermajority required to convict, 35-19. Ten days later, articles two and three of impeachment were voted on and again, the vote failed by the same vote. The hearings were adjourned, and the Senate would never vote or rule on the remaining eight articles of impeachment.

Surprisingly, on one evidentiary ruling, in which Chase ruled testimony about the cabinet's advising the president the Tenure Act was unconstitutional to be admissible, he was overruled by the Senate, 29-20.[27]

Chief Justice Chase presided over the first of only two impeachments of the president of the United States in our nation's history and only the sixth impeachment at the federal level. His great grandfather, Samuel Chase, was the first and only justice of the Supreme Court to be impeached. Samuel was acquitted of charges that he had ruled with a

---

26. http://www.famous-trials.com/johnson/488-home.
27. *Id.*

political bias and in an arbitrary manner, although the Senate voted by a majority to convict Samuel on three of the eight charges against him. Samuel and Chief Justice Chase are those of only a handful of justices in the Court's history to be related.[28]

Similar laws to the Tenure of Office Act were enacted. In 1926, the Supreme Court decided *Myers v. United States*,[29] a case that involved a statute similar to the Tenure of Office Act. In *Myers*, Chief Justice Howard Taft wrote (in dicta)[30]:

> "When, on the merits, we find our conclusion strongly favoring the view which prevailed in the First Congress, we have no hesitation in holding that conclusion to be correct, and it therefore follows that the Tenure of Office Act of 1867, insofar as it attempted to prevent the President from removing executive officer who had been appointed by him by and with the advice and consent of the Senate, was invalid, and that subsequent legislation of the same effect was equally so.

---

28. The other related justices in the Court's history were:

- John Marshall Harlan and John Marshall Harlan II (grandfather/grandson)
- David Brewer and Stephen Field (nephew/uncle)
- Lucius Q.C. Lamar, Joseph R. Lamar, and John A. Campbell (cousins).

Cotter, available at https://www.chicagolawbulletin.com/archives/2016/03/02/dan-cotter-forum-03-02-16.

29. *Myers v. United States,* 272 U.S. 52 (1926).

30. The terms, dictum and dicta (plural of dictum), refer to a judge's opinion that goes beyond the facts before the court and do not embody the resolution of the actual case. Dicta are not binding on judges or citizens.

"For the reasons given, we must therefore hold that the provision of the law of 1876, by which the unrestricted power of removal of first class postmasters is denied to the President, is in violation of the Constitution, and invalid. This leads to an affirmance of the judgment of the Court of Claims"[31]

Chief Justice Chase and His Legacy

Chase took his judicial oath on December 15, 1864. Shortly after, on February 1, 1865, the first African American lawyer was admitted to the Supreme Court bar. John S. Rock was moved to admission by Senator Charles Sumner on the day after Congress submitted the Thirteenth Amendment ending slavery to the states for ratification. Rock was also a doctor, becoming one of the first African Americans to earn a medical degree. Unfortunately, Rock became sick soon after his admission to the Supreme Court bar and died less than two years later. Samuel Lowry reportedly was the first African American to argue before the Supreme Court in 1880, although no record of what case he argued is available.

The Chase Court addressed a number of important cases during Chase's tenure as chief justice. The first major decision issued likely was *Ex Parte Milligan*, 71 U.S. 2 (1866), a

---

31. *Myers*, 272 U.S. at 176.

case that addressed the question of whether a civilian could be tried by a wartime military commission.[32] The Court held that "neither the President nor Congress had the power to authorize wartime military commissions to try civilians in an area where civil courts were open and functioning."[33] The Court unanimously found President Lincoln's suspension of the writ of habeas corpus went too far:

> "The unanimous Supreme Court held that the President had gone too far. The Court stressed that Indiana was not under attack and that Milligan was not connected with Confederate military service, nor was he a prisoner of war. He was arrested at home, not on a military maneuver. Even more important, the courts in Indiana were open and functioning normally during the war. The government could have charged him with treason and tried him in the courts, where he would have had the right to a jury and the right to a fair trial, under the Constitution."[34]

Chief Justice Chase dissented only regarding the ability of Congress to institute military commissions, writing:

---

32. *See* "Ex parte Milligan." *Oyez,* 9 Jun. 2018, available at www.oyez.org/cases /1850-1900/71us2.

33. Fridlington, p. 74.

34. Key Supreme Court cases, American Bar Association, available at https:// www.americanbar.org/groups/public_education/initiatives_awards/students _in_action/milligan.html.

"The power of Congress to authorize trials for crimes against the security and safety of the National forces may be derived from its constitutional authority to raise and support armies and to declare war, if not from its constitutional authority to provide for governing the National forces."[35]

The *Milligan* decision was not well received at the time.[36] Military tribunals were not uncommon before the end of the war and after.[37] *Milligan* continues to be cited for a variety of reasons, including martial law, military commissions, and other subjects. The decision does not seem as controversial in retrospect as was apparently the case when it was decided.[38]

The Chase Court issued a number of other decisions, but two stood out: (1) the *Slaughter-House Cases* and (2) *Texas v. White.* In *Texas*, the Supreme Court dealt with the issue of secession and whether Texas, which had joined the Confederate States of America during the Civil War, was able to seek redress in the Supreme Court.[39] The Chase Court

---

35. Warren, Vol. 2, p. 427.

36. For a detailed narrative about some of the concerns expressed at the time of the decision, *see* Warren, Vol. 2, pgs. 427–45.

37. For an excellent discussion of the *Ex parte Milligan* case and the use of military tribunals during the Civil War, *see* Bradley, available at file:///C:/Users/DCott/Downloads/SSRN-id1015618.pdf.

38. For an excellent narrative on the current use of *Milligan*, *see* Barry, available at file:///C:/Users/DCott/Downloads/20475-Article%20Text-45436-1-10-20151201.pdf.

39. The Supreme Court retains original jurisdiction in some limited cases, including this instance.

held that Texas never lost its status once it joined the Union and despite joining the Confederate States, holding:

> When, therefore, Texas became one of the United States, she entered into an indissoluble relation. All the obligations of perpetual union, and all the guaranties of republican government in the Union, attached at once to the State. The act which consummated her admission into the Union was something more than a compact; it was the incorporation of a new member into the political body. And it was final. The union between Texas and the other States was as complete, as perpetual, and as indissoluble as the union between the original States. There was no place for reconsideration, or revocation, except through revolution, or through consent of the States.

> Considered therefore as transactions under the Constitution, the ordinance of secession, adopted by the convention and ratified by a majority of the citizens of Texas, and all the acts of her legislature intended to give effect to that ordinance, were absolutely null. They were utterly without operation in law. The obligations of the State, as a member of the Union, and of every citizen of the State, as a citizen of the United States, remained perfect and unimpaired. It certainly follows that the State did not cease to be a State, nor her citizens to be citizens of the Union. If this were otherwise, the State must have become foreign, and her citizens

foreigners. The war must have ceased to be a war for the suppression of rebellion and must have become a war for conquest and subjugation.

Our conclusion therefore is, that Texas continued to be a State, and a State of the Union, notwithstanding the transactions to which we have referred. And this conclusion, in our judgment, is not in conflict with any act or declaration of any department of the National government, but entirely in accordance with the whole series of such acts and declarations since the first outbreak of the rebellion.[40]

Any state since that has asserted it is seceding from the Union has been reminded of this 150-year-old decision that makes it clear that secession is not a permissible way for a disgruntled state to proceed.

The *Slaughter-House Cases* was the first opportunity for the Supreme Court to consider the language and intent of the Fourteenth Amendment, particularly Section 1, which provides:

All persons born or naturalized in the United States and subject to the jurisdiction thereof, are citizens of the United States and of the State wherein they reside. No State shall make or enforce any law which shall abridge the privileges or immunities of citizens of the

---

40. *Texas v. White,* 74 U.S. 700, 726 (1869).

United States; nor shall any State deprive any person of life, liberty, or property, without due process of law; nor deny to any person within its jurisdiction the equal protection of the laws.[41]

The underlying facts involved the Louisiana legislature passing a law granting a monopoly to the Crescent City Livestock Landing & Slaughterhouse Company to run slaughterhouses in the New Orleans area. Local butchers challenged the legislative enactment. The Supreme Court narrowly read the language of the Fourteenth Amendment, holding that the "privileges or immunities" applied only to areas that the Federal government specifically controlled, and did not apply to state actions. The Court would later find that most of the Bill of Rights were incorporated into this Section 1 of the Fourteenth Amendment. Associate Justice Stephen Field wrote a dissent with Chief Justice Chase joining.

Reconstruction

During Chase's tenure as chief justice, Congress passed three proposed amendments to the U.S. Constitution that addressed slavery and the results of the end of the Civil War, which were ratified. Collectively known as the "Reconstruction Amendments," the Thirteenth Amendment (1865),

---

41. U.S. Constitution Fourteenth Amendment, Section 1.

the Fourteenth Amendment (1868), and the Fifteenth Amendment (1870), they were first interpreted narrowly and addressed only state action. In addition, Congress utilized its power under the Exceptions Clause of Article III, Section 2 of the Constitution[42] to try to limit the Supreme Court's power to hear appeals involving the Reconstruction Amendments.

In *Ex parte McCardle*,[43] the main question before the Supreme Court was whether Congress had the power to withdraw appellate jurisdiction from the Supreme Court. Chase, writing for the Supreme Court, answered the question in the affirmative, stating in part:

> "We are not at liberty to inquire into the motives of the legislature. We can only examine into its power under the Constitution, and the power to make exceptions to the appellate jurisdiction of this court is given by express words."[44]

Congress had limited the Court's *habeas corpus* jurisdiction for fear the Supreme Court "would nullify the Reconstruction acts."[45] The Court would only regain its esteem and prestige at some point in the twentieth century.

---

42. U.S. Const. Art. III, Sec. 2. The "Exception Clause" provides: "In all the other Cases before mentioned, the Supreme Court shall have appellate Jurisdiction, both as to Law and Fact, with such Exceptions, and under such Regulations as the Congress shall make."

43. *Ex parte McCardle,* 74 U.S. 506 (1869).

44. *Id.* at 514.

45. Magrath, p. 5.

Death

Chase died on May 7, 1873, of a stroke. Upon his death, the Supreme Court of the United States began the tradition of hanging black wool crepe over the justice's chair and in front of the bench where the justice sat, along with hanging the same crepe over the Court's entrance. An interesting note about him is that Chase National Bank was named in honor of Chase, although he had no financial or other interest in the bank. The search for a replacement for Chase would be a long one, as we see in the next chapter.

Chapter Nine

Morrison Waite: Narrow Interpreter of Thirteenth, Fourteenth, and Fifteenth Amendments

Nominated by President Ulysses S. Grant
Confirmed by Senate, 63-0, on January 21, 1874
Tenure: March 4, 1874 to March 23, 1888 (Died)
Presidents During Tenure
 Grant
 Hayes
 Garfield
 Arthur
 Cleveland

Upon Chase's death in 1873, President Ulysses S. Grant had to replace Chase. The person who eventually was nominated, Morrison R. Waite, was not the first or second choice. He would be the seventh choice. Morrison Remick Waite, like Chase, was an attorney who

*practiced in Ohio and who had a private practice
mixed with political service. He practiced from 1839
until 1874. In 1846, he was mayor of Maumee, Ohio,
and, in 1849–50, served as a member of the Ohio
General Assembly. In 1871, he was appointed co-counsel
at the Geneva Arbitration Tribunal, where he won a
substantial award on claims against Great Britain for
reparations stemming from the Civil War. In 1873, he
was elected president of the Ohio Constitutional
Convention.*

*President Ulysses S. Grant nominated Waite to the
position of chief justice in January 1874. The nomination followed a number of others where the person
either declined or withdrew for various reasons,
including corruption. Waite was relatively unknown
and not considered a top legal mind, but the Senate
unanimously approved his nomination.*

*The Waite Court was a busy one, deciding more than
3,000 cases in his fourteen years. He viewed the Reconstruction Amendments narrowly. In matters of commerce, he believed in broad national powers, and his
1877 decision for the court in Munn v. Illinois was
relied on by President Franklin D. Roosevelt's New
Deal to support the administration's views on matters
of economics and contracts.*

*In Santa Clara County v. Southern Pacific Railroad Co.
(1886), dictum in one of the headnotes by the court*

reporter may have been the first real instance of corpo-
rations being recognized by the court to have legal rights
of a person. It was referenced in subsequent court opin-
ions and relied on for support.[1] Waite served for four-
teen years, until his death on March 23, 1888.

Early Life and Career

Waite was born in Lyme, Connecticut on November 29, 1816, to Henry Matson Waite, an attorney, and his mother, Maria (nee Selden). Mr. Waite served as a judge for many years, including as an associate judge of the Supreme Court of Connecticut, then chief judge of the same court. After high school at a private academy, Waite attended Yale University, where he graduated in 1837. Waite then became a clerk to his father. Waite moved to Maumee, Ohio, where he apprenticed to a local attorney, Samuel L. Young. After admission and spending five months at Young's office, Waite and Young became partners in a law firm that focused primarily on business and property law.[2] Waite was an active oral advocate and became "a learned chancery lawyer, expert in real estate law and the history and status of legal titles."[3] Waite also served one term as mayor of

---

1. For an excellent discussion of the rights of corporations, including the headnote that led to real corporate rights and liberties, *see* Winkler, *We the Corporations: How American Businesses Won Their Civil Rights.*

2. Partnership formed on April 20, 1839. Magrath, p. 39.

3. Magrath, p. 39.

Maumee, Ohio and served from 1849 to 1850 in the Ohio House, having won by "a mere fifty-eight votes."[4]

In 1850, Waite moved to Toledo while maintaining his partnership with Young until Young retired, at which point Waite became partners with his brother, Richard Waite. Waite was opposed to slavery and joined the Republican Party soon after its formation. In 1851, Waite served one term on the Toledo City Council.[5]

In 1862, the Civil War being fought to save the Union, Waite was enlisted to run for a Congressional seat.[6] Waite ran on a platform of preservation of the Union, of immediate emancipation only in the event the president declared it necessary, and amendment of the Constitution to address slavery. Waite lost the election, and Ohio Governor Brough offered Waite a seat on the Ohio Supreme Court, which Waite declined.[7]

Waite built a prominent practice and was a leader in the Ohio bar. While "Waite never became rich," he had a "very comfortable income."[8] In 1871, Waite and two other attorneys were invited to represent the United States at the Geneva Tribunal. Waite was successful at the Tribunal, winning a $15 million award for the United States.[9]

---

4. *Id.* at 62.
5. *Id.* at 66.
6. *Id.* at 67–68.
7. *Id.* at 71.
8. *Id.* at 49.
9. Magrath, pgs. 13–14.

Back from the Tribunal, Waite "found himself something of a hero."[10] The festivities included a parade. Waite's hometown of Toledo selected him to represent the town at a new constitutional convention, and both parties endorsed him. Waite won an uncontested election, and when he arrived at the convention in Columbus on May 13, 1873, he was selected to preside over the Ohio constitutional convention, which he did.[11] One of Waite's main contributions to the convention was with respect to the court system of Ohio. The Ohio Supreme Court had a busy docket and delays of years.[12] He supported limiting the jurisdiction of the Ohio Supreme Court, which the state adopted.

Supreme Court Nomination

While presiding over the Ohio constitutional convention, he was notified by President Grant via telegram that Grant was nominating him to the chief justice position vacated by the death of Chief Justice Chase.[13] On January 19, 1874, Grant officially nominated Waite. Waite was Grant's seventh choice. After waiting six months after Chase's death to nominate anyone, Grant first offered the seat to powerful U.S. Senator Roscoe Conkling. The New Yorker turned Grant down. Grant then offered the position to two other

---

10. *Id.* at 87.
11. *Id.* at 87.
12. *Id.* at 88.
13. *Id.* at 90.

Senators, who both declined. Secretary of State Hamilton Fish next declined, with Grant turning to his attorney general, George H. Williams. Williams withdrew his name when a corruption scandal emerged during his Senate confirmation process. Upon Williams withdrawing, President Grant nominated former attorney general, Caleb Cushing, whose nomination Grant withdrew when potential evidence emerged that Cushing had a relationship with former Confederate President Jefferson Davis. The Waite choice was a surprise to many, as "all of his predecessors had been selected from among former members of presidential cabinets."[14] As we have seen, prior chief justices were prominent politically and had the attention of the party and, more importantly, the attention of the nominating president. Waite was "a crony of Grant's Ohio friends, who had zero judicial experience," someone who was not well known beyond Ohio.[15]

On January 21, 1874, two days after receiving Waite's nomination, the Senate unanimously confirmed Waite, 63-0, and on March 4, 1874, Waite became the seventh chief justice.

Waite would serve the next fourteen years.

Waite's beginnings as chief justice were interwoven with senior Court members who believed "the Chief Justiceship rightfully belonged to them" and caused great jealousy.[16]

---

14. Kens, p. xii.
15. Schermerhorn.
16. Magrath, p. 94. Justices Miller and Swayne were the two senior justices.

Legacy

Most Supreme Court historians view the Waite Court (and Fuller) as transitional and forgettable. Waite came on the bench in 1874, almost a decade after the end of the Civil War. His tenure as chief justice spanned five presidents: Grant, Hayes, Garfield, Arthur, and Cleveland.[17] The Waite Court covered a period where:

> "The problems of the war and its aftermath had been largely settled before he came upon the Bench; but new and grave economic and social questions now presented themselves. These years saw the growth of the Western States and the immense development of the material resources of the country. . . ."[18]

In 1875, Waite was approached to potentially run for president. He turned down the approaches, noting that the Court and prestige of it could not be so easily set aside. Waite wrote:

> "The office came to me covered with honor, and when I accepted it, my chief duty was not to make it a stepping stone to something else, but to preserve its purity, and, if possible, make my name as honorable as that of my predecessors."[19]

---

17. Warren, Vol. 2, p. 562.
18. *Id.*
19. *Id.* at 564.

Not all of his successors would follow the same compass.

The biggest legacy of the Waite Court might well be upholding the narrow interpretation of the Fourteenth Amendment that the Supreme Court began with the *Slaughterhouse Cases* during Chief Justice Chase's last year. The Waite Court issued many decisions "severely limiting federal protections for newly freed slaves that the framers of the Fourteenth Amendment had sought to provide."[20] The Waite Court affirmed the finding of *Slaughterhouse,* finding that the right of suffrage was not a "right belonging to a citizen of the United States."[21] The Waite Court read the intent of the Fourteenth Amendment, finding that the "Privileges and Immunity Clause of the Amendment, as construed by the Court, afforded slight protection to an individual, and no protection to a corporation, affected by oppressive legislation."[22]

While the Fourteenth Amendment was narrowly interpreted by the Waite Court, in the realm of the states' abilities to regulate within their borders, the court found expansive powers, in a series of cases that have been labeled the *Granger Cases.*[23]

---

20. Stevens, p. 22.

21. Warren, Vol. 2, at 567. The case was *Minor v. Happerset,* 21 Wall. 162 (1875).

22. *Id.*

23. Granger laws were laws trying to regulate the cost of fares on railroads and for grain elevators by farmers mostly in the Midwest post-Civil War. The laws got their name from the group of farmers who were mostly behind the laws, the National Grange of the Order of Patrons of Husbandry.

The *Granger Cases* were decided on March 1, 1877, including *Munn v. Illinois*.[24] President Franklin Delano Roosevelt (FDR) would rely upon *Munn* when implementing his broad New Deal programs.

Munn involved the question of whether state-imposed rates on grain elevators violated the equal protection and due process clauses of the Fourteenth Amendment. Chief Justice Waite, writing for the majority, found that "when such regulation becomes necessary for the public good," states had the power to regulate private property. Associate Justice Stephen Field strongly dissented, stating:

> "The principle upon which the opinion of the majority proceeds is, in my judgment, subversive of the rights of private property, heretofore believed to be protected by constitutional guaranties against legislative interference, and is in conflict with the authorities cited in its support."[25]

Waite and the Supreme Court during his tenure interpreted the Reconstruction Amendments (Thirteenth, Fourteenth, and Fifteenth Amendments) very narrowly. One of the Waite Court's most notable cases in this vein was *U.S. v. Cruikshank*.[26] In *Cruikshank*, a group of white men killed more than one hundred African Americans in a

---

24. *Munn v. Illinois*, 94 U.S. 113 (1877).
25. *Munn*, 94 U.S. at 136.
26. *U.S. v. Cruikshank*, 92 U.S. 542 (1876).

political dispute. Three men were convicted of violations of the 1870 Enforcement Act, which was designed to combat attacks on African Americans trying to exercise their suffrage rights by groups such as the Ku Klux Klan.[27] The defendants argued that the First and Second Amendments did not apply to their actions. The Supreme Court agreed with the defendants, discussing dual citizenship and holding, "The Fourteenth Amendment prohibits a State from depriving any person of life, liberty, or property, without due process of law; but this adds nothing to the rights of one citizen as against another."[28] This narrow reading of the Fourteenth Amendment by the Waite Court "gutted the 14th Amendment's civil rights provisions, leading to the swift and violent rise of Jim Crow."[29] It also reflected a very narrow view of the incorporation doctrine.[30]

However, in the realm of vested property rights, the Waite Court would do much to expand such rights, especially as they applied to and protected business organizations. The Waite Court included Stephen Field, who was a big proponent of corporate rights, especially as they pertained to the railroads. To Fields, "it did not matter that the 'powerful'

---

27. https://www.fjc.gov/history/timeline/us-v-cruikshank.

28. *Cruikshank*, 92 U.S. at 554.

29. Schermerhorn.

30. The incorporation doctrine is a constitutional doctrine that the Bill of Rights are applicable to the states through the Due Process clause of the Fourteenth Amendment.

were corporations."[31] In *The Sinking Funds Cases*,[32] Field's opinion and the other opinions "reflected a debate about whether corporations are persons entitled to full protection of the Constitution."[33] Field believed that corporations were afforded the same rights as the individual with the corporation "having human attributes and therefore human rights."[34] Chief Justice Waite was not ready to equate corporations with individuals, but recognized that corporations had certain property rights. Over a period of time, as demonstrated in Adam Winkler's book on corporate rights, the Field view would fully prevail, not only in property rights but in personal liberties as well.

Involvement in an Election

The 1876 presidential election was one of the closest in history, with Samuel Tilden winning the popular vote but the electoral college "was the closest in history."[35] To complicate the outcome, twenty electoral votes were disputed, and the outcome would determine the victor.[36] Several states submitted contested returns, and the Congress was

---

31. Kens, p. 108.
32. *The Sinking Funds Cases*, 99 U.S. 700 (1879).
33. Kens, p. 108.
34. *Id.*
35. Magrath, p. 288.
36. *Id.*

split, with Democrats in the majority in the House and
Republicans in the majority in the Senate.[37] Congress agreed
to an Electoral Commission bill, which would settle the disputed election. Consisting of fifteen members, the Commission included five Congressional Democrats and five
Congressional Republicans, and also included five Supreme
Court Justices.[38] Waite was told that because he was such a
strong critic of Tilden, he could not be part of the committee. The Electoral Commission compromise ended up with
an eight to seven Republican majority, and Hayes won the
election. Democrats attacked Justice Joseph Bradley for
being the swing vote and siding with the Republicans
because he believed "Congress lacked constitutional power
to examine the disputed returns for possible fraud."[39] Chief
Justice Waite wrote about the attacks on Bradley and the
charges he was biased:

> "'Just at present our judges are severely criticized,
> but I feel quite sure time will bring us out all right.
> Wonderful partisans our Republicans are. Strange that
> no one ever thought such a thing of a Democrat.'"[40]

The Court's involvement and impact on the 1876 election
"only blurred further the distinction between politics and

---

37. *Id.* at 289.
38. *Id.* at 289–90.
39. Magrath, p. 293–94.
40. *Id.* at 294.

the rule of law."[41] More than one hundred years later, the Supreme Court entered the presidential kingmaker thicket again, albeit more directly, when it would rule in *Bush v. Gore*.[42] Chief Justice Rehnquist wrote about the 1876 election and the Supreme Court's role in it in a 2004 publication, *Centennial Crisis*.[43] Rehnquist started the book almost a year before the 2000 election in which he became centrally involved and made the comparison of the two elections clearly in the book's prologue.[44]

Death

Waite's wife was vacationing in California in early March 1888.[45] Waite had completed his decision in the *Telephone Cases*,[46] which "climaxed the longest and perhaps most complex case in the first one hundred years of the Court's history"[47] and came to the Court on March 20 to read the decision. He was suffering from a bout of pneumonia that nobody knew was serious and was not able to read the opinion at Court.[48] Waite died three days later, nearly broke and bankrupt.

---

41. Kens, p. xii.
42. *See infra at* p. 375–76.
43. Obermayer, p. 98.
44. *Id*. at 98–99.
45. Cushman, p. 215.
46. *The Telephone Cases,* 126 U.S. 1 (1888).
47. Cushman, p. 215.
48. *Id*.

Waite by all accounts is not considered a great justice. At the same time, his tenure as chief justice was during the period of Reconstruction and while the country was trying to come back together as a union, it continued to struggle with race questions, because while the institution of slavery ended in 1865, the violence, hatred, and bigotry against African Americans did not stop at the end of the Civil War. The Waite Court had to review the civil rights legislation that had been enacted, including the Civil War Amendments (Thirteenth, Fourteenth, and Fifteenth Amendments). The Waite Court interpreted these amendments narrowly, finding that they did not extend to any power to enforce them against the states. Incorporation as a concept would come later.

Upon his death, one lawyer summed up the tenure of Chief Justice Waite:

"While impartial criticism may not assign to him the extraordinary rank in the esteem of the profession attained by his predecessors, yet it may be with entire truth be affirmed that in the soundness of his judgment, in the diligence of his research, in the clearness of his statements of legal principles and in the tact and skill displayed in the conduct of the business of the Court, he was a worthy successor. . . . It must be confessed that the period of service covered by his term was more fraught with difficulties, more full of new responsibilities and demanded more labor, learning and ability than in any previous period."[49]

The interpretation of the War Amendments, while in retrospect considered to be narrowly construed and not implementing their true intents, at the time was not considered to be out of line with how many viewed these amendments to be applicable. "In practical terms they show that the Court, in facing the Southern question, marched in step with the national mood."[50] By its various decisions, including the *Civil Rights Cases*, the Supreme Court was the "constitutional guardian of the Compromise of 1877."[51] In the *Civil Rights Cases*, Justice John Marshall Harlan published a strongly worded dissent that "ranks among the powerful dissents of Court history,"[52] in which he attacked the Supreme Court's narrow views of the Amendments, as well as blasting the Court for its decision in *Hall v. Decuir*.[53]

---

49. Warren, Vol. 2, p. 690 (quoting John Randolph Tucker).

50. Magrath, p. 133.

51. *Id.* at 142. The Compromise of 1877 was a bargain between the North and South that exchanged the peaceful seating of Hayes as president after the hotly contested election of 1876 for the withdrawal of federal troops from the South. It was for all intents and purposes a "rebuilding of the Republican Party." *Id.* at 138.

52. Magrath, p. 144.

53. Magrath, pgs. 143–45. *Hall v. Decuir*, 95 U.S. 485 (1878), was a case reviewing a civil rights statute passed by the Louisiana Reconstruction legislature that required public carriers to provide accommodations to all regardless of race. Chief Justice Waite wrote for the Court that a state had the power to regulate commerce wholly within its territory. Unless the activity involved interstate commerce, the state had exclusive jurisdiction. The immediate effect of the decision

Samuel A. Shellabarger, who spoke at the Bar Proceedings upon Waite's death, stated:

"When, therefore, Waite's great opinions construing these Amendments came, one in *Minor's Case* in 1874, holding that the Fourteenth Amendment does not add to the privileges and immunities of American citizens but simply adds guarantees for the protection of privileges theretofore existing, and especially when the great opinion appeared in 1876 in *Cruikshank's Case*, also holding that the Fourteenth Amendment adds nothing to the rights of one citizen against another, and ... that these framers did not design to enable Congress to legislate affirmatively and directly for the protection of civil rights, but only to use corrective and restraining legislation as against the States, ... many of the framers of these Amendments received information regarding their intentions, which was new ... succeeding decisions have explained and supplemented these early decisions and have guarded against what was believed to be their erroneous tendencies, that I am inclined to think the judgment of history will be, that he has been, in the main, steadily right regarding these Amendments."[54]

---

was that "[b]etween 1881 and 1889 nine Southern states hastened to pass Jim Crow laws segregating transportation." Magrath, p. 141.

54. Warren, Vol. 2, pgs. 690–92.

The Waite Court narrowly interpreted the Amendments to apply only to federal action, and not "for local breaches of the peace."[55] In *United States v. Cruikshank*[56] and the *Civil Rights Cases*,[57] the Waite Court found that the War Amendments were not intended to address state action or the conduct of private individuals. In *Cruikshank*, the Court held:

> "The only obligation resting upon the United States is to see that the States do not deny the right. This the amendment guarantees, but no more. The power of the national government is limited to the enforcement of this guaranty."[58]

The *Cruikshank* decision "revealed the Court's attachment to a model of federalism that existed before the Civil War."[59] When Waite began his tenure as chief justice, Associate Justice Stephen Field called Waite "an experiment which no President has a right to make with our Court."[60] Nothing suggests Field ever changed his assessment of Waite as "a man of fair but not great abilities."[61]

During Chief Justice Waite's tenure, Field wrote several opinions that expounded his views on the nation's founding

---

55. Magrath, p. 127.
56. *United States v. Cruikshank*, 92 U.S. 542 (1876).
57. *Civil Rights Cases*, 109 U.S. 3 (1883).
58. *Cruikshank*, 92 U.S. 542, 555.
59. Kens, p. 5.
60. Magrath, p. 107.
61. *Id.*

and most endearing principles. For example, in the case *Butcher's Union* (1884), Associate Justice Stephen Fieled provided an annotated Declaration of Independence to emphasize some points, writing:

> "We hold these trust to be self-evident"—that is, so plain that their truth is recognized upon their mere statement—"that all men are endowed"—not by edicts of emperors, or decrees of parliament, or acts of congress, but "by their Creator with certain inalienable rights"—that is, rights which cannot be bartered away, or given away, or taken away, except in punishment of crime—"and that among these are life, liberty, and the pursuit of happiness; and to secure these"—not grant them, but secure them—"governments are instituted among men, deriving their just powers from the consent of the governed." Among these inalienable rights, as proclaimed in that great document, is the right of men to pursue their happiness, by which is meant the right to pursue any lawful business or vocation, in any manner not inconsistent with the equal rights of others, which may increase their prosperity or develop their facilities.[62]

Associate Justice Stephen Field was one of the biggest early proponents of corporate rights under the Fourteenth Amendment:

---

62. *Id.* at 77.

"The Fourteenth Amendment guarantees due process to all 'persons,' and when, in 1883, Santa Clara County argued to Field, riding circuit, that corporations were not 'persons' under the Constitution, Field was practically scandalized. Behind every corporation, he said, a mere legal vehicle for holding wealth, were 'living human beings whom it represented.'"[63]

Perhaps part of Field's assessment of Waite is through the filter of Field's views of the Constitution and rights and the way Waite interpreted the same documents differently. Waite's War Amendments jurisprudence would remain in place for decades to come.

---

63. *Id.* at 79.

Part Five

The First Quarter of the Second Hundred Years of America

Reconstruction was over. The first hundred years of our great nation were behind it. It had survived continued International intrigue and war; it had fought an extremely horrific, bloody Civil War over the "peculiar institution" of slavery and was now looking to the turn of the centuries, and to the future. Upon the death of Morrison Waite, President Grover Cleveland had the opportunity to select the next chief justice of the Supreme Court. He turned to Melville W. Fuller. Fuller and the nation faced a time of "[r]apid industrialization, urbanization, and breakthroughs in science and technology" that "not only modernized society but brought a host of new issues before the Court."[1] The assessment of the Fuller and White Courts is one of conservatism and not very memorable for its jurisprudence.

---

1. Cushman, p. 249.

One of the cases from the Fuller Court, *Plessy v. Ferguson*, is considered one of the worst decisions in the history of the Supreme Court.

Chapter Ten

Melville W. Fuller: Equal Justice under Law, Separate but Equal

Nominated by President Grover Cleveland
Confirmed by Senate, 41-20, on July 20, 1888
Tenure: October 8, 1888 to July 4, 1910 (Died)
Presidents During Tenure
> *Cleveland*
> *Harrison*
> *Cleveland*
> *McKinley*
> *Teddy Roosevelt*
> *Taft*

Melville Weston Fuller was born into a family of law-yers and was raised by his maternal grandfather, who was a judge. After practicing law in Maine for a short period, Fuller moved to Chicago, where he practiced law from 1856 to 1888.

In 1860, he was the campaign manager for Stephen Douglas, who ran against Lincoln for president, and was a delegate to the Illinois Constitutional Convention in 1862. He was a member of the Illinois House of Representatives from 1863 to 1865. Fuller was president of the Illinois State Bar Association in 1886.

On April 30, 1888, President Grover Cleveland nominated Fuller to be chief justice. Republicans fought the nomination on various grounds, but he was confirmed by the Senate on July 20, 1888, by a vote of 41-20.

Fuller would serve the third longest tenure of any chief justice to date, just less than twenty-two years. The Fuller Court decided a number of memorable cases, including Caldwell v. Texas (1891) (which gave us the maxim "equal justice under law") and the much-criticized decision Plessy v. Ferguson (1896) ("separate but equal" doctrine upholding racial segregation in public facilities), which remained the law of the land until 1954 and set back the modest gains that had been made during Reconstruction.

Early Life and Career

Melville Weston Fuller was born on February 11, 1833, in Augusta, Maine, to Catherine Martin (nee Weston) and Frederick Augustus Fuller, a prominent attorney. Fuller's relatives were prominent in law—an uncle was a prominent attorney and both grandfathers were judges. His maternal grandfather was a Maine Supreme Court justice. When Fuller was a very young baby, his parents separated and divorced, and his mother won custody of Fuller and his brother. From the time of the divorce, Fuller's dad did not participate in Fuller's life at all.[1] Along with his mother, Fuller lived with his maternal grandfather, who was one of the Chief Judges of Maine. Fuller attended Bowdoin College, receiving his A.B. in 1853. After graduating from Bowdoin, Fuller apprenticed at a lawyer's office in Bangor, Maine. He also attended lectures at Harvard Law School in 1855 but did not obtain any degree from Harvard. That six-month lecture attendance made "Fuller the first Chief Justice of the United States to have any law school training."[2]

Toward the end of 1855, Fuller was admitted to the Maine bar. He worked a variety of jobs in Maine, including at a local newspaper and was elected to the Augusta common council as well as becoming the city solicitor. Fuller did not stay in Maine long. He headed west and settled in Chicago, where he would practice, initially at the firm of Pearson and Dow.

Fuller was interested in continuing his involvement in politics and devoted much time to those pursuits. Fuller became very active in Chicago politics and the Democratic Party. Fuller also helped Stephen Douglas in his

---

1. King, p. 11.
2. Cushman, p. 247.

1858 Senate reelection bid against Abraham Lincoln and, after Douglas won, Fuller returned to his law practice and politics. He was a member of the Illinois Constitutional Convention, playing a significant role, and in 1863, was elected to the Illinois House of Representatives. While a member of the Illinois House, Fuller opposed a number of President Abraham Lincoln's initiatives, including the Emancipation Proclamation.[3]

The death of his first wife due to tuberculosis in 1864 caused him to get serious about the law practice, with two young daughters to raise and extensive debt. Fuller remarried in 1866 and that marriage was a happy one and also increased his legal fortunes—his second wife was the daughter of a prominent Chicago banker.

One of Fuller's cases drew national attention when Fuller, a high Episcopalian, defended a minister who was accused of "low church practices." This case was instrumental in bringing the Reformed Protestant Episcopal Church in America into being.[4]

Supreme Court Nomination

On April 30, 1888, President Grover Cleveland discussed Fuller becoming chief justice of the Supreme Court with

---

3. Furer, p. 218.
4. Cushman, p. 248.

Fuller, after the death of Chief Justice Morrison Waite.[5]
Cleveland had tapped into Fuller's advice from the time of
Cleveland's election, and Cleveland had offered Fuller several positions. Fuller turned them all down, but when the
chance of becoming chief justice was presented, Fuller did
not refuse. As one biographer noted:

> "The rise of Fuller to the nation's highest judicial office
> is a story of the rewards of professional competence in
> ordinary affairs and also an illustration of the rule of
> chance in the selection of American judges."[6]

President Cleveland formally nominated Fuller on May 2,
1888.[7] The nomination faced some resistance by the Republican-dominated Senate, questioning his war record and
lack of military experience as well as his support and ties
to big corporations. After several months of delay, the Senate
finally confirmed Fuller on July 20, 1888, and he was sworn
in as the eighth chief justice on October 8, 1888.

Legacy

Fuller was a strict constructionist and a conservative.
Despite his longevity and service, unlike other chief justices
before and after him, he never really dominated the Court.

---

5. *Id.*
6. King, p. viii.
7. Warren, Vol. 2, p. 692.

"His primary contribution was as a moderator, very efficiently managing the administrative details of the Court and its conflicting personalities."[8] In addition, one lasting practice of decorum that Fuller initiated was each justice shaking hands before every oral argument session.[9]

The Fuller Court for much of his tenure steadily ruled regarding "the sanctity of private property, *laissez faire* economics, and limitations on the expansion of federal power."[10] The Fuller Court "methodically destroyed the regulatory authority of the states,"[11] with decisions that:

> "did away with the precedents established in *Munn v. Illinois* (1877), and made the concept of due process under the Fourteenth Amendment continually work on the side of corporate enterprise. . . . It was also applied in the freedom of contract cases such as . . . *Lochner v. New York* (1905). The Fuller Court's conservatism reached its height in 1895, when it struck down the income tax, *Pollock v. Farmers' Loan and Trust Company*, emasculated the Sherman Anti-Trust Act, *United States. E.C. Knight Company*, and upheld the use of federal injunctions in labor disputes, *In re Debs*. Fuller, and the Court, were fiercely denounced throughout the nation for these decisions."[12]

---

8. Furer, p. 218.
9. Stevens, p. 23.
10. Furer, p. 218.
11. *Id.*
12. *Id.* at 218–19.

As Justice Oliver Wendell Holmes asserted in his *Lochner* dissent, the Court during the Fuller Court had become too active and had usurped the legislature's powers:

> "But a Constitution is not intended to embody a particular economic theory, whether of paternalism and the organic relation of the citizen to the state or of *laissez faire*. It is made for people of fundamentally differing views, and the accident of our finding certain opinions natural and familiar, or novel, and even shocking, ought not to conclude our judgement upon whether statutes embodying them conflict with the Constitution of the United States."[13]

The *Lochner* decision and its resultant era were extremely conservative and prior to the current court, may have evidenced the most conservative court in our nation's history, which would last for several decades.

The Fuller Court looked to past decisions often to support its decisions and approaches. In addition, the Fuller Court, just post-Reconstruction, narrowly interpreted the meaning of the Fourteenth Amendment when it came to individuals and state rights. For example, in *In re Kemmler*,[14] Chief Justice Waite wrote:

---

13. *Lochner v. New York*, 198 U.S. 90 (Holmes, J., dissenting) (emphasis in original) (1905), as quoted by Maltz, pgs. 4–5.

14. In re Kemmler, 136 U.S. 436 (1890).

"The Fourteenth Amendment did not radically change the whole theory of the relations of the state and Federal governments to each other. . . . Protection to life, liberty and property rests primarily with the States . . ."[15]

The Fuller Court began to effectuate a significant expansion of the Commerce Clause.[16] One of the first such cases of the Fuller Court finding such extensive powers of the national government was the *Chinese Exclusion Case, Chae Chan Ping v. United States.*[17] In *Ping*, the Court held that an act of Congress that prohibited the entry of Chinese laborers was within the Congressional powers, despite the act being violative of a Treaty the United States had with China.

Fuller is the third longest serving chief justice, having served twenty-two years. One lasting legacy is the ascetic profile attributed to the justices. "As a result of the Court's growing caseload and his considerable administrative responsibilities, Fuller withdrew from active participation in the social life of the capital."[18]

---

15. *In re Kemmler*, 136 U.S. 436, 448 (1890).

16. The Commerce Clause is Article I, Section 8, Clause 3, and provides that the U.S. Congress has the power to "regulate Commerce with foreign Nations, and among the several States, and with the Indian Tribes."

17. *Chae Chan Ping v. United States,* 130 U.S. 581 (1889).

18. Cushman, p. 249. In recent decades, the Supreme Court justices have become much more engaged in social life and public appearances, including writing books and memoirs, appearing on TV and attending events of ideological organizations.

Fuller began the practice of all justices shaking hands with each other before private conference and before sitting on the bench, camaraderie efforts that have continued to this day. What is a tribute to Chief Justice Fuller is his assessment as "the most successful Chief Justice" by two associate justices who served under other chief justices.[19]

Fuller was approached by President Cleveland in 1892 to become secretary of state but turned it down to avoid diminishing the stature of the chief justice position. In 1899, Fuller did serve as a member of the Venezuela-British Guiana Border Commission, and also represented the United States on the Permanent Court of Arbitration at the Hague from 1900 to 1910.

Fuller was a conservative judge with a "reputation of a jurist who favored a strict construction of governmental powers and the defense of federal power as against the rights of the states."[20]

On July 4, 1910, Fuller died suddenly of a heart attack. President William Howard Taft would need to fill the vacancy, and he would turn internally to existing members of the Supreme Court to fill the vacancy.

Despite serving the third longest tenure to date as chief justice, his tenure was one that did not develop an exciting or strong legacy, other than being the first of

---

19. *Id.*
20. Highsaw, p. 69.

three consecutive conservative courts, and has been characterized as a tenure that was "predominantly flat, perhaps even a trough."[21] One Philadelphia newspaper wrote about Fuller after he died:

> "He was a modest man and as had the assignment of opinions . . . he selected other Justices . . . to . . . give the argument for the decision reached."[22]

Other newspapers tended to agree. His taking a back seat to his associate justices likely was due in part to his views of the judiciary and his comity among justices, for example, the shaking of hands that endures to this day. However, one should not read into such statements a chief justice who did not provide his fair share of the Court's writing. During his twenty-two years, Fuller wrote more than 17% of all opinions of the Court (840 of 4,823).[23] In addition, Fuller might be best known for the efficiencies with which he administered the business that is the Supreme Court:

> "But Fuller's most remarkable abilities were largely unknown to the country. They lay in his great skill as an executive in managing the business of the Court. When he became Chief Justice, the Court was clogged

---

21. King, pgs. ix–x.
22. *Id.* at 333.
23. *Id.* at 339 (Appendix I—Opinions of the Court).

with cases; it was more than four years behind in its work. In a few years, by securing the passage of the Circuit Court of Appeals Act, he brought the calendar almost up to date."[24]

The most famous case during the Fuller Court era may have been the income tax case, *Pollock v. Farmers' Loan & Trust Company*.[25] In *Pollock*, the Supreme Court ruled that the Income Tax Law of 1804 was unconstitutional.[26] But there are other cases decided during the Fuller Court that at best would be labeled infamous, including *Plessy* and the *Chinese Exclusion Case*.

While the Fuller Court may not have expanded the Court's influence and began what is known as the *Lochner Era*,[27] the country during Fuller's lifetime saw incredible sevenfold growth:

---

24. *Id.* at 333–34. The Circuit Court of Appeals Act, or Judiciary Act of 1891, eased the burden on the Supreme Court by creating the "United States circuit courts of appeals" and shifting some jurisdiction. The number of cases appealed to the Supreme Court was reduced and cases could be appealed for consideration by the Supreme Court by "writ of certiorari." *See* 26 Stat. 826.

25. *Pollock v. Farmers' Loan & Trust Company*, 157 U.S. 429 (1895).

26. King, p. 193.

27. The *Lochner Era* derives its name from a decision of SCOTUS in *Lochner v. New York*, 198 U.S. 45 (1905), which held that limitations imposed on employees' working time was a violation of the Fourteenth Amendment. From this decision and for some time thereafter, the SCOUTS invalidated federal and states laws that regulated working conditions. The period lasted until 1937, when the Court decided *West Coast Hotel Co. v. Parrish*, 300 U.S. 379 (1937).

"When he was born, Andrew Jackson was President and there were only 13,000,000 in the country. Now William Howard Taft presided over 91,000,000."[28]

Fuller's term also coincided with "a period of unprecedented National growth" and a period that found the United States as "a world power and in control of territorial possessions" that now had to deal with "the complex social and economic problems of modern times."[29] From all accounts, the Fuller Court had minimal impact on such growth or on the overall legacy and status of the Court.

---

28. *Id.* at 336.
29. Warren, Vol. 2, p. 693.

Chapter Eleven

Edward Douglass White: An Elevation from Associate Justice

Nominated by President Taft
Confirmed by Senate Acclamation
   on December 12, 1910
Tenure: December 19, 1910 to May 19, 1921 (Died)
Presidents During Tenure
   Taft
   Wilson
   Harding

When Fuller died in July 1910, Edward White was elevated from associate justice to chief that December. Sixty-five years old at the time of his nomination and a Democrat appointed by Republican President William Howard Taft, his selection was not well received. However, he was confirmed by the Senate by voice vote on the same day he was nominated.

Prior to his becoming an associate justice in 1894, he was an attorney and politician. He practiced in New

Orleans and had been a lieutenant in the Confederate Army and held captive by the Union Army prior to becoming a lawyer.

If critics at the time of his elevation were correct, Taft appointed him with the hopes he would not serve as chief for long: He served for ten and a half years, until his death on May 19, 1921. The White Court decided the case Standard Oil Company of New Jersey v. U.S. (1911), which found Standard Oil guilty of monopoly, as well as Arver v. U.S. (1918) (the "Selective Draft Law Case" upholding conscription into military service). It also continued what had become a very conservative Court.

Early Life and Career

White was born November 3, 1845, on the family plantation near Thibodaux, Louisiana, to Edward White Sr., a governor of Louisiana, and Catherine Sidney Lee (nee Ringgold). At the young age of 6, White was sent to a prep school run by Jesuits, and "the moral precepts of Jesuit instruction" he was exposed to at the school "were later to become apparent and marked in the Chief Justice."[1] After attending prep school in New Orleans at another Catholic institution, Ned (as he was known as a boy and young man) attended Georgetown University. The Civil War interrupted

---

1. Highsaw, p. 18.

White's studies. White returned home intent on joining the war but was too young to enter the war. White's family did not approve of his interest in joining the military.[2] White ran away and joined the Confederate Army as a private.[3]

White joined General W.N.R. Beal's staff at Port Hudson, Louisiana. White became a prisoner of war when Port Hudson surrendered on July 8, 1863. White would recall his capture and imprisonment:

> "Like everyone else in my environment, as a little boy, I went into the army on the side that didn't win . . . I was taken prisoner . . . and my mother went to the officer in charge of the prison and asked permission to come to see me. . . ."[4]

Post war, White apprenticed to Edward Bermudez in New Orleans. White was admitted to the bar in 1868 and began practicing law.

White's practice thrived, and he also became involved in local politics. White was elected to the Louisiana Senate in 1874, and after supporting the successful gubernatorial candidate, he became a member of the Louisiana Supreme Court. White lost a power struggle when the governor he supported lost and was removed from the bench when a minimum age law was passed.[5]

---

2. *Id.* at 19.
3. *Id.*
4. *Id.* at 20.
5. Cushman, p. 272.

White returned to private practice and thrived again. He also was very involved in the funding and creation of Tulane University, serving as its legal adviser.

In 1891, White was appointed a U.S. Senator from Louisiana. He served for three years and was a vigorous defender of "states' rights against the federal government's powers."[6]

Supreme Court Calling

While a Senator and embroiled in debate over a tariff reform bill, President Grover Cleveland summoned White to the White House.[7] To White's surprise, Cleveland informed White he was nominating him to the Supreme Court of the United States as an associate justice. White was appointed and confirmed on February 19, 1894, while continuing his work in the Senate against the president's tariff bill. White would serve the next almost seventeen years as an associate justice, voting with the majority in *Plessy v. Ferguson* and dissenting in the *Lochner v. New York* case.

Supreme Court Nomination to Chief Justice

At the time of Fuller's death in 1910, White had already served for almost seventeen years as an associate justice of

---

6. *Id.*
7. *Id.*

the Supreme Court when President William Howard Taft elevated White to the chief judgeship to fill the vacancy created by Fuller's death.

When White was confirmed as chief justice, he became the first sitting associate justice to be elevated to the chief justice position.[8] Taft, who wanted to be chief justice, selected White over fellow Associate Justice Hughes, whom he had promised the chief justiceship to just a few months earlier.[9] The reason for selecting White over Hughes may well have been the ages of the two being considered.[10]

While the reasons why Hughes was passed over in favor of White may not be known, Taft's Attorney General, George Wickersham, may have provided some insight to Taft's biographer, Henry F. Pringle. Wickersham told Pringle about the discussion Taft and Wickersham had when Wickersham brought White's commission to Taft to be signed:

"'There is nothing I would have loved more than being chief justice of the United States,' he mourned. 'I cannot help seeing the irony in the fact that I, who desired that office so much, should now be signing the commission of another man.'"[11]

---

8. Cushman, p. 271. However, he was not the first former associate justice to be elevated—Rutledge had resigned his initial associate justice position before becoming the second chief justice as a recess appointment.

9. *See* chapter on Justice Hughes.

10. Cushman, p. 274.

11. Pringle, Vol. 1, p. 535.

On December 12, 1910, Taft submitted the nomination of White, who was confirmed on the same day by the Senate. A week later, on December 19, 1910, White took his judicial oath as chief justice of the Supreme Court.[12] The elevation of White by Taft was at first well received, but the "appointment may have politically damaged Taft's chances of a second presidential term of office."[13] White would serve the next decade as chief justice.

Legacy

The Conservative Court of the era from 1910 to 1930, which saw White then Taft as chief justices, is not a time of the Court where significant developments in Constitutional law were often found—rather, they were few and far between. It would be the chief justices and Courts after Taft that would move the jurisprudence significantly on Constitutional law. White is remembered when he is as his "rule of reason" approach to law in antitrust matters. The Sherman Anti-Trust Act, which was enacted in 1890, was designed to address concerns raised over monopolies. Prior Supreme Court decisions, such as *United States v. E.C. Knight Co.* (1895), found no violation of the Act. When President Theodore Roosevelt came into the White

---

12. *Id.*
13. Highsaw, p. 59.

House, one of the cornerstones of his administration was prosecuting monopolies and trusts. In *Standard Oil Co. v. United States*,[14] the White Court found that Standard Oil had violated the Act and ordered that Standard Oil be dissolved. In his opinion, White in dicta set forth the "rule of reason," which provided "unreasonable" monopolies would be found to have violated the Act and "reasonable" monopolies not found to have restrained trade would be legal.[15]

One thing that White brought to the Supreme Court from his earlier experience on the Louisiana Supreme Court was the format of his decisions:

> "This style consisted of a brief statement of the case and its issues, followed by conclusions which were fortified as they were announced and supported by citations drawn from history and the legal writers and jurisprudence...."[16]

This style of reported decision has been fairly consistent since the White Court. On May 19, 1921, Chief Justice White died while having an operation performed.[17] Taft's appointment of White rather than Hughes paid off, as Taft would become the first and only former president to

14. *Standard Oil Co. v. United States*, 221 U.S. 1 (1911).
15. Bindler, p. 59.
16. Highsaw, p. 26.
17. Pusey, Vol. 2, p. 429.

become a justice of the Supreme Court. However, as previously noted, White's appointment also "may have politically damaged Taft's chances of a second presidential term of office."[18]

---

18. Highsaw, p. 59.

Chapter Twelve

William Howard Taft: A Former President Achieves His Goal

Nominated by President Warren G. Harding
Confirmed by Senate Acclamation on June 30,
*   1921*
Tenure: July 11, 1921 to February 3, 1930 (Retired)
Presidents During Tenure
*   Harding*
*   Coolidge*
*   Hoover*

After graduating with his bachelor's in law degree
from Cincinnati Law School, Taft became the
assistant prosecuting attorney for Hamilton County,
Ohio.[1]

---

1. Much of the introduction for this chapter and the next one was from an article in the *Chicago Daily Law Bulletin*, "The president and the governor who later became chief justices," *Chicago Daily Law Bulletin, Cotter's Corner*, February 10, 2015, available at https://www.chicagolawbulletin.com/archives/2015/02/10 /dan-cotter-forum-02-10-2015

The son of a prominent attorney and judge, Alphonso Taft, his ambition was to become a Supreme Court justice. He would do that and much more in his varied career. He remains the only person to lead both the executive and judicial branches of our federal government.

He practiced law in Cincinnati after his years as prosecutor until he became a judge of the Ohio Superior Court in 1887. He then became U.S. solicitor general and is the only former holder of that position to become a U.S. president.

In 1892, he was appointed to the Sixth U.S. Circuit Court of Appeals and during part of that tenure served as a law professor and dean at the University of Cincinnati. In 1901, he became the governor general of the Philippines and then was named secretary of war. (He and James Monroe are the only presidents to also serve as secretary of war.)

In 1909, he became president. Best friends with Theodore "Teddy" Roosevelt, Taft's administration did not go very well. He broke with Roosevelt on a variety of issues and served one term. Taft was said to hate the presidency and was a reluctant politician.

Associate Justice Felix Frankfurter once remarked to Justice Louis Brandeis that it was "difficult for me

*to understand why a man who is so good a Chief
Justice . . . could have been so bad as president." He
would fulfill his aspiration to be on the court and loved
his job as chief justice.*

*Taft became president of the American Bar Associa-
tion after being president of the United States, serving
1913–14. He also became the Chancellor Kent Professor of Law at Yale University, a post he held from 1913
to 1921. On June 30, 1921, Harding nominated him for
the Supreme Court, and he easily was confirmed by
voice vote, with only four senators voting against his
nomination.*

*Taft would serve for more than nine years and his
court would issue a number of notable decisions. One
of Taft's dissents challenged the court's upholding of
the Lochner doctrine, established in the 1905 Lochner
v. New York case. In Lochner v. New York, the court
ruled 5-4 that a state law that limited working hours
for bakers was unconstitutional because it interfered
with freedom of contract that is protected by the
Constitution.*

*In his dissent in Adkins v. Children's Hospital, Taft
stated, "It is not the function of this court to hold
congressional acts invalid simply because they are
passed to carry out economic views which the court*

believes to be unwise or unsound" Adkins v. Children's Hospital, 261 U.S. 525, 562 (Dissent 1923). Years later in 1937, the court would break with the Lochner doctrine. Taft also created the Judicial Conference of the United States in 1922.

He resigned on February 3, 1930 and died on March 8, 1930.

Early Life and Career

William Howard Taft was born on September 15, 1857, to Alphonso Taft, a prominent attorney and ambassador, and Alphonso's second wife, Louisa Maria (nee Torrey), in Cincinnati, Ohio. After attending public high school, Taft obtained his undergraduate degree from Yale and then studied at Cincinnati Law School, where he graduated. During law school, Taft had taken a position as reporter of legal affairs at the *Cincinnati Commercial*.[2] Taft was admitted to the Ohio bar in 1880. While building a successful legal practice, Taft also was very interested, and engaged, in national politics from early in his career. His political interests would pay off handsomely over the years.

Taft began his public service when he became assistant prosecuting attorney for Hamilton County, Ohio. He then

---

2. Cushman, p. 342.

became assistant county solicitor. Taft was appointed to the Ohio Superior Court, and he loved judging. However, his wife "had her eye on the presidency and spent her energies steering him toward a political career."[3] His track toward that goal of his wife would soon begin in earnest.

President Benjamin Harrison appointed Taft to the position of U.S. solicitor general. After serving in that role for two years, Taft sought a position on the Sixth Circuit, a newly created circuit established by Congress. The Sixth Circuit would be an amazing feeder court for the Supreme Court of the United States.

Sixth Circuit as a Feeder Court[4]

The Sixth Circuit was established on December 10, 1869, and covers Kentucky, Michigan, Ohio, and Tennessee. Five judges have sat on the U.S. Supreme Court, including the first four judges in the Sixth Circuit's history.

The most recent Sixth Circuit judge to sit on the Supreme Court was Potter Stewart, who was elevated in 1958. The circuit courthouse, located in Cincinnati, is named the Potter Stewart U.S. Courthouse in honor of him.

---

3. *Id.*

4. Much of the narrative for this section originally appeared in a a column in the Chicago Daily Law Bulletin on December 11, 2017, Two stories a century apart: Dark money and bench; 6th Circuit court feeder, available at https://www.chicagolawbulletin.com/archives/2017/12/11/dark-money-judiciary-6th-circuit-12-11-17.

The Sixth Circuit was established pursuant to the Judicial Circuits Act of 1866. The Evarts Act of 1891 established nine circuit courts of appeal, including the Sixth Circuit. After enactment of the Evarts Act, Howell Edmunds Jackson was reassigned by the act from the Sixth Circuit to the Sixth Circuit Court of Appeals.

Jackson became the first judge to serve on the Sixth Circuit, serving from 1891 to 1893, when he was nominated by President Benjamin Harrison to serve on the U.S. Supreme Court.

The Senate confirmed Jackson by acclamation. Jackson had expertise in patent law and the Supreme Court at the time had a backlog of patent cases before it. Jackson took his oath on March 4, 1893, but contracted tuberculosis shortly after becoming a Supreme Court justice, serving only until 1895 when he died.

In his short tenure, he issued forty-eight majority opinions for the court and four dissents. His most famous opinion was a harsh dissent in the 1895 decision, *Pollack v. Farmers' Loan & Trust Co.*, which addressed Congress's ability to impose taxes. Jackson argued that the majority decision striking down the tax powers was "the most disastrous blow ever struck at the constitutional power of Congress."

The second judge appointed to the Sixth Circuit was William Howard Taft, who served on the court for one year with Jackson before Jackson was elevated. Taft served on the Sixth Circuit until 1900, when he resigned at the request of

President William McKinley in order to become governor general of the Philippines.

McKinley promised Taft the next Supreme Court judicial vacancy; however, McKinley's death delayed Taft's trip to the high court.

Jackson was replaced on the Sixth Circuit by Horace H. Lurton. Lurton was nominated by President Grover Cleveland and served on the Sixth Circuit Court of Appeals from 1893 to 1909, when Taft nominated his good friend to a vacancy on the Supreme Court.

Taft's nomination surprised many, because Lurton was a Democrat and Taft Republican. On December 20, 1909, the Senate confirmed Lurton by acclamation. Lurton served only four years on the court due to bad health. He died on July 12, 1914, of a heart attack.

Lurton's most notable decision was in the 1911 case, *Coyle v. Smith*, where he wrote that Congress could not dictate where a state placed its capital.

In 1899, the third seat on the Sixth Circuit Court of Appeals was established. McKinley nominated William R. Day to fill this third seat. Day served from 1899 to 1903, so for a brief period of time, the Sixth Circuit Court of Appeals consisted of Taft, Lurton, and Day.

Day was nominated by President Theodore Roosevelt to the Supreme Court to fill the vacancy created by the resignation of George Shiras Jr. in 1903, and the Senate confirmed Day on February 23, 1903 by acclamation. Day served until November 13, 1922, when he retired. Day wrote a number of important decisions for the Supreme Court during his tenure.

One is hard-pressed to find another example of four judges who served on a circuit court of appeals being elevated to the Supreme Court. The first two judges who served on the Sixth Circuit Court of Appeals and the judges who filled the first three seats on the Sixth Circuit Court of Appeals all served on the Supreme Court.

The route to the highest court in the land at the end of the nineteenth century/beginning of the twentieth century often passed through Cincinnati.

Given the increased number of circuits that exist and other factors, it is doubtful we will see a similar circuit dominance again.

Leaving the Bench

During his tenure on the Sixth Circuit, Taft taught at Cincinnati Law School and became the Dean of the law school. Taft left the bench in 1901, when President William H. McKinley asked Taft to help with the Philippines post-Spanish–American War. Taft became the governor general of the Philippines Protectorate and was considered to be excellent in this role.

When President McKinley died, President Theodore Roosevelt offered Taft a Supreme Court seat, which Taft turned down. However, in 1904, when asked to become secretary of war, Taft agreed. Taft "soon became one of Roosevelt's most trusted and respected cabinet advisers as well as his close friend."[5]

President Taft

President Roosevelt pushed Taft to be the Republican Party's nomination for president in 1908, and Taft won the election. During Taft's one term, he had the unique ability to appoint a majority of the Supreme Court,[6] including his selection of Edward D. White as chief justice. Taft "was most proud of his Supreme Court appointments."[7]

Despite the efforts of President Roosevelt to get Taft elected in 1908, by 1912, Roosevelt had a split with his chosen successor, and Roosevelt ran a hard-fought third-party campaign. With the Republicans fighting, Woodrow Wilson was able to capture the White House, leaving Taft a one-term president. Accounts strongly suggest that Taft did not enjoy being president, and his passion and interest continued to be the law and the judiciary.

During the 1908 campaign, Taft had the support of President Teddy Roosevelt behind him. However, that friendship deteriorated even before Taft resided at the White House, and series of "[p]olitical troubles . . . established the perception of ineptitude that Taft never overcame." The

---

5. Cushman, p. 343.

6. Presidents Washington and Lincoln and FDR also had this ability. *See* **Appendix B**.

7. Cushman, p. 343.

relationship between Roosevelt and Taft would completely
sever during the 1912 presidential campaign.[8]

Post-Presidency

Having failed in his bid for reelection, Taft became the
Kent Professor of Constitutional Law at Yale University. Taft
also became President of the American Bar Association. In
1920, President Warren G. Harding won the presidency
and, shortly after, Harding and Taft met to discuss the
Supreme Court, with President Harding informing Taft
"that he would be willing to give him the next available seat
on the Court."[9] Taft replied the only position he would consider agreeing to would be chief justice, "[H]aving appointed
three of the present bench and three others and having pro-
tested against Brandeis, I could not accept any place but
the chief justiceship."[10]

Taft would soon have that opportunity. On June 30, 1921,
Taft was confirmed as the chief justice to replace Chief
Justice White, who had died. Chief Justice Taft would continue the Court on its conservative path, although the
Court he presided over was way behind in its work and
divided. Taft's efforts paid off on the administrative side-
he reduced the backlog and was instrumental in passage of

---

8. Gould, p. 9.
9. *Id.* at 344.
10. Pringle, Vol. 2, p. 955.

the Judiciary Act of 1925. In the division, he was not quite as successful—on many issues, Justices Holmes and Brandeis submitted "critical dissents."[11]

On Commerce Clause jurisprudence, the Taft Court did strike a very conservative tenor. For example, in *Bailey v. Drexel Furniture Co.*, 259 U.S. 20 (1922), the Supreme Court ruled the 1919 Child Labor Tax Law unconstitutional. In another case, *Adkins v. Children's Hospital*, 261 U.S. 525 (1923), the Court struck down a District of Columbia minimum wage for women, citing to the recently ratified Nineteenth Amendment. Chief Justice Taft dissented in that case.

The Taft Court also tackled issues related to the Eighteenth Amendment (prohibiton).[12]

Legacy

Chief Justice Taft demonstrated his strong administrative experience when he became chief justice. "Taft used his personal and political clout—and his connections—to initiate and promote various kinds of judicial reform in an effort to simplify procedures, reduce political patronage, and eliminate the perpetual backlog of pending cases."[13]

---

11. Cushman, p. 345.
12. *Id.*
13. *Id.*

Taft established the Judicial Conference of the United States and was instrumental in making sure the Judiciary Act of 1925 passed.[14] The Judiciary Act permitted the Supreme Court greater discretion in what cases it would hear. Finally, Taft is responsible for the current Supreme Court Building, overseeing these efforts. He would not live to see its completion.

Resignation and Death

Chief Justice Taft experienced several debilitating strokes, and, on February 1, 1930, he submitted his resignation. His successor, Charles Evans Hughes, was a friend of Taft's and had been promised elevation at one time when Taft was president. Taft died on March 8, 1930, the only person to serve as head of both the executive and judicial branches of our government.

---

14. Stevens, p. 29.

Part Six

The Great Depression, a Crisis on the Court; New Deal; Lead-Up to War

When Chief Justice Charles Evans Hughes returned to the Supreme Court on February 24, 1930, it was a time "of the most serious and steadily worsening economic crisis in U.S. history."[1] More than 5,000 banks would fail in the period from October 29, 1929, "Black Tuesday," through 1932, and unemployment would reach almost a quarter of the U.S. population.

President Herbert Hoover would be blamed in large part for the economic woes, and President Franklin Delano Roosevelt would come to the White House in 1933 as a result. FDR went on to be the longest serving president in our nation's history. FDR implemented his "100 Day Plan" and followed it with his "New Deal." The conservative court would find many of his New Deal initiatives invalid, leading

---

1. Mayer, p. 7.

to a crisis for the Supreme Court. The president and Congress pushed for various ways to address the Court's positions, including FDR's "court packing plan," which failed. Thanks to the "switch in time that saved nine" of Associate Justice Owen Roberts, the Court began to find FDR's initiatives valid, and the crisis was averted.[2]

---

2. At press time, we have arguments once again of various measures that might be implemented to address the rightward ideology of the current Roberts Court. Whether anyone on the present court will become the second "switch in time" is open to debate. While it does not appear to be entirely likely, at times Chief Justice Roberts has shown some limited signs of potentially filling that role. Time will tell as this Court settles in with its newest additions. Among proposals being thrown out are each four-year term comes with a sixteen-year appointment, appointing an eighteen-year term jusice every two years, with there remaining nine justices, expanding the number of seats on the Supreme Court, and other measures. Many of the proposals would require a constitutional amendment, as Article III judges serve on good behavior, interpreted and applied to mean lifetime appointments.

Chapter Thirteen

Charles Evans Hughes: White House Ambitions

Nominated by President Herbert Hoover
Confirmed by Senate, 52-26, on February 13, 1930
Tenure: February 24, 1930 to June 30, 1941 (Retired)
Presidents During Tenure
　Hoover
　Franklin D. Roosevelt

Hughes Follows as Successor

Charles Evans Hughes was nominated as Taft's successor on February 3, 1930, and confirmed ten days later by a split Senate, with a vote of 52-26.

Hughes was born in upstate New York to a minister and his wife. Upon graduation from Columbia Law in 1884, he practiced law in New York City and would do so at various times in his career. He became a law professor and lecturer and, in 1907, became governor of New York.

On April 25, 1910, then-President Taft nominated Hughes to an associate justice position. In 1916, he resigned from the court to run for president as the Republican nominee. Following his defeat, he returned to private practice, until he was tapped for secretary of state. He then served on the Permanent Court of Arbitration and was a judge for the Permanent Court of International Justice at The Hague.

When Taft announced his resignation from the court, President Herbert Hoover nominated Hughes. Some senators believed Hughes to be too close with businesses.

The Hughes Court would be faced with the various cases brought before it involving the New Deal and struck down a number of pieces of New Deal legislation, until the "switch in time that saved nine" in West Coast Hotel v. Parrish (1937).

Justice Owen Josephus Roberts, who had previously been a swing vote and consistently voted against New Deal reforms, changed his jurisprudence in this case, which overturned the Lochner doctrine. Some historians believe Roberts' shift may have been strategic to prevent Roosevelt from expanding the Supreme Court to fifteen justices.

Hughes' court would decide cases such as Schechter Poultry v. U.S. (1935) and NLRB v. Jones & Laughlin Steel Co. (1937).

Hughes was the second chief who had earlier been an associate justice and left the court for a time (the first was John Rutledge.) Hughes retired, effective July 1, 1941, after the Senate had confirmed his successor, Harlan Fiske Stone, who is the only justice to have sat in each of the nine seats on the Supreme Court.

Early Life and Career

Charles Evans Hughes was born on April 11, 1862, to David Charles Hughes, a Methodist preacher, and Mary Catherine (nee Connelly) in Glen Falls, New York. Hughes at the age of 6 proposed a program of self-study to his parents, "The Charles Evans Hughes Plan of Study."[1] Hughes' parents agreed, and when they moved to New York City, Hughes graduated from high school at the age of 13. Hughes delivered the salutatory on the topic of "Self-Help."[2] Hughes enrolled at Madison College (now Colgate University) to study for the ministry, but transferred to Brown University, graduating in 1881 with the fourth-highest honors.[3]

---

1. Hendel, p. 2.
2. Pusey, Vol. 1, p. 21.
3. *Id.* at p. 3. Some writings describe Hughes as having third highest honors. For conservativeness, we have gone with the rank in the book close to the time of Hughes' completion of his tenure as chief justice.

Hughes decided law was his calling rather than the ministry but had no financial ability to pay. He taught for a year at a private academy in New Delhi, New York, and apprenticed at a lawyer's office.[4] Hughes then attended Columbia Law School on a scholarship, where he graduated at the top of his class, then reportedly scored a 99[5] on his New York bar exam. Hughes' parents were also instrumental in supporting his pursuit of a law degree, having accepted that Hughes would not become a minister as they had hoped for him.[5]

Hughes devoted himself to the private practice of law at a New York law firm, Chamberlain, Carter & Hornblower, led by Walter S. Carter, who became Hughes's father-in-law. Hughes worked at the firm during summers while a student at Columbia Law School, becoming a partner within five years and where he worked until 1891, when he resigned to become a law professor at Cornell Law School. The law firm relationship began with a three-year fellowship for having graduated with highest honors.[6] Hughes primarily practiced in the field of commercial law.[7]

Despite enjoying teaching, his law firm lured him back, but he continued to teach at Cornell as well as New York

---

4. While teaching at the Delaware Academy, Hughes started studying law at the law offices of William M. Gleason, "a lawyer of high repute in up-State New York." Pusey, Vol. 1, p. 66.

5. *Id.* at 67.

6. Hendel, p. 3.

7. Pusey, Vol. 1, p. 91.

Law School.[8] In 1905, Hughes was appointed as counsel to a New York legislative committee formed to look at utility rates. He found corruption and was widely praised for his service, discovering savings of more than $800,000 for city street lighting and other overcharging.[9] Hughes next was appointed to the Armstrong Committee involving insurance companies, and once again found a number of violations that the New York legislature addressed soon after Hughes' investigation was complete.[10] Hughes had "laid bare an organized scheme on the part of the big insurance companies to control legislation throughout the United States."[11] These "great investigations" made Hughes "a national figure."[12] Hughes would ride this new-found prominence and recognition to the governor's mansion. He ran on a platform of government that is not corrupt. In one of his campaign speeches, Hughes stated:

> "You may think that the Constitution is your security— it is nothing but a bit of paper. You may think the statutes are your security—they are nothing but words in a

---

8. His father-in-law wrote a series of letters addressing the significant difference in income from being a partner at the firm and being a professor. *See* Pusey, Vol. 1, pgs. 101–04.

9. Hendel, p. 4.

10. *Id.*

11. Pusey, Vol. 1, p. 154. Hughes' work on the insurance investigation led to some insurance laws in New York, which "were widely copied in other states and became the foundation on which modern insurance in America rests." Pusey, Vol. 1, p. 167.

12. *Id.* at p. 132.

book. . . . It is nothing at all unless you have sound and uncorrupted public opinion to give life to your Constitution, to give vitality to your statutes. . . ."[13]

In 1906, Hughes was elected Governor of New York. Hughes was the only Republican candidate to win statewide office during that election year.[14] Hughes took the oath of office on January 1, 1907. Hughes established a number of workers' rights as governor, and successfully ran for a second term. Among his achievements, Hughes oversaw the enactment of "pioneering" legislation that created two public service commissions.[15] This work and his efforts to remove the insurance superintendent appear to be closely connected to his work as a lawyer before becoming governor, trying to ferret out and remove graft, corruption, and problems.

Shortly after the public service commissions legislation passed, Governor Hughes gave a speech at Elmira, New York. He had prepared remarks, but after the speaker before him blasted the public commissions bill, Hughes delivered a response to the previous speaker's attack. He talked about his view of the courts and their role:

I have the highest regard for the courts. My whole life has been spent in work conditioned upon respect for

---

13. *Id.* at 175–76.
14. Perkins, p. 8.
15. *Id.* at 14–15.

the courts. I reckon him one of the worst enemies of the community who will talk lightly of the dignity of the bench. We are under a Constitution, but the Constitution is what the judges say it is, and the judiciary is the safeguard of our liberty and our property under the Constitution. I do not want to see any indirect assault upon the courts.[16]

Hughes then discussed his views of how administrative decisions are not the proper role of the judiciary. Hughes made similar comments about the Court's powers in other speeches that when he became an associate justice, then chief justice would be used against him to argue he was a judicial activist. Hughes defended his speech and the out of context reference used to attack him in his Biographical Notes, stating:

"The inference that I was picturing constitutional interpretation by the courts as a matter of judicial caprice was farthest from my thoughts.... I was speaking of the essential function of the courts...."[17]

Hughes was independent as a governor, and carefully reviewed everything submitted to him. In his first year as

---

16. Speech before the Elmira Chamber of Commerce, May 3, 1907, available at https://books.google.com/books?id=pMNQGAeeaTkC&pg=PR4&lpg=PR4&dq =elmira+speech+1907+hughes&source=bl&ots=SeHl8ZkEwO&sig=XVfbrpFal 3z0MBa1gpSu7xWjOqk&hl=en&sa=X&ved=0ahUKEwi0j4i6lq_cAhUL9IM KHTX4C6oQ6AEIRDAG#v=snippet&q=under%20a%20constitution&f=false.
17. Pusey, Vol. 1, p. 204 (quoting Hughes' Biographical Notes).

governor, "he vetoed 297 bills and various items in six appropriation measures."[18] Hughes as governor passed a number of labor legislation bills, including the first workmen's compensation laws in the United States.[19]

Hughes' name was mentioned to be the Republican nominee for president of the United States, but Taft received the party's nomination on the first ballot, with 702 votes. Taft reached out to Hughes via telegram to be his vice president on the ticket, but Hughes saw nothing to recommend the spot and did not have the capacity to make financial sacrifices to do it.[20]

Hughes did not wish to seek a second two-year term as New York Governor, but at the Saratoga convention, Hughes on the first ballot had 827 votes versus 151 for his closest challenger, and the convention made it unanimous.[21] The September 17, 1908 edition of the *Nation* crowed:

> "The renomination of Governor Hughes must be reckoned as one of the most significant political events in the last quarter century."[22]

---

18. *Id.* at 210.
19. *Id.* at 212.
20. *Id.* at 239.
21. Pusey, Vol. 1, p. 246.
22. *Id.* (quoting the *Nation*).

Associate Justice of the Supreme Court of the United States

In March 1910, President William Howard Taft visited Albany, where Hughes hosted him at the Executive Mansion. The visit impressed favorably on Taft, who wrote to Archie Butt after his visit about Hughes:

> "I don't know the man I admire more than Hughes. If ever I have the chance I shall offer him the Chief Justiceship."[23]

The opportunity to nominate Hughes to a seat on the Supreme Court quickly arose, when Associate Justice David J. Brewer died. Hughes would not run for a third term as governor, with many in the party lamenting his acceptance of the Supreme Court position because Hughes was so effective in fighting corruption in New York.[24]

On April 25, 1910, President William Howard Taft nominated Hughes as an associate justice of the Supreme Court. President Taft announced:

> "I am very much delighted to secure Governor Hughes for the Supreme Court Bench. He is a man of wide experience, and it is a mighty valuable thing to have on that bench a man of affairs."[25]

---

23. *Id.* at 268.
24. *Id.*
25. Hendel, p. 13.

Former President Theodore Roosevelt was generally satisfied with the nomination of Hughes, with a warning of hope attached to it, writing to Henry Cabot Lodge:

"Hughes' nomination is excellent, and I think he will make a fine judge. I only hope that he has awakened to the fact that unless we are content to face disaster to the judiciary in the future, there must be a very radical change in the attitude of our judges to public questions. I verily believe that the conduct of the bench, in failing to move with the times, and in continually sticking on minor points of law rather than turning to broad principles of justice and equity, is one of the chief elements in producing the popular discontent."[26]

The confirmation of Hughes as an associate justice was a rather easy one, with the Senate confirming Hughes by acclamation on May 2, 1910. Hughes requested that he be allowed to wait until the beginning of the 1910 Supreme Court term to take his oath, in order to permit Hughes to focus on various matters as New York Governor.[27] Hughes was sworn in on October 10, 1910 as an associate justice of the Supreme Court and resigned his governorship the same day.

26. *Id.* at 13–14.
27. *Id.* at 15.

An Indirect Route to Chief

Hughes served as an associate justice from 1910 to 1916. One topic of focus for the Supreme Court during Hughes' relatively short term as associate justice was the regulation of interstate commerce. According to one law review author:

> "While these opinions were, of course, participated in by the other able members of the Supreme Court, the credit for them must be given in large part to the writer, and as to some of them it may safely be said that they rank among the most important and able pronouncements upon the principles of constitutional law that have come before the Supreme Court during its entire history."[28]

Heady words about Hughes the associate justice, but his nomination was only a beginning to what President William Howard Taft had in mind for the former New York Governor. When President Taft nominated Hughes on April 25, 1910 to fill the vacancy created by Associate Justice David Brewer, Taft told Hughes, "The Chief Justiceship is soon likely to be vacant and I should never regard the practice of never promoting associate justices as one to be followed."[29] Taft continued:

---

28. Allen, p. 566.
29. Pusey, Vol. 1, p. 271.

"Don't misunderstand me as to the Chief Justiceship. I mean that if that office were now open I would offer it to you and it is probable that if it were to become vacant during my term, I should promote you to it, but, of course, conditions change, so that it would not be right for me to say by way of promise that I would do it in the future."[30]

Hughes did not put much stock in the promise of a potential seat as chief justice, but in his April 24 response to Taft he wrote, "What right have I to refuse this opportunity of public service which is now presented by you and upon what ground could I justify myself in turning aside from such a plain path of usefulness?"[31] Hughes turned down potential income in private practice in the low to mid-six figures for a position that paid $14,500.[32] Hughes was confirmed by voice vote on May 2, 1910, taking his seat on October 10, 1910, after his resignation as governor.

Like other presidents and promises made, promises not always kept, President Taft did not follow through on his promise to Hughes for the chief justice seat. After Hughes was confirmed by the Senate but before he took his judicial oath, Chief Justice Melville Fuller passed away, and the expectation was that the promise made less than two weeks before would become reality. However, it did not turn out

30. Cushman, p. 308.
31. Pusey, Vol. 1, p. 272.
32. *Id.* at 273, 271.

that way. Instead, President Taft turned to the current members of the Supreme Court and selected sitting Associate Justice Edward D. White to succeed Fuller as chief justice.[33] But the process was not without intrigue, and on Sunday, December 11, Hughes received a call from the White House asking him to come to see the president. As he prepared to head to the White House, he received a second call cancelling the visit.[34] The next day, Hughes read in the newspapers that White had been selected. Had Hughes become chief justice in 1910, who knows if he would have run for president in 1916, or if Taft would have become chief justice if he appointed Hughes.

Despite this slight, Hughes served the Court admirably, and was a busy contributor to the Court, writing "151 opinions including 32 dissents."[35] In his time on the Supreme Court as an associate justice, Hughes adopted the views of Associate Justice Oliver Holmes in a dissent by Holmes in a 1905 case when it came to invalidating state legislation— just say no.[36] Despite being on the same side in that particular case, Holmes and Hughes often were on opposite sides, but "in the memorable cases in which they differed it has been Hughes' viewpoint which has thus far weathered the test of time."[37]

---

33. *See* chapter on Edward D. White for more details about his nomination.
34. Pusey, Vol. 1, p. 278.
35. Cushman, p. 308.
36. Perkins, pgs. 38–40 (describing Hughes' approach to such cases).
37. Pusey, Vol. 1, p. 294.

Hughes had often been named as a potential presidential candidate. Hughes was approached in 1912, but rejected the invite, writing to Republican National Convention Chairman Elihu Root:

> "The Supreme Court must be kept out of politics. I must add, to avoid all possible misunderstanding, that, even if nominated, I should decline."[38]

Hughes joined his colleagues on the Supreme Court in "a broad interpretation of the commerce clause."[39] For example, in the *Minnesota Rate Cases*,[40] Hughes wrote an opinion that gave Congress broad oversight of interstate commerce, writing in part:

> "The power of Congress to regulate commerce among several States is supreme and plenary. . . . There is no room in our scheme of government for the assertion of State power in hostility to the authorized exercise of Federal power. The authority of Congress extends to every part of interstate commerce. . . ."[41]

A Presidential Nomination

Finally, in 1916, the Republicans nominated Hughes as their presidential nominee. While Hughes "made no effort

---

38. *Id.* at 301 (quoting Hughes' letter to Root).
39. *Id.* at 303.
40. *Minnesota Rate Cases*, 230 U.S. 352 (1913).
41. *Id.*

to obtain the nomination, he was unwilling to oppose it,"[42] and, not following the views of Waite and despite his note to Root in 1912, Hughes accepted the party's nomination and resigned from the Court to run against Woodrow Wilson, resigning on June 10, 1916.[43] What may have influenced his final decision in part was a long plea from William Taft to Hughes arguing that the party needed him and would likely nominate Hughes unless he clearly declined. In one of the closest elections in history, Wilson won the electoral college, 277-254, and the popular vote, 9,126,300 to 8,546,789.[44] President Hughes' run for the position of president of the United States would end here. By most accounts, "there has rarely been a more ineptly conducted political conflict" than the one that Hughes conducted in 1916.[45] Despite his losing the race, Hughes never did "give way either to bitterness or to public lamentation," and wondered later if Wilson was a better person to be "able to unite the country."[46]

Return to Practice

After his presidential defeat, Hughes returned to New York City and private practice, as a member of the law firm

---

42. Hendel, p. 68.
43. Pusey, Vol. 1, p. 330.
44. *Id.* at 309.
45. Perkins, p. 55.
46. *Id.* at 64.

of Hugh, Rounds, Schurman, and Dwight, focusing his practice on corporate work. At the same time, Hughes was often involved in various efforts at public service, including being chairman of the District Draft Appeals Board for New York City.[47] One matter that Hughes became very involved in at the local level was the New York State Assembly. Five Socialist members were elected from the City of New York and took their seats. However, the New York Speaker informed the five they were to be excluded from the legislature pending an investigation into them.[48] Many lawyers and others did not intervene or get involved. But Hughes spoke up, sending the Speaker a letter, arguing that implementing such a step as excluding the duly elected assemblymen was a denial of peaceful government by the "masses of our citizens combined for political action."[49] While he lost the battle, "he had spoken out in behalf of traditional American ideals."[50]

President Warren G. Harding brought Hughes back to public service, appointing Hughes to the position of secretary of state on Harding's first day as president, March 4, 1921. Hughes was an active Secretary and gets high praise according to Perkins.[51] One activity that occupied much of

---

47. *Id.*

48. *Id.* at 68.

49. *Id.* at 68–69 (quoting Hughes' letter).

50. *Id.* at 70.

51. Perkins, p. 138. Author Perkins describes a survey he sent to "a group of distinguished students of American diplomatic history" and in that survey, Hughes

his time at the front end of his service was the League of Nations and whether the United States should join. Post-World War I, he worked on various treaties and at the Washington Conference on armaments, he gave an opening speech that was widely hailed for its contents. The four years spent as secretary of state were very busy ones for Hughes.

When President Harding died on August 2, 1923, Hughes advised President Calvin Coolidge to "take the oath of office and come to Washington at once."[52] For the next two years, Hughes worked closely with President Coolidge, "being consulted on all the important issues relating to the welfare of the country."[53] Remarkably, in the four years that Hughes served as secretary of state, "sixty-nine treaties were negotiated, not counting a few insignificant ones that were later withdrawn."[54]

In 1925, Hughes submitted his letter of resignation to the president, to take effect on March 4, 1925. After a spring and summer of relaxation with his family, Hughes once again returned to private practice to make some money[55] and focus on commercial clients and their needs. Hughes also made significant money giving speeches to groups

---

was the person ranked third overall, thus permitting Perkins to conclude "Hughes is clearly one of the very eminent Secretaries." *Id.* at 139.

52. Pusey, Vol. 2, p. 563.

53. *Id.* at 565.

54. *Id.* at 611.

55. According to Hendel, Hughes wanted to "recoup his fortune." Hendel, p. 77.

such as the American Society of International Law.[56] In the mid-1920s, Hughes thrived, with his income "as high as $400,000 a year."[57] Hughes was "the acknowledged leader of the American bar. He represented some of the most important corporate interests in the country. . . ."[58] Hughes served as the president of the American Bar Association as well.[59] Hughes appeared before the Supreme Court on several occasions to argue cases before it.[60]

In 1928, Hughes was elected to a position as a judge on the Permanent Court of International Justice.[61] The Permanent Court was designed to promote the cause of international justice and Hughes and Root had been instrumental in getting the United States into the Court. Hughes served in this position until 1930, when President Herbert Hoover tapped Hughes to replace Chief Justice Taft,[62] who announced his retirement on February 3, 1930, due to poor health, President Hoover named Hughes to succeed Taft. The "nomination drew strong opposition from progressive and southern Democratic senators."[63] Hughes resigned from the World Court on the same date, saving a potential

---

56. Pusey, Vol. 2, p. 619.
57. Perkins, p. 141.
58. Hendel, p. 77.
59. Pusey, Vol. 2, p. 620.
60. *Id.* at 625.
61. Perkins, p. 140.
62. *Id.* at 142–43.
63. *Id.*

showdown with his wife, who did not enjoy living abroad.[64] Hughes was coming to the chief justice position "in the hour of the court's greatest need for leadership."[65] His leadership skills would be tested as chief justice of a highly split Court during a time of U.S. struggle through the Great Depression and the New Deal of President Franklin Delano Roosevelt.

Chief Justice Hughes and Legacy

On February 3, 1930, President Hoover nominated Hughes as chief justice of the Supreme Court of the United States, and Hughes was confirmed, 52-26, on February 13, 1930. But despite the margin of the vote, the Senate had a heated debate over the nomination of Hughes to chief justice of the Supreme Court. The supporters of Hughes knew they had the votes to carry the nomination. However, the debate went on for some time, with opponents of the nomination expressing concerns over Hughes' resignation from the Court to run for president and also because of his practice with big corporate organizations, including some in the oil industry immediately after resigning from his post as secretary of state. Senator George Norris, for example, expressed concern that "such a precedent would encourage political activity on the part of Supreme Court judges" and also

---

64. Pusey, Vol. 2, p. 646.
65. *Id.* at 648.

expressed concerns that Hughes' "viewpoint is clouded" by representing "untold wealth" and he had "lived in luxury."[66] The debate was healthy:

> "But the importance of the debate, from the point of view of the Senate liberals, lay not in the hope of immediate success in blocking the confirmation but in the educational value in expounding to the Senate and to the nation the nature of the issues being decided by the Court and the considerations which controlled its decisions. These issues, the liberals insisted, were largely economic, and the considerations which decided them were fundamentally based not upon the law of the Constitution but the preference of the Justices."[67]

While the efforts did not affect the confirmation of Hughes as chief justice, one of President Hoover's nominees, Judge John J. Parker, was rejected by a vote of 41-39, based in part on the preferences argument made in the Hughes confirmation hearing.

As a lawyer, Hughes had summed up the role of chief justice that he would now assume:

> "Popular interest naturally centers in the Chief Justice as the titular head of the Court. He is its executive officer; he presides at its sessions and at its conferences,

---

66. *Id.* at 655.
67. Hendel, p. 89.

and announces its orders. By virtue of the distinctive function of the Court he is the most important judicial officer in the world; he is the Chief Justice of the United States."[68]

On the same date that Hughes was confirmed, Hughes' son, Charles Evans Hughes Jr., resigned his position as solicitor general. Hughes generally was admired and respected by the legal community. Felix Frankfurter, who joined the Supreme Court in Hughes' final years, had written about Hughes becoming chief justice:

"with a mastery . . . unparalleled in the history of the Court, a mastery that derived from experience as diversified, as intense, as extensive, as any man every brought to a seat on the Court, combined with a very powerful and acute mind that could mobilize these vast resources in the conduct of the business of the Court."[69]

Hughes demonstrated the abilities Frankfurter described most notably during the 1930s, when two factions, the "Four Horsemen" made up of conservatives (Willis Van Devanter, James C. McReynolds, George Sutherland, and Pierce Butler), and the liberal group, worked at opposites to invalidate much of the New Deal initiatives implemented by Congress and President Roosevelt. Hughes

---

68. Pusey, Vol. 2, p. 663.
69. Cushman, p. 310.

generally had sided with the conservatives and wrote the majority opinion invalidating the National Industrial Recovery Act.

On February 5, 1937, in response to the Supreme Court blocking FDR's efforts to address the Great Depression through various legislative initiatives that are referred to as the "New Deal," which the Four Horsemen and the Supreme Court invalidated on numerous occasions early in FDR's first term, FDR proposed a court packing plan that permitted a president to appoint one member to the Court for every justice over the age of 70 who did not retire.[70] The idea generally was not well received and that led to the Court pushing back on the initiative. For example, on March 21, 1937, Chief Justice Hughes wrote Senator Burton K. Wheeler a letter debunking that the Supreme Court, due to the age of the justices, was unable to keep up with the workload, writing:

> "The Supreme Court is fully abreast of its work. When we rose on March 15 (for the present recess) we had heard argument in cases in which certiorari had been granted only 4 weeks before, . . . There is no congestion of cases upon our calendar. . . . An increase in the number of Justices of the Supreme Court, apart from any question of policy, which I do not discuss, would not promote the efficiency of the Court."[71]

---

70. Urofsky, Division, p. 4.
71. Pusey, Vol. 2, p. 756.

However, more important than the pushback, Hughes worked with Associate Justice Owen Roberts to back off of some of the Court's hardline positions on the New Deal initiatives and began to find some of FDR's New Deal legislation valid, beginning in 1937 with *West Coast Hotel Co. v. Parrish.*[72]

The Four Horsemen[73]

As noted, the Four Horsemen were a conservative voting bloc that were very effective in overturning much of the New Deal legislation passed during the Great Depression, effectively calling into question whether FDR would be able to implement programs to address the economic challenges facing the nation.

During the 1932 through 1937 terms, the Four Horsemen effectively thwarted President Franklin Delano Roosevelt's agenda. Seldom in the history of the Supreme Court has a voting bloc been memorialized by a group name like the Four Horsemen earned.

---

72. *West Coast Hotel Co. v. Parrish,* 300 U.S. 379 (1937).

73. Much of the narrative in this section originally appeared in Constituting America's 90 Day Study: A History of Our Country's Judicial System. Cotter, *Justice George Sutherland (1862-1942),* available at https://constitutingamerica .org/justice-george-sutherland-1862-1942-guest-essayist-daniel-a-cotter/, as well as in a Chicago Daily Law Bulletin article that appeared in the October 10, 2016, edition, available at https://www.chicagolawbulletin.com/archives/2016/10/10/scotus -4-horsemen-10-10-16.

When Van Devanter and McReynolds were joined by
Sutherland and then Butler in early 1923, they formed a
powerful conservative bloc on the court, first under Chief
Justice Taft and then under Chief Justice Charles Evans
Hughes.

In the 1932 term, their cohesiveness resulted in the nickname the Four Horsemen from the national press (a reference
to the Four Horsemen of the Apocalypse in the Bible—
Death, Famine, War, and Conquest). From 1932 to 1937, they
(together with Hughes and Justice Owen J. Roberts) invalidated many of Roosevelt's New Deal initiatives, including
the Agricultural Adjustment Act, the Federal Farm Bankruptcy Act, the Railroad Act, and the Coal Mining Act.

The Four Horsemen also ruled with justices Roberts and
Hughes that the National Industrial Act and minimum
wage laws for women and children were unconstitutional.

The Four Horsemen rode together to the Supreme Court
every day to discuss strategy and positions and were
opposed to laws regulating labor as well as state economic
regulation.

The Supreme Court's invalidation of much of the New
Deal led to a potential constitutional crisis when Roosevelt
proposed his court-packing.

The Constitution does not specify the number of justices who sit on the Supreme Court, and the current com-
position of nine justices, which was also in effect at the
time of Roosevelt's proposal, was set by the Judiciary Act
of 1869.

The crisis was averted when Roberts voted to uphold a Washington state minimum wage law in *West Coast Hotel v. Parrish*.[74] Known as the "switch in time that saved nine," recent scholars have concluded that Roberts actually cast his vote in this case before the court-packing legislation was introduced, rather than as a result of political pressure stemming from Roosevelt's effort to reconstitute the court. Whatever the reasons behind his change, a crisis was averted. Two weeks after the *West Coast* decision, the Supreme Court "upheld the National Labor Relations Act in the *Jones & Laughlin* case."[75]

On May 18, 1937, Van Devanter retired from the Supreme Court due to health issues. He had stated that but for his concerns about the New Deal legislation, he might have retired much sooner.

Van Devanter was replaced by Hugo Black. Sutherland retired on January 17, 1938, replaced by Stanley Reed. The Four Horsemen were no more, and Roosevelt saw a number of New Deal victories from the Supreme Court over the next several years during the Hughes Court.

The Supreme Court has not seen such a consistent voting bloc since the Four Horsemen and one wonders if we will see such a bloc again.[76] One reason that the blocs might

---

74. *West Coast Hotel Co. v. Parrish*, 300 U.S. 379 (1937).

75. Irons, p. 73.

76. The current Court's quartet of Alito, Thomas, Gorsuch and Kavanaugh (joined by Chief Justice Roberts often) might be such a bloc, and perhaps might earn a label in the future such as "Four Horsemen of the FedSoc."

have thrived was Hughes' views on a divided Court and his thoughts on how best to address it:

> "Hughes knew that a divided Court is a Court which loses public confidence. But he had a deep respect for his colleagues, and he did not like to think in terms of judicial blocs."[77]

Hughes dealt with the difficult nature of the justices who sat with him as best he could. He was unable to have that undivided court that spoke with one voice, but he did much to improve the efficiency of the justice system. In 1938, he encouraged the Court to adopt new rules of civil procedure and also helped to ensure enactment of 1939 legislation that formed the Administrative Office of the U.S. Courts, which improved the administration of justice.

Hughes tightly controlled his Court—the oral arguments never started late during his tenure as chief justice, "he held each speaker to exactly his allotted time," and he would let advocates know when no further argument was warranted.[78] According to Louis Brandeis, Hughes "was the greatest executive genius he had ever encountered in law, in business, or in government."[79] Unlike some of his successors, "Hughes often modified his own opinions in order to win additional support for them if that could be done without compromising the integrity of the position the majority

---

77. Perkins, p. 146.
78. Pusey, Vol. 2, pgs. 664–65.
79. *Id.* at 673.

had taken."[80] Hughes strived always to "enhance public confidence in the entire court as an independent and impartial tribunal."[81] One of the difficult obligations Hughes encountered was visiting the elderly Justice Oliver Wendell Holmes to ask for Holmes' resignation. A majority of associate justices had made the request to Hughes.[82] On January 11, 1932, Hughes visited Holmes at Holmes' house and explained the purpose of his visit. Holmes asked for the language of the statute and wrote his resignation.[83] Holmes was replaced by Benjamin Cardozo, and for the next five years, the same Court would be intact.

Death

Perhaps no chief justice has "showed more executive talent than Hughes" and perhaps "none realized more acutely that the delay of justice is often its denial."[84]

Perhaps no better epitaph is available than the one that Samuel Hendel wrote in his Preface to his book in 1950:

---

80. *Id.* at 677. Especially in the last two Courts (Rehnquist and Roberts), we don't often (if ever) see a chief changing an opinion or softening it to gain votes or an acceptable compromise decision. The one exception might be in the decision that Chief Justice Roberts wrote in the Affordable Care Act case, which has been written about extensively. According to numerous reports, Roberts originally was on the other side of that decision but changed his vote late in the process. We may some day have full insight into what transpired, but likely not during the author's lifetime.

81. Pusey, Vol. 2, p. 679.

82. *Id.* at 681.

83. *Id.*

84. Perkins, p. 147.

"[N]o man ever brought greater wealth and diversity of experience to the Chief Justiceship than he did; and in this experience, sometimes in obvious and palpable ways, and sometimes in subtle and imponderable ways, had a profound effect upon his decisions. Primarily, however, this book will be concerned with an analysis of the contributions of Associate Justice and later Chief Justice Hughes to the solution of important *constitutional* issues that came before the Supreme Court. So delimited, the area to be canvassed is still large because the two periods of Mr. Hughes' service on the Court were periods of great ferment in American history."[85]

In the present, we talk much about a Supreme Court justices' ideology and whether they are liberal or conservative. At least one biographer has described Hughes as someone more in the middle, straddling those two positions:

"The major problem of politics is the problem of a just balance between conservatism and liberalism. While it would be too much to say that Charles Evans Hughes attained that balance to perfection, he surely represented in his strong will and clear mind the desire to see that balance attained."[86]

---

85. Hendel, pgs. vii–viii.
86. Perkins, p. xiii.

Hughes definitely aspired to that impartiality and to the balance between states' rights and nationalism. He believed also in a living Constitution, one that could be (and must be) adaptable to the exigencies of the times. In an address to the federal judges of the Fourth Circuit at Asheville on June 9, 1932, Hughes spoke "words that should long be remembered":[87]

> "The supreme exercise of the judicial power of the United States is in maintaining the constitutional balance between State and Nation and in enforcing the principles of liberty which the Constitution safeguards against arbitrary power. . . . We should be faithless to our supreme obligation if we interpreted the great generalities of the Constitution so as to forbid flexibility in making adaptations to meet new conditions, and to prevent the correction of new abuses incident to the complexity of our life, or as crystallizing our own notions of policy, our personal views of economics and our theories of moral or social improvement. . . . It is permeated with American ideals, infused with an American conception of liberty."[88]

Hughes "was destined to adapt the great charter to the bewildering requirements of an economic and social

---

87. Pusey, Vol. 2, p. 692.
88. *Id.* at 692–93.

transition," and he did so admirably.[89] Hughes was also a champion of First Amendment rights and personal liberties.

As noted earlier, the Four Horsemen had voted as a bloc against much of the New Deal legislation that President Roosevelt had implemented in an attempt to address the economic conditions of the nation resulting from the Great Depression. The matter came to a head on May 27, 1935, when the Supreme Court issued three unanimous decisions striking down various administration initiatives.[90] Chief Justice Hughes expressed concern about releasing "three such jolts" on the same day, but did so, and President Roosevelt spoke of the Court action a few days later, asserting "that the destruction of the NRA was the most important Supreme Court ruling since the Dred Scott case precipitated the Civil War."[91] Over the next few years, Hughes and his fellow justices would fight the court packing plan and continue to overturn New Deal legislation. However, in 1937, Justice Roberts informed Hughes he was changing his vote on an important case, and the switch has been hailed as the "switch in time that saved nine." According to Hughes, "The President's proposal had not the slightest effect on

---

89. *Id.*, at 704.

90. The three cases decided that day were *Schechter v. U.S.*, 295 U.S. 495, *Louisville Joint Stock Land Bank v. Radford*, 295 U.S. 555, and *Humphrey's Executor v. U.S.*, 295 U.S. 602.

91. Pusey, Vol. 2, p. 742.

our decision."[92] While many theories of what happened have been offered, the actual "reasons for the Court's apparent transformation remain controversial, and some scholars have argued that 1937 was a year of evolution rather than revolution."[93]

Retirement

On Jun 2, 1941, Chief Justice Hughes wrote President Franklin D. Roosevelt that he was retiring, effective July 1:

> "Considerations of health and age make it necessary that I should be relieved of the duties which I have been discharging with increasing difficulty. For that reason I avail myself of the right and privilege granted by the Act of March 1, 1937, 28 U.S. Code, Section 3758, and retire from regular active service on the Bench as Chief Justice of the United States, this retirement to be effective on and after July 1, 1941."[94]

President Roosevelt immediately wrote back Chief Justice Hughes:

> "I am deeply distressed by your letter of June 2 telling me of your retirement on July first from active

---

92. *Id.* at 757.
93. Ross, p. 134.
94. Letter from Hughes to President Franklin Roosevelt, June 2, 1945, available at http://www.presidency.ucsb.edu/ws/index.php?pid=16123.

service as Chief Justice of the United States. This comes to me, as I know it will to the whole Nation, as a great shock for all of us had counted on your continuing your splendid service for many years to come. My every inclination is to beg you to remain; but my deep concern for your health and strength must be paramount. I shall hope to see you this coming week in Washington."[95]

Speculation on Hughes' replacement focused on two potential replacements: Attorney General Robert Jackson and Associate Justice Stone. The latter would be nominated, in no small measure due to President Roosevelt's lunch meeting with Hughes, where "Hughes strongly recommended Stone."[96] Stone wrote Hughes:

"When I reflect upon the fact that I have taken it [oath of office] as your successor and upon the great service which you have rendered as Chief Justice, to the country and the Court, I bow my head in humility and pray that I may in some moderate degree prove worthy to be your successor."[97]

Hughes would remain in Washington for the rest of his life, dying on August 27, 1948.

---

95. Letter from President Franklin Roosevelt to Chief Justice Hughes, June 2, 1945, available at http://www.presidency.ucsb.edu/ws/index.php?pid=16123.
96. Pusey, Vol. 2, p. 787.
97. *Id.* at 788.

Part Seven

Intermezzo: A Period of "Division and Discord"[1] and Transition

In the Editor's Preface to a book by Melvin I. Urofsky, a statement is made about the next two chief justices that is something of note, that the Stone and Vinson Courts "share the unenviable distinction of being perhaps the least collegial and most internally vindictive periods of the Court's history."[2] These two Courts witnessed "animosity and personality clashes among its members."[3] Strong personalities among the associate justices contributed some to that division and discord.

At the same time, the Supreme Court was dealing with large issues on the national and world stage. World War II was looming and, soon after Stone became chief justice,

---

1. The quoted language is from the title of a book by Melvin I. Urofsky, "Division and Discord: The Supreme Court under Stone and Vinson, 1941–1953."

2. Urofsky, p. ix.

3. *Id.*

the Japanese bombed Pearl Harbor. The Supreme Court would have to address the Japanese internment, the Rosenbergs spying case, and other matters. Stone would die on the Court to be replaced by Vinson, who would also be chief justice for a relatively short period of time. Segregation and treatment of blacks would be big issues during Vinson's tenure as chief justice, and the United States would engage in another war, the Korean War, that would bring issues to the Supreme Court regarding presidential powers during wartime.

The Stone and Vinson Courts in many ways are seen as a transition period between two chief justices that sandwiched them: Hughes and Warren. Their courts did include "some of the most important figures in our judicial history—Hugo Black, Felix Frankfurter, William O. Douglas, and the underrated but very important Robert Jackson."[4] Perhaps these strong individuals had much to do with their inability to have a unified voice for the Supreme Court and contributed to the division and discord.

---

4. *Id.* at xiii.

Chapter Fourteen

Harlan F. Stone: Playing All Positions

Nominated by President Franklin D. Roosevelt
Confirmed by Senate Acclamation on June 27, 1941
Tenure: July 3, 1941 to April 22, 1946 (Died)
(Served as an associate justice, March 2, 1925
*   to July 3, 1941, when he became chief justice)*
Presidents During Tenure
*   FDR*
*   Truman*

Stone became chief justice during World War II. Less
than six months after becoming chief, Pearl Harbor
was attacked by Japan and for much of Stone's tenure,
the United States would be at war.[1] *Stone taught high*

---

1. Much of the introduction for this chapter and the next one was from an article in the *Chicago Daily Law Bulletin*, "How a school teacher and a semi-pro baseball player became chief justices," *Chicago Daily Law Bulletin, Cotter's Corner,* March 12, 2015, available at https://www.chicagolawbulletin.com/archives/2015 /03/12/dan-cotter-forum-03-12-2015

school in Massachusetts for one year after completing his bachelor's degree. He then went on to Columbia Law School, graduating in 1898. He immediately became a full-time professor at Columbia while also practicing law in New York City. In 1910, he was named dean of the law school, a post he held for more than a dozen years, until he became U.S. attorney general in 1924.

In January 1925, President Calvin Coolidge nominated Stone for associate justice. He served the U.S. Supreme Court in that post for sixteen years, and though he was a Republican who campaigned for Coolidge's reelection, Stone eventually aligned himself with Justices Louis Brandeis and Benjamin Cardozo in supporting New Deal programs, voting to uphold the Social Security Act of 1935 and a national minimum wage, for example.

Stone's pro-regulation stance caught the attention of Roosevelt, who nominated him to replace Hughes and become the nation's twelfth chief justice. Stone was the second of three chiefs to be elevated from sitting associate justice to chief. (Edward Douglass White and William H. Rehnquist also were promoted.)

Among the decisions he wrote during his more than two decades on the court, Stone is often remembered for the 1938 opinion in U.S. v. Carolene Products Co., which included the famous Footnote 4 that set forth a framework for enhanced judicial scrutiny in certain circumstances—what's now called strict scrutiny.

As chief, Stone's court in 1942 upheld the president's powers to try Nazi spies caught on U.S. soil (Ex parte Quirin), and he penned the famous International Shoe v. Washington decision that every law student since has read to learn the standards for state courts to exercise personal jurisdiction over litigants.

His tenure ended suddenly. During an open session of the court, Stone was reading a dissenting opinion when he suffered a cerebral hemorrhage. He died a short time later at his home on April 22, 1946. His term as chief justice was the third shortest of the seventeen who have served.

Early Life and Career

Harlan Stone was born in Chesterfield, New Hampshire, on October 11, 1872, to Fred Lauson Stone and his wife, Ann Sophia (nee Butler). Fred followed many generations of Stones before him and was a farmer. When Stone was two years old, they moved to a farm near Amherst, Massachusetts. He was educated in Amherst, graduating from the public high school there. After first attending the Massachusetts Agricultural College (today, the University of Massachusetts), from which Stone was kicked out due to rowdyism,[2] he attended Amherst College, where he graduated Phi Beta Kappa.[3] Stone also received a master's degree from Amherst College two years later.

When Stone graduated from Amherst College in 1894, he became a natural science teacher at Newburyport High School in Massachusetts.[4] While in Newburyport, Stone found his calling in the law after attending several sessions of the superior court.[5] He met William H. Moody, the district attorney, with whom he became friends. (Moody would later be appointed to the Supreme Court of the United States as well.)[6]

After a year of teaching and coaching football at Newburyport, Stone pursued his interest in law by enrolling at Columbia Law School, where he earned his L.L.B. in 1898. To help pay for this first year of law school. Stone also was an instructor of history at Adelphi Academy in Brooklyn.

Stone was admitted to the New York Bar in 1898 and, in the Fall of that year, Stone became a lecturer on bailments and insurance at Columbia Law School.[7]

---

2. Stone was accused of five violations of college regulations. While specifics are not widely known, it appears they were minor transgressions. See Mason, p. 39 (describing the dismissal and setting forth all minutes of the trustees of the college discussing Stone).

3. Mason describes a plea to a cousin to speak with Stone's dad to permit Stone to attend Amherst College. Mason, p. 41.

4. Id. at 65–66.

5. Cushman, p. 362.

6. Id.

7. Mason, p. 74.

Upon his law school graduation, Stone became a clerk at the New York law firm of Sullivan and Cromwell.[8] The next year, "he became connected with Wilmer and Canfield."[9] In 1905, Stone joined the firm, and eventually, that firm would be named Wilmer, Canfield, and Stone.[10]

In December 1906, Stone was made an offer to be a professor and dean of the Columbia Law School, but, in early 1907, withdrew his name when a promise he had been made was not kept. But after events unfolded at Columbia Law School, the Board of Trustees nominated Stone Professor of Law and Dean of the Law Faculty, effective July 1, 1910.[11] From 1910 to 1923, Stone held that position, while he also practiced law during that period.

While serving at Columbia Law School in those roles, for a brief period of time during World War I, Stone served on a board of inquiry along with Major Richard C. Stoddard (who was replaced by Major Walter G. Kellogg) and Federal Judge Julian Mack. The board of inquiry's responsibility was to review those who had claimed conscientious objector status under the Selective Service Act.[12]

On February 21, 1923, Stone submitted his formal letter of resignation effective on or before September 15, 1923.[13]

---

8. *Id.* at 77.
9. *Id.*
10. Cushman, p. 362.
11. Mason, pgs. 81–82.
12. *Id.* at 102.
13. *Id.* at 137.

The letter was the culmination of a long dialogue with the school, in which they discussed emerging divergent views about the school and the position Stone held.

Stone returned full-time to the practice of law, becoming a partner at Sullivan and Cromwell, where he headed the litigation department.[14]

However, his private practice return was not to be a long one. The U.S. attorney general, Harry M. Daugherty, was embroiled in scandal. Daugherty, who had been appointed by his good friend, President Warren D. Harding, engaged in a variety of wrongdoing. After Harding died and being pressured to do so, Daugherty resigned his post when Calvin Coolidge became president. President Coolidge, a classmate of Stone's at Amherst, asked Stone to replace Daugherty. Despite a large deduction in his salary (from $100,000 to $12,000), Stone accepted on April 1, 1924, after a White House meeting with President Coolidge and some Senators.

As attorney general, one of the major matters Stone worked on was finding a replacement for the head of the Bureau of Investigation, William J. Burns, eventually hiring a twenty-nine year old by the name of J. Edgar Hoover.[15] Stone also initiated an antitrust action against the Aluminum Company of America, a company owned by Andrew Mellon.[16] When the Supreme Court nomination came

---

14. Cushman, p. 362.
15. Mason, pgs. 149–50.
16. *Id.* at 179.

shortly thereafter, some speculated that the cause was to get Stone away from that prosecution and his aggressive cleaning out of the Department of Justice.

Nomination to Associate Justice

Shortly after Coolidge successfully ran for reelection, he nominated his attorney general to the Supreme Court of the United States as an associate justice to replace the retiring Justice Joseph McKenna. In a letter to his son, Marshall, in late December 1924, Stone wrote:

> "*Confidentially* there is much prospect that I may go on to the Supreme Court by the first of the year. . . . But he also feels that I am the man he wants on the Court. I have some doubt about taking it but it is a place of great dignity and public usefulness—a life position."[17]

The contents of the letter would become reality and public on January 5, 1925, when President Coolidge announced his nomination of Stone to the Supreme Court. The reaction to the announcement was well received generally:

> "Throughout the country newspapers hailed Stone's appointment, describing him as practical and level-headed, well-equipped for his job, a brilliant addition to the Court."[18]

17. *Id*. at 179.
18. *Id*. at 181.

Despite the general approval of his nomination by the press, Stone's antitrust efforts as attorney general, and his perceived deep ties to Wall Street, as well as his case against Senator Wheeler in Montana, caused concerns about his nomination. On January 28, 1925, Stone became the first Supreme Court nominee to personally appear before the Senate Judiciary Committee to answer questions and address the Senators.[19] Of the cross-examination and questioning he faced, Stone later wrote, "The coyotes have been trying to bite me, but I think they have only broken their teeth."[20] On February 5, 1925, the Senate easily approved Stone's nomination by a vote of 71-6, and Stone took his judicial oath on March 2, 1925. For the next sixteen years, Stone would serve as associate justice.[21] Stone was President Coolidge's only Supreme Court nomination.

Associate Justice Stone

Stone joined the Taft Court, which was heavily focused on business and how it interacted with government. Just before Stone took his oath, Congress helped the Supreme Court when it passed the Judiciary Act of 1925 (also known

---

19. Ninety years later, every Supreme Court nominee (and other Article III judicial nominees) appears before the Senate Judiciary Committee.

20. Mason, p. 197 (quoting a letter from Stone to William S. Booth).

21. When Chief Justice Taft retired, many thought that Stone would be elevated at that time, but instead, Charles Evans Hughes was nominated by President Hoover. Many expressed concerns about the ability of Stone to gather a majority on important decisions.

as the Judge's Bill because three associate justices had proposed the changes), which gave the Court significant discretion in which cases it heard going forward.[22]

After Stone was assigned a bankruptcy case to write shortly after becoming a Justice, his "first draft drew sharp comments."[23] Despite being a conservative and appointed by a Republican president, Stone soon joined with the "liberal" faction of the Court, often dissenting in police power cases.

During the Great Depression and President Franklin D. Roosevelt's New Deal program, Stone consistently aligned in a very fractured court with two other "liberal justices" who supported the New Deal—Justices Louis Brandeis and Benjamin Cardozo. The three became known as the "Three Musketeers," a bloc that to some extent was able to counter the work of four conservative Justices who became known as the "Four Horsemen"—Justice Van Devanter, Butler, McReynolds, and Sutherland. The Four Horsemen "believed that the government could do only what the Constitution expressly permitted it to do."[24] Stone was a strong supporter of government regulation of the economy.[25]

Perhaps Stone's most famous decision from his time as associate justice was his decision for the Court in *United*

22. Judiciary Act of 1925, 43 Stat. 936.

23. Mason, p. 213.

24. Urofsky, Division, p. 3.

25. Renstrom, p. 22 (citing that for the 1935–1936 term, Stone voted 97.7% of the time in favor of such government regulation).

States v. Carolene Products Co.,[26] which set forth scrutiny differences for various forms of discrimination in the decision's well-known Footnote 4, which stated in part:

There may be narrower scope for operation of the presumption of constitutionality when *legislation appears on its face to be within a specific prohibition of the Constitution*, such as those of the first ten amendments, which are deemed equally specific when held to be embraced within the Fourteenth. . . .

It is unnecessary to consider now whether legislation which restricts those political processes which can ordinarily be expected to bring about repeal of undesirable legislation, is to be subjected to more exacting judicial scrutiny under the general prohibitions of the Fourteenth Amendment than are most other types of legislation. . . .

Nor need we inquire whether similar considerations enter into the review of statutes directed at particular religious . . . or nations . . . or racial minorities . . .: whether prejudice against *discrete and insular minorities* may be a special condition, which tends seriously to curtail the operation of those political processes ordinarily to be relied upon to protect minorities, and

---

26. *United States v. Carolene Products Co.*, 304 U.S. 144 (1938).

which may call for a correspondingly more searching judicial inquiry. . . .[27]

That footnote 4, one of the most famous footnotes in Supreme Court jurisprudence history, would be the process by which civil rights and so many other future matters of import to the nation would be reviewed by the Supreme Court. To this date, Stone's categorizing of liberties and rights is looked to by the Court to determine what level of scrutiny is appropriate to the case at hand.

Nomination to Chief Justice

On June 2, 1941, Chief Justice Hughes wrote to President Franklin D. Roosevelt that he intended to retire, effective July 1.[28] Ten days later, on June 12, 1941, President Franklin D. Roosevelt nominated Stone to become chief justice.[29] President Roosevelt had passed over Attorney General Robert Jackson in favor of Stone, a Republican, who owed nothing to Roosevelt.[30] World War II was in full swing, but the United States would not join the war until later in 1941. The nomination of Stone to chief justice generally received universal acclaim. "Seldom has a presidential appointment

---

27. *Id.*, Footnote 4. (Italics added, citations in the Footnote omitted.)
28. Mason, p. 563.
29. Renstrom, p. 3.
30. Mason, p. 568.

evoked such a wave of public approval."[31] However, his colleague, Associate Justice William O. Douglas, expressed doubt over the nomination to his Supreme Court colleague, Hugo Black, noting, "it will not be a particularly happy or congenial atmosphere in which to work."[32] On June 27, 1941, Stone was confirmed by Senate acclamation and he took his judicial oath as chief justice on July 3, 1941.[33] On October 6, 1941, Stone took his position in the center of the bench as chief justice.[34] His tenure as chief justice was less than five terms. Almost the entire time that Stone was chief justice, the United States was involved in World War II.

Legacy

On April 22, 1946, while reading a dissent in *Girouard v. United States*,[35] Stone suddenly became ill. Court was adjourned for the day and Stone later died at his house in Washington, D.C. As noted, to date, Stone served the third shortest tenure of any chief justice. However, his tenure when combined with his service as an associate justice places him fortieth in terms of overall longevity in the

---

31. *Id.*

32. Urofsky, Division, p. 9 (quoting a letter from Douglas to Black dated June 22, 1941).

33. Mason, pgs. 572–73.

34. Urofsky, Division, p. 13.

35. *Girouard v. United States*, 328 U.S. 61. Various writings state that Stone was either in the process of reading or had just completed reading his dissent.

history of the Supreme Court. The Stone Court "left an imprint" when it "affirmed the conclusion reached during the last years of the Hughes Court that the Constitution permitted the federal government to engage in extensive regulation of the national economy and private property."[36]

Stone was the first chief justice who never served in elected office prior to his Supreme Court service. Stone was the second of three chief justices to be elevated directly from associate justice to chief justice.[37]

During Stone's tenure as chief justice, his most famous opinion that he wrote is probably *International Shoe Co. v. Washington*,[38] a case in which the Court addressed what was required for a state to have personal jurisdiction over a defendant and established a "minimum contacts" test.

The Stone Court was called upon to hear cases during wartime concerning FDR's expansive assumption of authority and his policies regulating the economy during wartime, but "the wartime Court validated every federal economic measure brought before it, including price controls, rent controls, and restrictions on profiteering."[39]

---

36. Renstrom, p. xi.

37. The first was Edward Douglass White, and the third was William Rehnquist. Two other chief justices, John Rutledge and Charles Evans Hughes, held associate justice positions, but left the bench before returning as chief justice.

38. *International Shoe Co. v. Washington*, 326 U.S. 310 (1945).

39. Urofsky, Division, p. 50.

The Stone Court also decided two cases of note with respect to World War II—*Ex parte Quirin*[40] and *Korematsu v. United States*.[41] In the first, the Supreme Court held that German saboteurs could be tried by a U.S. military tribunal. The Court, in a per curiam opinion,[42] found that:

> "By universal agreement and practice, the law of war draws a distinction between the armed forces and the peaceful populations of belligerent nations and also between those who are lawful and unlawful combatants. Lawful combatants are subject to capture and detention as prisoners of war by opposing military forces. Unlawful combatants are likewise subject to capture and detention, but in addition they are subject to trial and punishment by military tribunals for acts which render their belligerency unlawful. The spy who secretly and without uniform passes the military lines of a belligerent in time of war, seeking to gather military information and communicate it to the enemy, or an enemy combatant who without uniform comes secretly through the lines for the purpose of waging war by destruction of life or property, are familiar examples of belligerents who are

---

40. *Ex parte Quirin*, 317 U.S. 1 (1942).

41. *Korematsu v. United States*, 323 U.S. 214 (1944).

42. A per curiam opinion is one in which it is made by the court rather than identified by the judges' names who wrote it. Literally, it means "by the court" in Latin.

generally deemed not to be entitled to the status of prisoners of war, but to be offenders against the law of war subject to trial and punishment by military tribunals."[43]

Of the seven Nazis prosecuted, six were executed within days of the decision. The seventh was given a life sentence, and an eighth, who had not appealed to the Supreme Court, was given a sentence of thirty years at hard labor.[44] The *Quirin* decision has been cited in recent times to address enemy combatants held in Guantanamo and the use of military tribunals.[45]

In the second case, the Supreme Court of the United States had to determine whether a Japanese American individual, Fred Korematsu, was rightly punished for refusing to comply with President Franklin D. Roosevelt's Executive Order 9066 to relocate. The Supreme Court, in a 6-3 decision, held that the evacuation order was a valid one. The case has been criticized since, including because the Justice Department had provided false information to the Court.[46]

---

43. *Ex parte Quirin,* 317 U.S. at 30–31.

44. Mason, p. 657.

45. *See, e.g., Hamdan v. Rumsfeld,* 548 U.S. 557 (2006) (finding military commissions for Guantanamo Bay detainees invalid under the Geneva Conventions and the Uniform Code of Military Justice).

46. For an excellent fictional rendition of the case (the book is based primarily on truth), consider reading Kermit Roosevelt III's excellent book, *Allegiance.* The author wrote a review of the Roosevelt book for the Chicago Daily Law Bulletin on September 28, 2015, Cotter, *Chicago Daily Law Bulletin, Cotter's Corner,* "Japanese-American internment and U.S. loyalty."

In a 2018 decision, *Trump v. Hawaii,*[47] Chief Justice Roberts addressed a fiery dissent that referred to *Korematsu* and did a "soft" overturning of the decision (although he did not explicitly overturn it—perhaps because the question was not before the Court), writing:

> Finally, the dissent invokes *Korematsu* v. *United States*, 323 U. S. 214 (1944). Whatever rhetorical advantage the dissent may see in doing so, *Korematsu* has nothing to do with this case. The forcible relocation of U. S. citizens to concentration camps, solely and explicitly on the basis of race, is objectively unlawful and outside the scope of Presidential authority. But it is wholly inapt to liken that morally repugnant order to a facially neutral policy denying certain foreign nationals the privilege of admission. See *post,* at 26–28. The entry suspension is an act that is well within executive authority and could have been taken by any other President—the only question is evaluating the actions of this particular President in promulgating an otherwise valid Proclamation.

"The dissent's reference to *Korematsu,* however, affords this Court the opportunity to make express what is already obvious: *Korematsu* was gravely wrong the day it was decided, has been overruled in the court

---

47. *Trump v. Hawaii*, 585 U.S. ____ (2018).

of history, and—to be clear—'has no place in law under the Constitution.' 323 U. S., at 248 (Jackson, J., dissenting)."[48]

As the two cases (*Korematsu* and *Quirin*) indicate, and as previously noted, the Stone Court five-year period was during World War II, and so much of the decisions and issues facing the Court (and the nation) during this time related to the war and security of the United States, with "many of the Stone Court's most important decisions focused either directly or indirectly on the dimensions of the government's war power."[49]

In addition to *Korematsu* and *Quirin*, other national emergency cases "such as *Yamashita, Hirabayashi . . .*"[50] are part of the Stone Court legacy and have not been treated kindly in retrospect.

The Stone Court is also the first Supreme Court in which a "majority of the Court's decisions—58 percent—came down with divided opinions."[51]

The Stone Court's legacy is one "of unmet expectations, and it is a legacy without significant consequence until the second decade of the Warren era."[52] A combination of factors contributes to that unsatisfactory legacy, including the

---

48. *Id.*
49. Renstrom, p. 179.
50. *Id.*, p. 180.
51. Urofsky, Division, p. 42.
52. Renstrom, p. 180.

exigencies of war, a relatively short tenure as chief justice, and a change in most of the justices on the Court during the first term of President Roosevelt all contributed to the results that were the Stone Court.

Justice Frankfurter, in a June letter to Justice Frank Murphy, described the five-term period that Stone was chief justice harshly:

1. Never before in the history of the Court were so many of its members influenced in decisions by considerations extraneous to the legal issues that supposedly control decisions.
2. Never before have members of the Court so often acted contrary to their convictions on the governing legal issues in decisions.
3. Never before has so large a proportion of the opinions fallen short of requisite professional standards.[53]

Assessments of Stone are that "he was an exceptionally poor presiding officer during the Court's deliberations in conference."[54]

When Taft announced his retirement in 1930, "many expected that Stone would succeed him."[55] However, the thing that proved to be true when he did eventually get

---

53. Urofsky, p. 137.
54. Stevens, p. 36.
55. Cushman, p. 363.

elevated to the Supreme Court- that he could not effectively control the Court- was a concern in 1930, and so Hughes was chosen instead.[56]

While reading a dissent on April 22, 1946, Stone experienced a cerebral hemorrhage and died that night.[57]

Stone was followed by the fifth shortest serving chief justice in the Court's history, Fred Vinson.[58]

---

56. *Id.*
57. *Id.* at 365.
58. The chief justices in order of length of service are (shortest to longest):

1. John Rutledge
2. Oliver Ellsworth
3. Harlan Fisk Stone
4. John Jay
5. Fred Vinson
6. Salmon Chase
7. William Howard Taft
8. Edward Douglass White
9. Charles Evans Hughes
10. John Roberts
11. Morrison Waite
12. Earl Warren
13. Warren Burger
14. William Rehnquist
15. Melville Fuller
16. Roger B. Taney
17. John Marshall

The list includes only service as chief justice. Roberts will, if he remains chief justice and does not retire any time in the foreseeable future, surpass Waite and Warren, another two years surpass Burger, and then another year, be longer serving than Rehnquist. If he remains sixteen more years, he would become the longest serving chief justice in our nation's history, surpassing John Marshall. At 64 in 2019, he would be 79 or 80 then.

Chapter Fifteen

Fred M. Vinson: The Last Democratically Appointed Chief

Nominated by President Harry S. Truman
Confirmed by Senate Acclamation on June 20, 1946
Tenure: June 24, 1946 to September 8, 1953 (Died)
Presidents During Tenure
   Truman
   Eisenhower

After graduating from Centre College in Danville, Kentucky, where he played on championship baseball teams, Vinson took a turn at semi-professional ball. The shortstop shifted his attention, however, to legal studies at Centre and began practicing law in 1911 at the age of 21.

Vinson interspersed periods of private practice with other positions. From 1917 to 1919, he served as a private in the U.S. Army and an officer trainee. After World War I, he was elected the commonwealth attorney for the Thirty-Second Judicial District of Kentucky. He served two stints as a U.S. representative for Kentucky, putting in a total of twelve years.

Afterward, Vinson became a judge on the U.S. Court of Appeals for the D.C. Circuit. He was the first chief to have previously served on that court.

During his time in Washington, he became friends with Harry S. Truman, who as president counted Vinson as a trusted adviser and named him treasury secretary and, ultimately, chief justice.

Vinson joined the high court at a difficult time in its history, with the sitting justices deeply at odds. The acrimony had been so severe that Justices Hugo Black and Robert H. Jackson each allegedly warned Truman that he would resign should the other be named chief. But the job went to Vinson, who is credited with mending relations between the factions.

In the meantime, a different divide faced the nation. The Vinson court addressed racial discrimination, ruling in Sweatt v. Painter, for instance, that states that employed racial segregation must provide truly equal facilities and, in the particular case, had failed.

Those cases were some of the building blocks that Thurgood Marshall and the NAACP argued leading up to Brown v. Board of Education. (When Vinson died suddenly of a heart attack on September 8, 1953, Brown had been set for reargument. A decision waited until Vinson's successor, Earl Warren, became chief justice.)

In other areas of the law, the Vinson court's legacy includes Youngstown Sheet & Tube v. Sawyer, which limited the president's powers. In the midst of the Korean War and facing a strike by the United Steelworkers of America in 1952, Truman wanted to take control of U.S. steel mills in the interests of national security.

Vinson dissented from the 6-3 majority decision, taking great umbrage at his colleagues and giving a history of presidential seizures. The decision in favor of the steelmakers was a blow to Truman.

Vinson was the fourth, and to date last, chief justice appointed by a Democratic president.

Early Life and Career

Fred Vinson was born on January 22, 1890, in Louisa, Kentucky, to James Vinson and Virginia (nee Ferguson). James was the town and county jailer in the small town.[1] Vinson was a smart kid, and after high school, graduated

---

1. Cushman, p. 421.

from Kentucky Normal College, then worked his way through Centre College, where he was both an athlete and a scholar.[2] Vinson helped the Centre College baseball team have successful seasons and also played some semiprofessional baseball. He tried out for the Cincinnati Reds, but did not make the team.[3] In 1911, Vinson graduated from Centre College with his L.L.B. as well. Upon graduation and admission to the Kentucky bar, Vinson entered private practice. His private practice would not be a big part of his career, as he would serve as the City Attorney of Louisa, then in the U.S. Army during World War I when drafted, then spent the bulk of his legal career in public positions. Postwar duty, Vinson served as the Commonwealth's Attorney for the Thirty-Second Judicial District of Kentucky, winning election in 1921.[4]

In 1924, Vinson ran for the U.S. House of Representatives in a special election to complete an unexpired term. He would serve from 1925 until 1929, then again from 1931 to 1938, when he resigned to become a federal judge. The gap from 1929 to 1931 was due to a Republican landslide in the 1928 elections. In the interim between service, Vinson focused on strengthening his political organization.[5] While in the House, Vinson became a leading Representative on the very powerful House Ways and Means Committee.

---

2. Mayer, p. 259.
3. Cushman, p. 422.
4. *Id.*
5. *Id.*

Vinson also became friends with Senator Harry S. Truman from Missouri, who would nominate Vinson to the Supreme Court.

Vinson was rewarded for his work on the House Ways and Means Committee and on coal and tax issues by President Roosevelt, who nominated Vinson to a seat on the U.S. Court of Appeals for the District of Columbia Circuit.[6] Vinson was nominated on November 26, 1937, and was confirmed by the Senate on December 9, 1937, receiving his commission a few days later, on December 15.

During World War II, President Roosevelt appointed Vinson the chief judge of the U.S. Emergency Court of Appeals. Vinson held the judicial roles until May 28, 1943, when he resigned to become the Director of the Office of Economic Stabilization, a position to which he was appointed because President Roosevelt was impressed "with Vinson's administrative ability."[7]

In July 1945, his friend from his House of Representatives days, President Truman, appointed Vinson the Secretary of the Treasury, a position he held for just under one year, from July 23, 1945, until June 23, 1946.[8] President Truman had a higher position in mind for Vinson when Chief Justice Stone died—chief justice of the Supreme Court.

---

6. Mayer, p. 260.

7. *Id.*

8. Cushman, pgs. 423–24.

Supreme Court Nomination

On April 20, 1946, Chief Justice Stone died. President Truman recognized the Supreme Court "was riven by infighting" and "rather than elevating a sitting justice," he had to choose someone who "would have to be a peacemaker."[9] President Truman's friend, Vinson, "seemed ideally suited to that role."[10] On June 6, 1946, Truman submitted Vinson's nomination to the Senate and, on June 20, 1946, by voice vote, the Senate confirmed Vinson.[11] Vinson took his judicial oath on June 24, 1946.[12] From April 22, 1946, until June 23, 1946, Associate Justice Hugo Black served as acting chief justice.

The Vinson Court and Legacy

Chief Justice Vinson possessed a strong view "in the need for a powerful national government that could solve the country's problems the way he and other federal officials had done during World War II."[13] However, despite his personality and generally being liked by his fellow justices,

---

9. Belknap, p. 39.

10. *Id.*

11. McMillion & Rutkus, available at https://fas.org/sgp/crs/misc/RL33225 .pdf.

12. Belknap, p. 39.

13. *Id.* at 41.

the chief justice's efforts at compromise and seeking more unified decisions failed.[14]

Although generally liked, "some of his colleagues would not even treat him as a first among equals."[15] Vinson worked hard to reduce the Court's workload, believing the justices had been overworked (and "had contributed to the untimely death of [Justice] Wiley Rutledge"), so reduced the number of written opinions from more than 200 decisions to just over 100.[16]

The Vinson Court is not considered one of the great tenures in our Supreme Court's history. As noted, when Vinson joined the Court there was a great deal of infighting, with Associate Justice Felix Frankfurter being part of the cause for such tensions. The basis for why the Court was so unremarkable has been simply stated:

> "Fred Vinson was not a great Chief Justice. Nor was the Supreme Court he headed from 1946 to 1953 a great Court. Indeed, both were at most mediocre. The Vinson Court was a produce of an anxious era after World War II, when the euphoria inspired by the greatest military triumph of the United States gave way to

---

14. *Id.* at 40. In his first three terms, the number of unanimous decisions declined from year to year, and are low by historical standards at 36%, 26%, and 19%, respectively. *Id.*

15. *Id.*

16. *Id.*

uncertainty and fear aroused by a developing Cold War between this country and the Soviet Union."[17]

Part of the reason for mediocrity of the Vinson Court was President Truman's nominees who sat on the bench—in addition to Vinson, Truman during his presidency added Justices Tom Clark, Sherman Minton, and Harold Burton.[18] The mediocre court assessment was not the only negative one about Vinson. In then-Chief Justice Rehnquist's book about the Supreme Court,[19] Rehnquist wrote about the three chief justices that presided during the New Deal Court that spanned the Roosevelt presidency:

> "Hughes was an outstanding administrator and an able judge; Stone was an able judge, but not an outstanding administrator; Vinson was neither."[20]

In Vinson's relatively short tenure as chief justice, perhaps his most famous decision is that in *Dennis v. United States*.[21] In *Dennis*, several members of the Communist Party were convicted of violating the Smith Act by teaching and advocating the violent overthrow of the government.[22] Vinson, for a 6-2 Court, held that the Smith Act did not violate the First Amendment. His decision in *Dennis* was not

---

17. Belknap, p. xi.
18. *Id.* at xii.
19. Rehnquist, "The Supreme Court."
20. *Id.* at 149.
21. *Dennis v. United States*, 341 U.S. 494 (1951).
22. Belknap, p. 42.

surprising—his "decisions earned him a reputation as an enemy of civil liberties and a jurist of rather modest ability," someone who favored federal power over that of the states and government over the individual.[23] In the period he served as chief justice, Vinson voted against a finding of a civil liberty in the case 83% of the time.[24] In his jurisprudence and that of the Supreme Court, "Vinson successfully checked the trend toward judicially enforced civil liberties due to what he considered a grave Communist threat."[25]

The Vinson Court spanned the Cold War and Korean War, and the "Red Scare" of Communism. Part of the judicial conservatism demonstrated by the Vinson Court might be committed to two tenets of the New Deal and time in our nation's history. A majority of the Vinson Court justices:

"[They] believed in the goodness of government, and they also believed that unelected judges should not use their power to thwart the initiatives of politically responsible legislators and executive officials."[26]

---

23. *Id.* at 36.
24. Urofsky, Division, p. 158.
25. Mayer, p. 261.
26. *Id.*, p. xii. The tenets sound very much like the principles of the *Chevron Doctrine*, which recently confirmed Supreme Court justice, Brett Kavanaugh, has challenged. Kavanaugh joins others on the court, including Chief Justice Roberts and Associate Justices' Gorsuch, Alito, and Thomas, who have all questioned the agency deference that is part and parcel of these two tenets.

During the Cold War and with respect to reviewing a series of loyalty cases that came before the Supreme Court, the Court "got caught up in the anticommunism fever of the times."[27]

The extent to which the executive branch had power to act was tested in a case that faced the Supreme Court in 1952, *Youngstown Sheet and Tube Co. v. Sawyer*,[28] aka "The Steel Seizure Case." During the Korean conflict, United Steel Workers threatened to strike when a wage dispute could not be settled.[29] In response to the threatened strike, Truman issued Executive Order 10340, permitting his Secretary of Commerce to seize the mills, and informed Congress he had done so, inviting Congress to act if they deemed it to be an appropriate response.[30] The Supreme Court decided against Truman, asserting he had exceeded his executive powers, by a 6-3 decision. Justice Black's opinion required the president have explicit constitutional authority to act, while Justice Frankfurter thought the president had broader powers than Black's opinion. In another concurrence, Justice Jackson set forth a test that has been used in subsequent Supreme Court decisions to determine the extent to which a president has power to act. Jackson's concurrence stated:

---

27. Urofsky, Division, p. 161.
28. *Youngstown Sheet and Tube Co. v. Sawyer*, 343 U.S. 579 (1952).
29. Belknap, p. 23.
30. *Id.*

1. When the President acts pursuant to an express or implied authorization of Congress, his authority is at its maximum, for it includes all that he possesses in his own right plus all that Congress can delegate. In these circumstances, and in these only, may he be said (for what it may be worth) to personify the federal sovereignty. . . .

2. When the President acts in absence of either a congressional grant or denial of authority, he can only rely upon his own independent powers, but there is a zone of twilight in which he and Congress may have concurrent authority, or in which its distribution is uncertain. Therefore, congressional inertia, indifference or quiescence may sometimes, at least, as a practical matter, enable, if not invite, measures on independent presidential responsibility. . . .

3. When the President takes measures incompatible with the expressed or implied will of Congress, his power is at its lowest ebb, for then he can rely only upon his own constitutional powers minus any constitutional powers of Congress over the matter. Courts can sustain exclusive presidential control in such a case only by disabling the Congress from acting upon the subject.[31]

---

31. *Youngstown*, 343 U.S. 579, 635–38. (Footnotes deleted.)

The Supreme Court most recently has used this three-pronged Jackson test in the context of President Obama's and President Trump's use of executive orders in various areas, where Congress has spoken or considered a particular course of action, which puts the president at the "lowest ebb."

The Vinson Court generally rejected the incorporation doctrine with respect to the Fourteenth Amendment making the Bill of Rights applicable to the states,[32] despite efforts of Justice Black to move the court there. For example, in *Adamson v. California*,[33] the majority of the Court rejected Black's argument that the "Fourteenth Amendment had made the Bill of Rights applicable to the states."[34] Black in dissent wrote:

> "My study of the historical events that culminated in the Fourteenth Amendment, and the expressions of those who sponsored and favored, as well as those who opposed, its submission and passage persuades me that one of the chief objects that the provisions of the Amendment's first section, separately and as a whole, were intended to accomplish was to make the Bill of Rights, applicable to the states. With full knowledge

32. The incorporation doctrine is a constitutional doctrine that certain of the Bill of Rights are applicable to the states through the Due Process Clause of the U.S. Constitution. The Court started to use what is known as "selective incorporation," making certain parts of the amendments applicable to the states.

33. *Adamson v. California*, 332 U.S. 46 (1947).

34. Belknap, p. xiii.

of the import of the *Barron* decision, the framers and backers of the Fourteenth Amendment proclaimed its purpose to be to overturn the constitutional rule that case had announced. This historical purpose has never received full consideration or exposition in any opinion of this Court interpreting the Amendment."[35]

The Vinson Court did, however, incorporate the Establishment Clause into the Due Process Clause.[36] The Warren Court would implement selective incorporation with respect to many of the criminal justice provisions contained in the Bill of Rights.

The Vinson Court "had been chipping away at the separate-but-equal rule" for several years when Vinson died suddenly, but what may well be the enduring legacy of the Vinson Court is what was not decided–*Brown v. Board of Education*. When Vinson died suddenly on September 8, 1953, of a heart attack, *Brown* had been set for reargument.

---

35. *Adamson*, 332 U.S. 46, 71–72. (Footnote omitted.) Black is noted as one of the only pure "originalists" in the Court's history, with his strong argument that the First Amendment beginning that "Congress shall make no laws" is absolute. His assessment and arguments to date have not been successful. However, one of the interesting phenomena of the Roberts Court is how often the First Amendment has been used to justify various decisions. Some have argued that the First Amendment is the current version of the extent to which the Commerce Clause was used to justify laws and decisions in prior years by previous Courts. In his *Adamson* dissent, Black cites to *Ex parte Bain*, 121 U.S. 1 (1887), which stated: "It is never to be forgotten that in the construction of the language of the Constitution here relied on, as indeed in all other instances where construction becomes necessary, we are to place ourselves as nearly as possible in the condition of the men who framed that instrument." *Bain*, 121 U.S. 1, 12.

36. Belknap, p. xiii.

According to Justice Felix Frankfurter and other accounts, had Vinson lived, the decision in *Brown* might have turned out differently, perhaps a 5-4 decision upholding "separate but equal." What we do know is that the Vinson Court "did not handle [civil liberties cases] very well."[37] We also know that "Vinson liked whenever possible to resolve cases on the basis of precedent, and he thought change should be evolutionary rather than revolutionary."[38] We will never know the outcome if Vinson had lived, but we do know that the next term, Vinson's successor, Earl Warren, was able to obtain a unanimous decision. Despite the open question on *Brown*, Vinson did advance race relations and civil rights, writing the unanimous decisions in *Shelley v. Kraemer* (1948) (racially restrictive covenants unenforceable),[39] *McLaurin v. Oklahoma State Regents* (1950) (admitted black students could use all facilities at a state university),[40] and *Sweatt v. Painter* (1950) (black law student could not be denied entry to law school even if "black" law school available).[41]

Chief Justice Fred Vinson "is remembered mainly as an almost dogmatic supporter of the government who damaged civil liberties while failing to unify his badly divided

---

37. *Id.* xi.
38. *Id.* at 43.
39. *Shelley v. Kraemer,* 334 U.S. 1 (1948).
40. *McLaurin v. Oklahoma State Regents,* 339 U.S. 637 (1950).
41. *Sweatt v. Painter,* 339 U.S. 629 (1950).

Court."[42] His philosophy was "an unabashed belief in strong government by the executive and a more deferential role for the judiciary."[43] Perhaps the final word on Vinson is:

> "Vinson had neither the intellectual nor the political skills to lead the Court, and with the exception of the communist cases, he played a relatively minor role in shaping the Court's jurisprudence."[44] The Vinson Court truly reflected its chief- in his time on the Court, his "tight control over opinion assignments" and "bending to the will of the majority" meant that he was on the winning side an astonishingly high "86 percent of the time."[45]

---

42. Belknap, p. 43.
43. Cushman, p. 424.
44. Urofsky, Division, p. 8.
45. Belknap, p. 40.

Chapter Sixteen

Earl Warren: *Brown v. Board of Education,* Civil Rights, and Criminal Rights

Nominated by President Dwight D. Eisenhower
Confirmed on March 1, 1954, by Senate
Acclamation
Tenure: October 5, 1953 to June 23, 1969 (Retired)
Presidents During Tenure
Eisenhower
Kennedy
Johnson
Nixon

Nine chief justices and nearly 120 years separate John Marshall from Earl Warren.[1] *While each chief has added something to the Supreme Court and helped to*

---

1. The introduction to this chapter in italics is based on an article that originally appeared in the *Chicago Daily Law Bulletin* on March 24, 2015, Cotter, "California governor and 14th chief justice."

develop the continuum, Warren and Marshall are often mentioned together as the greatest of the seventeen chiefs.[2]

Between their respective terms, while some definite movement in certain areas took place and major constitutional law was developing, it was a long stretch of time between Courts that could truly be labeled game changing. Much of the work of the Courts in between eventually was pulled back, if not outright reversed (Lochner, Dred Scott, Plessy, to name a few examples).[3]

Early Years

When Warren graduated from the University of California, Berkeley, he went into private practice for a few years in the San Francisco Bay Area. In 1917 at the height of World War I, he joined the Army.

Warren stayed stateside, and the young lieutenant returned to civilian life after a year. From the time he

---

2. In a C-Span interview with Chief Justice Roberts, he cited Chief Justice Marshall as the "most important" predecessor and ranked Chief Justices Rehnquist and Warren as the "most influential" modern chief justices. *See* Lamb, pgs. 4 and 5, video available at https://www.c-span.org/video/?193515-1/chief-justice-interview-constitution, transcript at http://www.scotusblog.com/movabletype/archives/Robertts%20interview%20transcript.doc.

3. My son, John, who read the book and provided extensive editing assistance, perhaps summed that thought best, noting in his editing work, "It seems to me that the Court had a rather large identity crisis and stagnated for the better part of 100 years."

was discharged until his retirement in 1969, Warren's career would be devoted to government service.

Back in California, Warren became deputy city attorney for Oakland, and then after that, deputy district attorney for Alameda County. Gaining attention in the right quarters, he was appointed Alameda County district attorney in 1925 and won three successive elections to the post.

In 1938, he successfully ran for California attorney general. Near the end of his one term as attorney general, and in the shadow of the Pearl Harbor attack, Warren pushed for the internment of Japanese Americans living on the West Coast, an effort Warren said in his 1977 memoirs that he "deeply regretted."

Warren was hugely popular among California voters, who sent him to the governor's mansion in 1942. His 1946 reelection was remarkable in that the Republican governor was nominated to run on all three tickets: Republican, Democratic and Progressive. He won a third term in 1950.

In 1948, Warren debuted on the national stage as the Republican nominee for U.S. vice president, running with Thomas Dewey against Harry S Truman. It would be his sole electoral loss.

Four years later, Warren was a contender to be the GOP candidate for president. However, on the train ride to the Republican National Convention in Chicago, Warren learned of backroom dealings by Richard M. Nixon, who would throw his support from Warren to Dwight D. Eisenhower.

Following the GOP victory in 1952, Eisenhower agreed to appoint Warren to the Supreme Court. When Chief Justice Fred M. Vinson died suddenly in September 1953, Warren reminded the president of their deal.

Ike balked at first, arguing that the deal was for associate justice, but Warren stood firm. He received a recess appointment on September 30, 1953, and was confirmed on March 1, 1954, on a voice vote by the Senate.

Chief Justice

Warren's first case in 1953 was Brown v. Board of Education, which was heard earlier that year, but the justices had asked for a rehearing to address specific questions. The court was divided over the case, and Justice Felix Frankfurter used the rehearing to buy the court time. Meantime, Vinson had died and Warren became chief.

After the rehearing, Warren, who had supported the integration of Mexican American students into California schools while governor, masterfully worked the justices in conference and throughout the process of the court arriving at its decision.

Early on, he did not allow a straw vote during the justices' conferences but argued that racial segregation violated the Constitution. Eventually, he convinced all justices to join the opinion, with Stanley F. Reed from Kentucky being the final justice to agree.

Although Warren was seen not as a legal scholar on the level of Frankfurter, he was a masterful coalition builder who found ways for the justices to reach common ground.

The Warren Court would tackle a host of watershed cases, dealing with racial equality and discrimination, voting rights, criminal procedure, and many other subjects. Underlying those decisions is the principle that rights established by the Constitution apply to the states and their residents, and many cases would enter the popular lexicon:

- *Brown v. Board of Education (1954), striking down the doctrine of separate but equal in public education.*
- *Baker v. Carr (1962), holding that legislative apportionment was a justiciable issue.*
- *Miranda v. Arizona (1966), requiring that individuals interrogated by police be notified of their right to counsel and protection against self-incrimination under the Fifth Amendment.*
- *Gideon v. Wainright (1963), holding that the Sixth Amendment right to counsel in criminal cases extends to defendants in state courts.*

Even so, the Brown decision, among others, would spark outrage in some quarters and would be the catalyst for "Impeach Warren" billboards that sprouted throughout the South.

The Warren Court was very active and set new courses in many areas. When Warren retired, Justice William J. Brennan would remain for a number of years, and the Warren Court in many ways would continue through Warren E. Burger's tenure as chief justice.

Warren's sixteen years on the court and the decisions it rendered put him at the top of the chief justices list, right after Marshall. Warren is fascinating and one of the reasons I proposed teaching a course on judicial biography.

While he was an advocate for the interment of the Japanese Americans, he supported integration of the California schools and led the court to the unanimous Brown decision; though his father was murdered when Warren was DA and the case never solved, his court was strong on rights of defendants; and while his office as DA was part of questionable interrogation practices, his court decided Miranda.

In law school, we never learn about the person behind the judge. It is worthwhile to understand the justices' pasts as part of understanding the court.

Early Life and Career

Earl Warren was born in Los Angeles, California on March 9, 1891, to Mathias and Crystal (nee Hemlund). Mathias was a longtime Southern Pacific Railroad employee who was blacklisted for joining in a strike, and the family when Warren was very young moved to Bakersfield, California, where Warren would grow up. After attending the local public high school, Warren attended the University of California, Berkeley, where he received his B.A. Warren then attended UC Berkeley Law School (Boalt Hall), where he received his J.D. in 1914. Warren was not a great student, as he often admitted. After being admitted to the California bar, Warren worked briefly for the Associated Oil Company, then joined the Oakland law firm of Robinson & Robinson. Warren served in private practice until 1917.

When World War I came, Warren enlisted in the Army, hoping he would see action overseas. However, Warren remained stateside at training camps, and never saw active combat. Shortly after Armistice Day, Warren was discharged, with the rank of First Lieutenant.

Returning to California, Warren spent a year as a legislative aide for the California State Assembly as Clerk for the California Assembly Judiciary Committee. Warren next moved to the position of Deputy City Attorney of Oakland, California, in 1919. After a year in that role, Warren became the deputy city attorney in Alameda County and, in 1925, after serving five years as deputy, Warren was appointed as the District Attorney of Alameda County, a position to which he would be reelected to three four-year terms.[4]

While serving in his role as Deputy City Attorney, his father, Mathias, was murdered on May 14, 1938. Mathias was found bludgeoned to death in his home and, while several suspects were questioned, the case was never formally solved.[5]

Also, as Deputy City Attorney, getting ready to run for Attorney General, Warren faced "the most controversial case of his career as district attorney of Alameda County."[6] The "Point Lobos" case, as it is known, involved a murder on a freighter that was off the California coast.[7] The chief engineer's body was found stuffed in a bunk on the freighter, and Warren and his team believed the engineer had been murdered for firing Communists.[8] After finding an informant with perhaps evidence of who committed the crime, Warren's investigator and chief deputy together planted a microphone in the hotel room the suspects shared.[9] Some alleged that the defendants were wrongly convicted and the case has been used to show the "ironies"

4. White, p. 25.

5. See, e.g., https://cdnc.ucr.edu/cgi-bin/cdnc?a=d&d=MT19380516.2.2, contemporaneous reporting in the Madera Tribune in 1938; see also Cray, p. 94 (describing the gruesome death of Matt Warren, found in his blood at his own home).

6. White, p. 34.

7. Id.

8. Cray, p. 83.

9. Id.

of Warren, given his work twenty years later on the Supreme Court around rights of criminal defendants.[10]

Attorney General

On February 17, 1938, Warren announced his candidacy for the position of California attorney general.[11] Given California's somewhat unique election system, Warren filed for the nomination of all three parties and was nominated from each.[12] Warren easily won the election.[13] During his tenure as attorney general, another irony of Warren and how he decided as chief justice came to be—after the invasion of Pearl Harbor, Warren was extremely active and approving of "securing the exclusion of those of Japanese ancestry from the West Coast after the invasion."[14]

California Governorship

In 1942, Earl Warren was elected Governor of California.[15] This would be his last elected position, one he held for the next eleven years. During his time as governor, Warren was instrumental in his work resulting in the state

---

10. White, p. 36.
11. *Id.*
12. *Id.* at 45.
13. *Id.* at 46.
14. Cushman, p. 437.
15. *Id.*

government reorganization and securing many reform legislation victories.[16] Warren was a popular governor who over the years became more aligned with the progressives in his Republican Party. Many of those progressive ideals would be reflected in his tenure as chief justice of the Supreme Court.

As governor, in a precursor of his work in *Brown v. Board of Education*, Warren had a role in Mexican students' desegregation in California. The case, *Méndez v. Westminster School District of Orange County*, involved segregation of California schools that had long existed. The U.S. Circuit Court for the Ninth Circuit found such segregation unconstitutional.[17] Governor Warren signed a bill two months after the Ninth Circuit decision ending school segregation in public schools, the first state in the nation to do so.

In 1948, Warren was the Republican nominee for vice president of the United States, on the ticket with Thomas E. Dewey. Dewey lost a very close election to President Harry S. Truman. The race was so close that the *Chicago Tribune* ran the headline "Dewey Beats Truman" that was incorrect.

In 1952, Warren was considered a frontrunner for the presidential nomination. However, he discovered on a train ride to the convention in Chicago with Richard Nixon that there was duplicity afoot, and Nixon informed Warren that

---

16. *Id.*
17. https://blogs.loc.gov/law/2014/05/before-brown-v-board-of-education -there-was-mendez-v-westminster.

the nomination had "come down to Taft and Eisenhower."[18] Warren eventually gave up his delegates to Eisenhower, whom he viewed to have very similar political views to his own. While he anticipated being rewarded the vice president nomination, that was not to be. When Eisenhower won, speculation began about a Cabinet position for Warren, but Warren was concerned about Cabinet pay and also his skills and experience.

In late November 1952, President-elect Eisenhower phoned Warren to inform him that Eisenhower "intend[ed] to offer [Warren] the first vacancy on the Supreme Court."[19] Eisenhower responded to Warren's expression of gratitude for the kindness by informing Warren it was Eisenhower's commitment.[20] Warren would not forget, and the commitment was soon due.

Supreme Court Nomination

When Warren was overlooked for the position of vice president on the Eisenhower ticket, he struck a deal for "the first Supreme Court vacancy"[21] and as it turned out, that position was the chief justice position when Chief Justice Vinson died unexpectedly. President Dwight D. Eisenhower at first tried to reject Warren's demand, but made Warren

---

18. Cray, p. 233.
19. *Id.* at 247.
20. *Id.*
21. Cushman, p. 438.

a recess appointment on October 5, 1953, the beginning of the Supreme Court term.[22] Warren would be confirmed on March 1, 1954, by unanimous voice vote.

The first case that Warren had to tackle as chief justice was *Brown v. Board of Education*, a case that had been set for rehearing in the previous term. At the first conference as chief justice, Warren presented the matter "in terms of racial inferiority," challenging the Justices to think about the case in those human terms:

> "He told the justices that segregation could be justified only by belief in the inherent inferiority of blacks and, if the cases upholding segregation were to be followed, it had to be upon that basis."[23]

In this book, few cases are discussed at great length. The focus is on the chief justices, not their jurisprudence. While we look at their legacy briefly, and the times they were in, or the courts that they led, we have not made this a traditional law school casebook- intentionally. However, *Brown v. Board* and Warren's efforts in it are worth the telling. It is a story of how a chief justice can lead the Court to a decision. A few chiefs have had that ability—Marshall, Warren for sure. The case, its history, and its outcome follow.

---

22. Cray, p. 260.
23. Cushman, p. 438.

Brown v. Board of Education[24]

On May 18, 1896, a nearly unanimous U.S. Supreme Court in *Plessy v. Ferguson* upheld the constitutionality of state laws requiring "separate but equal" facilities in places of public accommodation.

On May 17, 1954, one day short of fifty-eight years after the *Plessy* decision, Chief Justice Earl Warren stated for the unanimous Supreme Court in *Brown v. Board of Education*: "We conclude that, in the field of public education, the doctrine of 'separate but equal' has no place. Separate educational facilities are inherently unequal."

The intent of the Supreme Court in issuing its holding in *Brown*, a combination of cases from four states and the District of Columbia, was to put an end to racially segregated public schools. Sixty-two years later, the jury remains out on the effectiveness of desegregation efforts in American schools.

The Case Background

On June 7, 1892, Homer Plessy, a man of mixed race, purchased a first-class ticket and boarded a "whites only" railcar in New Orleans. The railroad company knew Plessy was planning to board the car, and a committee of New Orleans

---

24. Much of the narrative in this section orginally appeared in a Chicago Daily Law Bulletin article, Supreme Court makes seismic shift 58 years after Plessy v. Ferguson, on June 6, 2016, available at https://www.chicagolawbulletin.com /archives/2016/06/06/plessy-v-ferguson-update-6-6-16.

citizens hired a detective to ensure Plessy was arrested for violating Louisiana's Separate Car Act, which required him to sit in the "blacks only" car. Plessy was removed from the train and arrested.

At trial, Plessy's attorneys argued that his thirteenth and fourteenth Amendment rights had been violated. Plessy was convicted and fined $25, which was upheld on appeal by the Louisiana Supreme Court.

The U.S. Supreme Court affirmed the conviction in a 7-1 decision written by Justice Henry B. Brown, considered by many to be one of the worst decisions ever issued by the Supreme Court.

The Supreme Court upheld the "separate but equal" doctrine in a number of subsequent decisions, which resulted in state-sanctioned racial segregation continuing unabated for generations.

Courts and much of the public paid little attention to the reality that the separate facilities in no way could be considered "equal."

Justice John Marshall Harlan issued a dissent in *Plessy* in which he strongly declared the Constitution favored no race: "Our Constitution is color-blind and neither knows nor tolerates classes among citizens." His dissent would become the law as applied to education in 1954—but the road to *Brown* was not a direct one.

Beginning in the 1930s, the National Association for the Advancement of Colored People (NAACP) and its Legal Defense and Education Fund implemented a strategy to attack racial inequality in education. The NAACP, under the leadership of Charles Hamilton Houston and Thurgood Marshall, successfully challenged "separate but equal" practices in a number of lawsuits dealing with segregation in higher education.

This series of victories led the NAACP to take up the challenge of "separate but equal" at the grammar and high school level.

The Tide Shifts

Brown v. Board of Education was the consolidation of five separate cases and was initially argued before the Supreme Court in December 1952. In its briefs, the NAACP asserted that racial discrimination was unreasonable and that segregation did great harm to African American students.

With regard to the court's prior ruling in *Plessy*, the NAACP argued that rather than expressly overruling it, the court should ignore that ruling as being irrelevant because it involved segregated transportation. Marshall and the Legal Defense Fund argued that the Supreme Court had never found the doctrine of "separate but equal" constitutional in the context of education, citing recent decisions of the Supreme Court.

At the 1953 term's end, the Supreme Court announced that the cases would be reheard in the 1954 term with the parties to focus on the Fourteenth Amendment's equal protection clause. (In the spring of 1953, the Court was divided and many predicted the Court would rule that "separate but equal" applied to education as well.)

In September 1953, Chief Justice Fred M. Vinson died and former California Governor Earl Warren was appointed as his replacement. The case was reargued before the court on December 8, 1953. After the rehearing, Justice Felix Frankfurter wrote Marshall a letter informing him that his rebuttal argument was the "most appropriate and the most forceful argument I have ever heard in any appellate court."

Warren mustered support for a unanimous decision, which was not easy because many justices feared the backlash and turmoil that would ensue.

In a meeting of the justices, Warren indicated that the only way to uphold segregation would be to find that African Americans were inferior. On May 17, 1954, Warren announced the unanimous decision of the court: "We conclude that in the field of public education the doctrine of 'separate but equal' has no place. Separate educational facilities are inherently unequal." Warren had achieved an amazing result, which was "a direct result of Warren's considerable efforts."[25]

The Supreme Court returned the consolidated cases to the docket to allow the parties to present positions on how to implement the desegregation ruling:

"On reargument, the consideration of appropriate relief was necessarily subordinated to the primary

---

25. *Id.*

question—the constitutionality of segregation in public education. We have now announced that such segregation is a denial of the equal protection of the laws."

Brown Comes Back

The issue facing the Supreme Court when the case returned to the docket was the method that would be used to implement the *Brown* decision. On May 31, 1955, the court issued its decision in *Brown II*, holding that the constitutional principles announced in *Brown I* "may require solution of varied local school problems" and remanded the cases back to the original courts "to take such proceedings and enter such orders and decrees consistent with this opinion as are necessary and proper to admit to public schools on a racially nondiscriminatory basis with all deliberate speed the parties to these cases."

"With All Deliberate Speed"

Although *Brown I* is seen as one of the great decisions in the Supreme Court's history and a correction of *Plessy*, the Warren Court received much criticism for its *Brown II* decision—chiefly that the directive that schools integrate "with all deliberate speed" imposed no time limit or potential sanctions on recalcitrant local authorities.

The Warren Court, sensitive to the local resistance and opposition to the Court's decision the previous term, intended to allow localities to fashion their own approaches to school integration.

Currently, the Department of Justice has more than 100 open desegregation cases that it is monitoring and enforcing. The LDF continues to oversee more than one hundred school desegregation cases.

For example, recently *CBS News* reported that a federal court in Cleveland, Mississippi, ordered schools in the district to be integrated.

The order met with local resistance. Another example is the case of *Thomas v. School Board of St. Martin Parish*, a lawsuit that LDF initiated in Louisiana in 1965 to end the segregation taking place in the school district. A Federal Court of Appeals decision in 2014 finally led the district to take steps to ameliorate the segregation that was still taking place.

In Chicago, it wasn't until 2006 when U.S. District Judge Charles P. Kocoras ruled that the Chicago Public Schools' desegregation plan could finally be partially removed from federal oversight.

Supreme Court Legacy

The Warren Court was an activist Court, perhaps "the most activist, law-changing Court in the Nation's history."[26] The Warren Court "had a more profound impact

---

26. Rice, p. x.

on American political and social life than at any other time in its existence, except for when the great John Marshall served as head of the tribunal during the first third of the nineteenth century."[27]

The Warren Court developed and expanded jurisprudence in three distinct areas: "civil rights, criminal justice, and legislative apportionment."[28] When asked what he believed his most important decision to be from his tenure as chief justice, *Brown* was mentioned second and Gideon third, but "he regarded his reapportionment decision to be the most important contribution he made. . . ."[29] The fifteen years of the Warren Court left legacies in a host of discrete areas:

> "[B]anned racial segregation in the public schools; prohibited racial discrimination in voting, in the use of places of 'public accommodation,' such as stores, restaurants, hotels, and theaters, and in the use of bus, railroad, and airline facilities; strengthened the right of persons to be secure against unreasonable searches and seizures; bolstered the right of a suspect in a crime of access to counsel; declared the 'one person, one vote' principle in elections to state legislatures; precisely and strictly defined the nature of 'subversive' activities

---

27. *Id.* at ix.
28. *Id.* at x.
29. Tributes, p. 97. The case Warren is referring to is of course *Baker v. Carr*, 369 U.S. 186 (1962), which held the famous rule "one person, one vote."

against the federal government; restricted the government's power to penalize an individual for his beliefs or associations; barred compulsory religious exercise in the public schools; secured the right to disseminate and obtain birth control information; effected the binding on the states themselves of most of the guarantees to individuals contained in the Bill of Rights."[30]

"Warren would face calls for his impeachment, with billboards along highways in the South. Despite promises by President Nixon and other Republican presidents to undo much of the Warren Court's decisions, many of them have survived."[31]

The Warren Court is remembered for its work in the three areas mentioned *infa*, and for being a pioneering court in many respects. However, Warren was never considered "a profound legal scholar,"[32] but made up for that lack of scholarship with "his leadership abilities and skill as a statesman" that "made him one of the most effective chief justices in the Court's history."[33]

---

30. *Id.*

31. As we go to press, there is a continued dialogue about President Donald J. Trump's latest Supreme Court nominee, Brett Kavanaugh, and how with this new conservative justice, some cases from the Warren Court and Burger Court may finally be formally overturned. Time will tell if rumors of certain decisions' demise are exaggerated.

32. Cushman, p. 438.

33. *Id.*

In 1968, Warren announced his retirement. Part of his thought likely involved his calculation that Johnson would win reelection and could select the next chief either before the election or post-election. Johnson picked his friend and a current associate justice, Abe Fortas, to succeed Warren. However, things did not turn out that way—Johnson announced he would not seek a second full term, and Nixon won the presidency. The nomination of Fortas as chief justice quickly came apart, when it was discovered that Fortas had received money from former clients, including someone being investigated by the Securities and Exchange Commission. A future associate and chief justice, Rehnquist, would be involved in the efforts to make sure that Fortas was removed completely from the Supreme Court.[34] Nixon asked Warren to remain on the Court for another term, while he attended to replacing other vacancies on the Supreme Court, including that of Fortas.

Warren stayed on for the next year, finally retiring on June 23, 1969.[35] In May one of his grandsons wrote a letter urging Warren to remain as chief justice. Warren responded with a long letter explaining the "world was an imperfect place" and explained how things can go awry in a democratic republic:

> "Under a democratic form of government, people can vote for poor government as well as good, and, when

---

34. *See* Jenkins, pgs. 91–93.
35. Cray, p. 511.

they do, it often takes time and a lot of effort to undo the bad results."[36]

After the cases were handled on the last day of Chief Justice Warren's tenure, President Nixon approached the lectern and spoke, acknowledging Warren's service.[37] After President Nixon spoke, Warren gave a lecture directed at President Nixon about the importance of the Court, stating:

> "It is a responsibility that is made more difficult in this Court because we have no constituency. We serve no majority. . . . We serve only the public interest as we see it, guided only by the Constitution and our own consciences. . . . It is not likely ever, with human nature as it is, for nine men to agree always on the most important and controversial things of life. . . . But so long as it is manned by men like those who have preceded us and by others like those who sit today, I have no fear of that ever happening."[38]

Warren turned to writing his memoirs, something he had said he would not do for many years, and to travel. Later in life, Warren expressed regret to his former clerk about his

---

36. *Id.* at 511–12.
37. *Id.* at 513.
38. *Id.*

role in the evacuation of the Japanese in 1942 but would not formally apologize publicly.[39]

During his final days, he often made comments about his feelings about President Nixon, and also thought the National Court of Appeals idea was a bad one, as well as worrying about the Nixon subpoena.[40] On July 8, 1974, Arthur Goldberg visited Warren in the hospital and they talked about the Nixon tapes. Warren told Goldberg, "No man, not even a king, can put himself above the law. I am confident the Court will do its duty, and so will the nation."[41]

On July 9, 1974, Justice Bill Brennan and Bill Douglas visited and told Warren the Court had voted in conference, 8-0, compelling President Nixon to release the tapes.[42] A few hours after their visit, Warren gasped his last breath.

Arthur Goldberg spoke at a ceremony on June 29, 1969, to honor Chief Justice Warren's retirement. Goldberg spoke eloquently of his former boss, stating in part:

> "For Earl Warren, as Chief Justice of the United States, has also been a Great Emancipator. He has helped liberate the law from the bonds of judicial timidity, knowing, from the core of his being, that judicial timidity is far more likely to be the undoing of our beloved country than the faithful and courageous exercise of

---

39. Cray, p. 520.
40. *Id.* at 526–27.
41. *Id.* at 526.
42. *Id.*

judicial responsibility. . . . Like Abraham Lincoln was during his lifetime, the Chief Justice has been subjected to unparalleled abuse in the conduct of his office. . . . The Chief Justice . . . conceived that whatever the justification in other ages or times for seeking out ways of avoiding decisions on the merits of a case, the tenor of the modern world demands that judges, like men in all walks of public and private life avoid escapism and frankly confront even the most controversial and troublesome justifiable problems."[43]

When Earl Warren died, the *New York Times* ran a long obituary, again noting the achievements of the chief justice:

The impact of the Warren Court was cumulative, and Mr. Warren's stature grew perceptibly over sixteen years. The parts that constituted the whole were embodied in a series of decisions that had the collective effect of reinforcing popular liberties. Among these were rulings that:

Outlawed school segregation.
Enunciated the one-man, one-vote doctrine.
Made most of the Bill of Rights binding on the states.
Curbed wiretapping.

---

43. United States. 91st Congress, 2nd Session. "Tributes to the Honorable Earl Warren, chief justice of the United States, To Commemorate the Occasion of his Retirement from the Supreme Court, June 23, 1969," pgs. 96–98.

Upheld the right to be secure against "unreasonable" searches and seizures.

Buttressed the right to counsel.

Underscored the right to a jury trial.

Barred racial discrimination in voting, in marriage laws, in the use of public parks, airports and bus terminals and in housing sales and rentals.

Extended the boundaries of free speech.

Ruled out compulsory religious exercises in public schools.

Restored freedom of foreign travel.

Knocked out the application of both the Smith and the McCarran Acts—both designed to curb "subversive" activities.

Held that Federal prisoners could sue the Government for injuries sustained in jail.

Said that wages could not be garnished without a hearing.

Liberalized residency requirements for welfare recipients.

Sustained the right to disseminate and receive birth control information.

***

More than many Chief Justices, Mr. Warren removed himself from partisanship and political activity, but in one instance he felt obliged to take on, albeit reluctantly, an extra-judicial task. That was the chairmanship of the so-called Warren Commission, which investigated the assassination of President Kennedy in November, 1963, and concluded that Lee Harvey Oswald, acting alone, had shot the President.[44]

Warren's name is often listed just after Marshall as the greatest chief, considered "second in greatness only to John Marshall himself in the eyes of most impartial students of the Court as well as the Court's critics."[45] Warren "ushered the United States into the modern era of race relations and, in some deeper sense, saved the Supreme Court as an institution."[46] The praise is earned, "for his opinions interpreting the Constitution" in numerous instances "represented giant strides forward on the road to the formation of a more perfect union."[47]

---

44. Whitman, available at https://archive.nytimes.com/www.nytimes.com /learning/general/onthisday/bday/0319.html?mod=article_inline.

45. Cray, p. 531 (quoting Henry J. Abraham).

46. Toobin, p. 87.

47. Stevens, p. 98.

Chapter Seventeen

Warren E. Burger: A Minnesota Twin Goes to Bat, Expanding Warren Court Rulings

Nominated by President Richard Nixon
Confirmed by Senate, 74-3, on June 9, 1969
Tenure: June 23, 1969 to September 26, 1986
  (Retired)
Presidents During Tenure
  Nixon
  Ford
  Carter
  Reagan

When Earl Warren wanted to retire as chief justice in 1968, he sent word to President Lyndon B. Johnson (LBJ).[1]
LBJ picked his friend and adviser, Justice Abe Fortas,

---

1. The introduction to this chapter in italics is based on an article that originally appeared in the *Chicago Daily Law Bulletin* on April 7, 2015, Cotter, "Minnesotan rises to become chief justice."

to replace Warren before the presidential election. Fortas, however, faced stiff resistance in the Senate and ultimately withdrew himself from consideration.

As a result, Warren's retirement was delayed until 1969, when his nemesis Richard M. Nixon became president. Nixon would nominate Warren Earl Burger to be the fifteenth chief justice.

Early Career

Burger began his career with a life insurance company, attending law classes at night. Upon graduating from the St. Paul (now William Mitchell) College of Law in 1931, he joined a St. Paul, Minnesota, law firm and was in private practice for two decades. For many years, he also taught law at St. Paul and was active in Republican politics.

In 1953, Burger was named assistant U.S. attorney general of the Justice Department civil division, a reward from President Dwight D. Eisenhower for helping deliver the Minnesota delegation to Ike at the 1952 Republican National Convention.

Burger would hold the Justice Department post until his 1955 appointment to the U.S. Court of Appeals for the District of Columbia Circuit. The federal court has become a stepping stone to the Supreme Court in recent years.

After fourteen years on the D.C. Circuit, Nixon nominated Burger for chief justice of the Supreme Court. Burger, who had been a critic of the Warren Court, argued for a strict construction of the U.S. Constitution, and it was his conservative stance that had attracted Nixon. The Senate over-whelmingly confirmed Burger by a 74-3 vote.

Chief Justice

A year after taking the reins, Burger was joined on the court by Harry A. Blackmun, who had attended the same St. Paul grade school as the chief. The two Nixon nominees would be dubbed the "Minnesota twins." And, though friends, they would often be on opposite sides of a decision.

Burger was in the conservative bloc, Blackmun the liberal. Nixon would learn that his expectation of a Burger Court overturning the precedents of the Warren Court was unlikely.

For example, in Swann v. Charlotte-Mecklenberg Board of Education (1971), the court unanimously ordered busing of schoolchildren to address desegregation.

The next year, the court ruled the death penalty unconstitutional in three cases that were consolidated together in Furman v. Georgia (1972). While Burger and Blackmun both dissented (as did justices William H. Rehnquist and Lewis F. Powell Jr.), the majority declared the death penalty was cruel and unusual punishment in these particular cases.

The Burger Court decided a number of hot-button cases and, in many instances, set a new course for rights with decisions that were seen as extensions of the Warren Court, not strict construction.

Arguably, the most controversial case the Burger Court decided was Roe v. Wade (1973), which extended the right of privacy to bar states from prohibiting abortions. Burger was in the 7-2 majority; Rehnquist and Justice Byron R. White dissented from the decision to restrict state regulation of abortion to the third trimester of pregnancy.

Thirteen years later, however, Burger questioned the foundation of Roe and declared in Thornburgh v. American College of Obstetricians and Gynecologists (1986) that the decision should be reexamined.

In one of the most important cases ever involving the separation of powers, the court decided United States v. Nixon (1974), which would be the penultimate chapter in the Watergate scandal. Argued July 8, 1974, Nixon was decided sixteen days later.

Burger issued the opinion of the unanimous court, finding with respect to the president who appointed him, "Neither the doctrine of separation of powers nor the need for confidentiality of high-level communications, without more, can sustain an absolute, unqualified presidential privilege."

The top court ordered Nixon to hand over tapes sought by the special prosecutor in the Watergate investigation, and sixteen days after the ruling, the president resigned.

Burger is often remembered best as an effective administrator of the court, a part of the job he enjoyed.

He founded the Supreme Court Historical Society and was a large proponent of alternative dispute resolution.

Even so, in the book "The Brethren," Bob Woodward and Scott Armstrong assessed Burger as not well liked by his brethren. He allegedly would switch votes to be able to assign himself the majority opinion.

While there may be some truth to these assertions, in cases such as Nixon, he sought to limit the broadness of the court's opinions.

Burger resigned in 1986 and until 1992 worked full-time as chair of the Commission on the Bicentennial of the U.S. Constitution. President Ronald Reagan would nominate Justice Rehnquist to replace Burger.

Early Life and Career

Warren Burger was born in St. Paul, Minnesota, on Constitution Day,[2] September 17, 1907, to Katharine (nee Schnittger) and Charles, who was a traveling salesman as well as a railroad cargo inspector. Burger grew up on the family farm and after graduating high school, Burger attended the University of Minnesota while working part-time as an accountant at an insurance company.[3] Upon graduation, he attended law school at the St. Paul College of Law (currently William Mitchell College of Law), graduating *magna cum laude.* Upon graduation, Burger went to work at a law firm in St. Paul and became an adjunct professor of law at St. Paul College of Law, teaching contracts.[4] He would practice law at the firm for the next twenty-one years.

Burger was a Republican and helped on the Minnesota front to help get Harold E. Stassen elected Governor of Minnesota. In 1952, Burger attended the Republican National Convention, where he was instrumental in getting delegates

---

2. Given the day of his birth, his later appointments as chief justice of the Supreme Court and then to the Bicentennial Commission seem extra apropos.

3. Cushman, p. 482.

4. *Id.*

to vote for Dwight D. Eisenhower, who would go on to win the Republican nomination and the presidency.

Assistant Attorney General

Eisenhower rewarded Burger's efforts and loyalty by appointing him to the position of assistant attorney general for the Civil Division at the Justice Department.[5] During his two years at the Justice Department, Burger argued two cases before the Supreme Court of the United States, winning one and losing one.

DC Court of Appeals

In 1955, "just as Burger was preparing to return to his St. Paul partnership, a vacancy occurred on the U.S. Court of Appeals for the District of Columbia Circuit."[6] President Eisenhower nominated Burger to fill the vacancy and the Senate confirmed Burger. Burger served from March 29, 1956 until June 23, 1969, when he became chief justice of the Supreme Court of the United States.[7]

---

5. "Warren E. Burger." *Oyez*, August 12, 2018, available at www.oyez.org/jus tices/warren_e_burger.

6. Cushman, p. 482.

7. The D.C. Circuit has often been referred to as the "little Supreme Court" because it handles so many constitutional questions, many of which never are heard by the Supreme Court of the United States. In addition, in recent years, the D.C. Circuit has been referred to as a "feeder court" for the Supreme Court. While this certainly is true of the current court (with Kavanaugh's confirmation,

During his time on the D.C. Circuit, Burger was a strong "law and order" judge who was hard on criminal defendants.[8] Burger also took every opportunity to assail and attack the jurisprudence of the Warren Court, and that would come to the Nixon administration's attention when a chance to name a chief justice arose. However, despite those expressed views, the Burger Court would not significantly erode most of the decisions of the Warren Court.

Supreme Court Nomination

Burger's views on criminal defendants and the Fifth Amendment attracted the attention of President Richard Nixon when Chief Justice Earl Warren announced his retirement, and President Nixon nominated Burger, following through on his campaign promise to install "strict constructionist," "law and order" judges to the federal bench as vacancies occurred.[9] The nomination to replace the chief justice fell upon President Nixon because of problems that developed around the nomination by Johnson to replace

the total former D.C. Circuit judges who are on the Supreme Court will reach four—Ginsburg, Roberts, Thomas, and Kavanaugh, and Scalia also was a D.C. Circuit Court judge just before the Supreme Court), only seven total D.C. Circuit Court judges have sat on the Supreme Court, including the current four.

8. "Warren E. Burger." *Oyez,* August 12, 2018, available at www.oyez.org /justices/warren_e_burger.

9. "Burger's service on the Court of Appeals ultimately drew attention to him as a leading federal judge with conservative inclinations, especially with respect to criminal matters." Galub, p. 334.

Warren with Associate Justice Fortas.[10] President Richard Nixon announced the nomination of Burger on May 21, 1969.[11] Burger was considered the ideal candidate by many— "[w]ith his wavy white hair, resonant baritone, courtly demeanor, and conservative views, he was right out of central casting."[12] Burger had been recommended to Nixon and his team by two others who had been asked to serve.[13] On June 9, 1979, by a Senate vote of 74-3, Burger was easily confirmed as the fifteenth chief justice of the Supreme Court of the United States.[14] Burger took his judicial oath as chief justice on June 23, 1969.[15]

The Burger Court would hear and decide many cases during his long tenure. In many areas, the Burger Court would disappoint- the "law and order" and anti-Warren hopes did not materialize in many ways as Republicans hoped when President Nixon made his appointments to the Supreme Court. Perhaps no Burger Court decision became as controversial long-term as the decision of the Burger Court in *Roe v. Wade*.[16]

---

10. *See supra.*
11. Halpern & Lamb, p. 129.
12. Jenkins, p. 94.
13. *Id.* at 93.
14. Cushman, p. 483.
15. Galub, p. 6.
16. *Roe v. Wade*, 410 U.S. 113 (1973).

Roe v. Wade

The Supreme Court initially heard this and the companion case, *Doe v. Bolton*,[17] in December 1971. The initial conference was held on December 16, 1971, and Justice Harry Blackmun, a Nixon appointee, received the assignment to write the majority opinions.[18] A slow writer, Blackmun's drafts were not ready to circulate until May 1972.[19] While Blackmun was drafting his opinion, which now appeared to have a solid five-person majority to overturn the laws, Burger was pushing for reargument, and Burger prevailed. The cases were reheard in 1973, and decisions issued. In a surprise majority of 7-2, the Supreme Court found the laws banning abortion unconstitutional, "with the majority including five of the Court's six Republican-appointed justices."[20] The justices, president who appointed them, and how they ruled were:

- Burger—Nixon—Unconstitutional
- Douglas—FDR—Unconstitutional
- Brennan—Eisenhower—Unconstitutional

---

17. *Doe v. Bolton*, 410 U.S. 179 (1973).

18. There was debate among the justices about the actual count and who had the power to appoint the opinion writer. Associate Justice Bill Douglas had counted four votes to strike down the laws and he was the senior justice in that position. However, once the liberal justices saw a draft of Blackmun's opinion, they accepted it and wanted to make sure it was finalized before the new Nixon appointees were on the Court. *See* Jenkins, pgs. 138–41.

19. Maltz, p. 248.

20. Graetz & Greenhouse, p. 133.

- Stewart—Eisenhower—Unconstitutional
- White—Kennedy—Constitutional
- Marshall—Johnson—Unconstitutional
- Blackmun—Nixon—Unconstitutional
- Powell—Nixon—Unconstitutional
- Rehnquist—Nixon—Constitutional

The *Roe* decision was one that did not per se give rights and did not grant "a right *to* anything but a right *against* something, the right not to be prosecuted for performing an abortion or obtaining one."[21] Today, *Roe* has become a litmus test for Supreme Court nominees[22] and remains for many a single issue upon which votes for candidates to various offices are determined. However, the backlash against *Roe* "actually took years to develop."[23] Surprisingly, in December 1975, during John Paul Stevens' confirmation hearings, Stevens was not asked any questions about his views on abortion.[24] More surprising still is that the support for abortion was apparently "stronger among Republicans than Democrats" and that the "Republican Party maintained a big-tent position on abortion until its 1980 convention, when Ronald Reagan won the presidential

---

21. *Id.* at 134 (emphasis in original).

22. For example, President Donald J. Trump with help from conservative think tanks and other groups developed a list of twenty-one potential Supreme Court nominees (expanded to twenty-five in late 2017), all of whom were vetted to agree to overturn *Roe v. Wade*, or at a minimum opposed to the decision.

23. Graetz & Greenhouse, p. 146.

24. *Id.* at 147.

nomination."[25] Despite the controversy that *Roe* eventually engendered, the Rehnquist Court upheld the main holding of *Roe* in a 5-4 decision, *Planned Parenthood v. Casey*,[26] in 1992, with Republican-appointed justices having the majority vote. The Court cited to the need for *stare decisis*,[27] recognizing its creditability:

> "The Court's claim to legitimacy, always fragile in a democratic society that has bestowed on life-tenured judges the extraordinary power to thwart the majority's

---

25. *Id.* The 1980 Republican National Convention included for the first time a platform position for the "appointment of federal judges who would vote to overturn *Roe*." *Id.*

26. *Planned Parenthood v. Casey*, 505 U.S. 833 (1992).

27. The term, *stare decisis*, means "to stand by things decided." In law, it is intended to be a means of honoring precedent, although there cannot be blind adherence to the concept. As is often pointed out, a good example of the Supreme Court getting it wrong was in *Plessy v. Ferguson*. As Justice Brandeis eloquently stated in dissent, *stare decisis* "is not inflexible." *Burnet v. Coronado Oil & Gas Go.*, 285 U.S. 393, 406 (Brandeis, dissenting). He went on to discuss how *stare decisis* should be approached by the Supreme Court, stating:

Stare decisis is usually the wise policy, because, in most matters, it is more important that the applicable rule of law be settled than that it be settled right. This is commonly true even where the error is a matter of serious concern, provided correction can be had by legislation. But in cases involving the Federal Constitution, where correction through legislative action is practically impossible, this court has often overruled its earlier decisions. The court bows to the lessons of experience and the force of better reasoning, recognizing that the process of trial and error, so fruitful in the physical sciences, is appropriate also in the judicial function. . . . *In cases involving the Federal Constitution, the position of this court is unlike that of the highest court of England, where the policy of* stare decisis was formulated and is strictly applied to all classes of cases.

Id. at 406-410 (footnotes and case references omitted).

Unfortunately, no nominee for the Supreme Court of the United States (or other Article III judgeship) appears willing to express this approach, but rather state they will respect precedent.

will, is nonetheless the only currency the Court really has."[28]

Rehnquist was in dissent in *Casey*.

Criminal Procedure

The Warren Court handed down several decisions that were heavily criticized involving rights for criminal defendants, including the trilogy of *Miranda v. Arizona*,[29] *Gideon v. Wainright*,[30] and *Mapp v. Ohio*.[31] This may have been the Burger Court's biggest victory in rolling back Warren Court precedent, as "his opinions gave greater weight to law enforcement than had the Warren Court."[32]

Presidential Power

President Richard Nixon had appointed four Supreme Court Justices to the Court—Chief Justice Burger and Associate Justices Powell, Rehnquist, and Blackmun. As President Nixon challenged the investigation into his involvement and coverup of Watergate, Nixon fought hard against release of the recordings made in the White House. When the case arrived at the Supreme Court in 1974, Nixon likely expected

---

28. Jenkins, p. 144 (quoting Linda Greenhouse of the *New York Times*).
29. *Miranda v. Arizona*, 384 U.S. 436 (1966).
30. *Gideon v. Wainright*, 327 U.S. 335 (1963).
31. *Mapp v. Ohio*, 367 U.S. 643 (1961).
32. Cushman, p. 484.

that his nominees would try to save him and his presidency. However, that was not to be—in a unanimous decision, the Court ruled in *United States v. Nixon*[33] that Nixon "must surrender tapes of recorded conversations, which had been subpoenaed in a criminal conspiracy trial."[34] Nixon was finished, and seventeen days later, Nixon made history by resigning from the presidency.[35]

Legacy

When Earl Warren retired as chief justice, many expected a counter-revolution, overruling much of what the Warren Court had decided. However, that is not how things turned out with the Burger Court. While the Burger Court did start the trend toward a much more conservative Supreme Court (one that continues fifty years later), the Warren Court doctrines and decisions became "more securely rooted now than they were in 1969, accepted by the Burger Court as the premises of constitutional decision-making in those areas."[36] President Nixon campaigned on a ticket of "law and order" that included the overturning of many of the Warren Court decisions. In making the appointments of Blackmun and Burger, Nixon often referred to both as

---

33. *United States v. Nixon*, 418 U.S. 683(1974). Rehnquist recused himself, so it was an 8-0 decision.

34. Cushman, p. 484.

35. *Id.*

36. Blasi, p. vii (Foreword by Anthony Lewis).

"strict constructionists" who Nixon most assuredly had not expected *Roe* or other decisions to include the "Minnesota Twins" in the majority. Nixon also could not have anticipated that a Supreme Court that had so many of his appointees on it and a large majority of Republican-appointed justices on it would turn on him and find against him, but it did.[37] While the Burger Court did not have a counter-revolution and to a large degree portrays a time of status quo for the Supreme Court, the *Roe* case and others reflected a Burger Court that rather than reversing the work of the Warren Court, extended it in some instances, at least when it related to Constitutional issues.[38] At the same time, in areas such as discrimination and criminal procedure, the Burger Court in many cases eviscerated some Warren Court decisions if not outright overturning them. Finally, the Burger Court "made progress on the rights of women."[39]

---

37. *United States v. Nixon*, 418 U.S. 683 (1974) The Supreme Court Supreme Court ruled, 8-0, that President Richard Nixon must provide taped recordings and other subpoenaed materials. Nixon resigned a few days later. As this book goes to press, much debate is being had about what impact Brett Kavanaugh would have on any decision that the Supreme Court might render should President Donald J. Trump be subpoenaed in the Special Counsel Robert Mueller investigation. This decision should give those concerned some comfort that the Supreme Court would order Trump to respond to a subpoena, but if and when the question arrives at the Supreme Court, we will see if the Roberts Court is as definitive in the number of justices voting for or against disclosure and compliance.

38. Although Graetz & Greenhouse make a strong case that while the Burger Court is assessed to be one that did not change any of the Warren Court jurisprudence in important substantive areas, the Burger Court did in fact eviscerate many of the prior Court's decisions, especially in criminal matters.

39. Sexton, p. 174.

Burger also cared deeply about the institution that is the Supreme Court and the justice system, creating among other things the Supreme Court Historical Society.[40]

In 1986, shortly after Chief Justice Burger retired, Associate Justice William Brennan was interviewed by *The New York Times Magazine*.[41] When asked about qualities that make for an effective chief justice, Brennan responded:

> "A conviction that you have to be fair in the assignment of opinions—this ensures good feelings all around—and an extraordinary capacity for persuading others to a point of view."[42]

Brennan went on to indicate that the contemporaneous and historical assessment of Burger would be that he lacked those qualities.[43] When asked whether the Burger Court had departed from the Warren Court, Brennan responded:

> "Perhaps in terms of direction and momentum, yes. But the times changed also. Of course there have been some erosions in some areas, for example the Fourth Amendment right not to be subject to unreasonable searches or seizures, but I don't think it's very accurate to speak of the Burger Court having unraveled the work of the Warren Court. Some important decisions

---

40. *Id.*

41. Leeds, available at https://www.nytimes.com/1986/10/05/magazine/a-life-on-the-court.html.

42. *Id.*

43. *Id.*

affirming personal liberties came down during Burger's years. The abortion decision was not a legacy of the Warren Court, but the Burger Court. The first case to strike down the death penalty in a number of states came out of the Burger Court. Also, important cases involving the separation of church and state- prayer in school in particular- and the affirmative-action cases this past term."[44]

Brennan, who served on the Supreme Court from 1956 until 1990, and who is considered one of the most influential justices in the history of the Supreme Court due to his ability to garner five-vote majorities for his opinions on a Court that became more right-leaning over those long years of service, likely has a large claim to be able to accurately reflect on the Burger Court legacy.

However, Burger's clerks also have a view of the man and justice, and their thoughts provide a different perspective.[45] John Sexton offers insights into Burger and his adherence to precedents, stating that he received a note in one case from Burger after proposing a solution in a religion case that stated, "But we are bound in this Court by our precedents, even those with which we disagree strongly."[46] While strict adherence to past precedents has its

---

44. *Id.*
45. *See, e.g.,* Fabrikant, p. 203; *see also* Sexton, p. 173.
46. Sexton, p. 176.

limits,[47] unfortunately we arguably have lost the adherence to precedent, and careful deliberations about overturning *stare decisis*. Sexton summed up Burger and his views:

> "What the Chief Justice expected and would expect from the Court is principled, reasoned decision-making based upon the hard, intellectual work of legal reasoning, not upon ideology or political belief. Though my observations may not be consistent with the consensus view, I can attest that he held himself to that standard."[48]

One lasting practice initiated by Chief Justice Burger is the reduction of oral arguments from two hours per case to one hour.[49]

Retirement and Death

On May 27, 1986, Burger visited the White House to meet with President Ronald Reagan.[50] Reagan's staff was reluctant to agree to the meeting, fearing Burger simply wanted more funds for the Bicentennial Commission, but he "dropped a bombshell. He intended to resign."[51] Burger retired on September 29, 1986, at the time serving the fourth

---

47. Taken to its logical conclusion, *Plessy* would remain the law because it is past precedent.
48. Sexton, p. 181.
49. Stevens, p. 119.
50. Jenkins, p. 209.
51. *Id.*

longest tenure as chief justice in the Supreme Court of the United States' history (Rehnquist, his replacement, would become the fourth longest serving chief justice).[52] Part of Burger's decision was to become Chairman of the Bicentennial Commission, a position he enthusiastically held. In modern times, Burger is one of the few chief justices (or associate justices, for that matter) who have retired while in good health to do something else. Burger died of congestive heart failure on June 25, 1995.[53]

---

52. Chief justices by tenure (shortest to longest):

1. Rutledge
2. Ellsworth
3. Stone
4. Jay
5. Vinson
6. Chase
7. Taft
8. White
9. Hughes
10. **Roberts (current)**
11. Waite
12. Warren
13. Burger
14. Rehnquist
15. Fuller
16. Taney
17. Marshall

Roberts has served as chief justice for almost fourteen years at the time of publication. If he serves eight more years, he would become the third longest serving chief justice in history. An additional seven years after that, he would become second longest, and if he can serve another six years after that, he would be the longest serving chief justice in history. If he were to achieve that, Roberts would be eighty-five years old.

53. Cushman, p. 485.

Part Eight

The Return of the Conservative Bench

The Burger Court did not end up being the revolutionary Court that was going to rollback the Warren Court precedents in criminal justice and other areas that President Nixon and the Republicans had expected. President Nixon appointed four justices to the Supreme Court, including Chief Justice Burger. President Ford appointed one justice, John Paul Stevens, to the Supreme Court. But the Burger Court did not reverse the work of the Warren Court, as outlined in Burger's chapter. With the retirement of Chief Justice Burger, President Ronald Reagan had an opportunity to replace Burger with someone who would more rigidly adhere to a view of original intention. Reagan's attorney general, Edwin Meese III, gave a speech to the American Bar Association on July 9, 1985.[1] The speech,

---

1. Speech available at https://www.justice.gov/sites/default/files/ag/legacy/2011/08/23/07-09-1985.pdf.

considered by many as the "speech of his career,"[2] advo-
cated for an approach of original intention. Meese quoted
Associate Justice Joseph Story, close to Chief Justice John
Marshall, about views of interpretation:

> "In construing the Constitution of the United States,
> we are in the first instance to consider, what are its
> nature and objects, its scope and design, as apparent
> from the structure of the instrument, viewed as a
> whole and also viewed in its component parts. Where
> its words are plain, clear and determinate, they require
> no interpretation. . . . Where the words admit of two
> senses, each of which is conformable to general usage,
> that sense is to be adopted, which without departing
> from the literal import of the words, best harmonizes
> with the nature and objects, the scope and design of
> the instrument."[3]

Rehnquist, while a strong conservative with strong views
on a variety of issues, "led a Court that put the brakes on
some of the excesses of the Warren era while keeping pace
with the sentiments of a majority of the country—generally
siding with economic conservatives and against cultural
conservatives."[4] Rehnquist was someone who did exercise

---

2. Clemetson, available at https://www.nytimes.com/2005/08/17/politics
/meeses-influence-looms-in-todays-judicial-wars.html.

3. Speech of Edwin Meese III, available at https://www.justice.gov/sites
/default/files/ag/legacy/2011/08/23/07-09-1985.pdf (quoting Justice Story).

4. Rosen, p. 180.

judicial restraint, with the belief the judiciary "should defer to the judgement of elected legislators" and, in so doing, "was the conservative justice who most consistently practiced what he preached."[5] Rehnquist's counterparts, Justices Thomas and Scalia, on the other hand, were judicial activists. The Court under Rehnquist definitely became more conservative, and with the additional justices that President Trump has added to the Roberts Court, we are in a period where the Court has become very conservative again, as discussed in the next two chapters.

---

5. *Id.* at 182.

Chapter Eighteen

William Rehnquist: A Clerk, an Associate Justice, a "Great Chief Justice"

Nominated by President Ronald Reagan

Confirmed by Senate, 65-33, on September 17, 1986

Tenure: September 26, 1986 to September 3, 2005 (Died)

Presidents During Tenure

Reagan

H.W. Bush

Clinton

W. Bush

William H. Rehnquist, a staunch conservative, joined the Supreme Court in 1971 as an associate justice, serving in that role for fourteen and a half years until President Ronald Reagan nominated him to replace

Warren Burger as chief justice.[1] *Rehnquist would serve as chief for nineteen years, the longest term since the late 1880s.*

Rehnquist died in September 2005, just as John G. Roberts Jr. appeared poised to join him on the court as an associate justice.

Nominated by President George W. Bush, Roberts was headed to Senate confirmation for associate justice when Rehnquist succumbed to thyroid cancer. Bush then revised Roberts' nomination, and he became the third youngest chief justice (after John Jay and John Marshall).

A Contentious Memo

After serving in the Army Air Corps, Rehnquist obtained his bachelor's degree from Stanford University, a master's from Harvard University, and then his law degree from Stanford University. Upon graduating, he became a clerk for Supreme Court Justice Robert H. Jackson.

While clerking, he wrote a memo titled "A Random Thought on the Segregation Cases," which would be a

---

1. The introduction to this chapter in italics is based on an article that originally appeared in the *Chicago Daily Law Bulletin* on May 7, 2015, Cotter, "Chief Justices Rehnquist, Roberts and a shift right."

point of controversy in his confirmation hearings. In the memo, Rehnquist, writing in the first-person states, "I think Plessy v. Ferguson was right and should be reaffirmed." He later claimed the memo was written from Jackson's point of view, not his.

After his clerkship, he moved to Phoenix, where he worked in private practice and became active in Republican politics, including Barry Goldwater's presidential bid.

When Richard Nixon became president, he appointed Rehnquist an assistant U.S. attorney general for the Office of Legal Counsel. After two justices retired, Nixon nominated Rehnquist. He was confirmed by a Senate vote of 68-26. He established himself as a conservative voice on the Burger Court.

When Burger announced his retirement in 1986, Reagan nominated Rehnquist for chief, and he was confirmed by a 65-33 Senate vote.

In each confirmation hearing, the 1953 segregation memo arose. Rehnquist read the Fourteenth Amendment narrowly. In Rostker v. Goldberg, 453 U.S. 57, 79 (1981), his opinion noted, "The Constitution requires that Congress treat similarly situated persons similarly, not that it engage in gestures of superficial equality."

Rehnquist was well liked and respected by his colleagues on the court. He also was a frequent author, and his book "The Supreme Court" is a leading title on the court through his tenure.

Rehnquist became only the second chief justice to preside over an impeachment trial when President Bill Clinton was impeached in 1999. Diagnosed with thyroid cancer in 2004, he missed many hearings that term.

When Justice Sandra Day O'Connor discussed her plans to retire, she did so after Rehnquist confirmed he intended to remain on the court. Shortly after, he would die in his home.

Early Life and Career

William Hubbs Rehnquist was born on October 1, 1924, in Shorewood, Wisconsin, a suburb of Milwaukee, to William Benjamin and Margery (nee Peck). William was a sales manager and Margery was the daughter of a local hardware store owner. From his childhood, Rehnquist was exposed to a very conservative viewpoint by his family. According to a report in the *Washington Post,* heroes of the "Rehnquist household were 'Republican standard bearers such as Alf Landon, Wendell Wilkie and Herbert Hoover.'"[2] After attending the local public high school in Shorewood, Rehnquist attended Kenyon College, where

---

2. Cushman, p. 496.

he quit after one semester to enter the U.S. Army Air Force. Rehnquist served in the Air Force from 1943 until 1946. After his discharge, and partially as a result of the G.I. Bill, Rehnquist attended Stanford University, where he obtained his B.A. and M.A. in political science in 1948.[3] Rehnquist then attended Harvard University, where he received a second M.A., this time in government. Rehnquist returned to Stanford University to obtain his law degree from the Stanford Law School. Rehnquist finished first in his class at Stanford Law School.[4]

Having met Associate Justice Robert Jackson when Jackson had visited Stanford Law School to dedicate a new building for the law school, Rehnquist obtained an interview to clerk for Jackson and, despite thinking the interview went terribly, Rehnquist was offered the clerkship.

Clerk for Robert Jackson

During the 1952 term, Rehnquist clerked for Robert Jackson. Some of Rehnquist's memos to Associate Justice Jackson raised questions about Rehnquist's views on race. In his memo on the *Brown v. Board of Education* case, Rehnquist wrote:

---

3. *Id.*
4. *Id.* His classmate and future fellow Supreme Court Justice, Sandra Day O'Connor, finished third in his class.

Urging a view palpably at variance with precedent and probably with legislative history, appellants seek to convince the Court of the moral wrongness of the treatment they are receiving. I would suggest that this is a question the Court need never reach; for regardless of the Justice's individual views on the merits of segregation, it quite clearly is not one of those extreme cases which commands intervention from one of any conviction. **If this Court, because its members individually are "liberal" and dislike segregation**, now chooses to strike it down, it differs from the McReynolds court only in the kinds of litigants it favors and the kinds of special claims it protects. To those who would argue that 'personal' rights are more sacrosanct than 'property' rights, the short answer is that the Constitution makes no such distinction. To the argument made by Thurgood Marshall that a majority may not deprive a minority of its constitutional right, the answer must be made that while this is sound in theory, **in the long run it is the majority who will determine what the constitutional rights of the minority are.** One hundred and fifty years of attempts on the part of this Court to protect minority rights of any kind—whether those of business, slaveholders, or Jehovah's Witnesses—have been sloughed off, and crept silently to rest. If the present Court is unable to profit by this example it must be prepared to see its

work fade in time, too, as embodying only the sentiments of a transient majority of nine men.

I realize that it is an unpopular and unhumanitarian
position, for which I have been excoriated by 'liberal'
colleagues, but I think *Plessy v. Ferguson* was right and
should be re-affirmed. If the fourteenth Amendment
did not enact Spencer's <u>Social Stations</u>, it just as surely
did not enact Myrddahl's <u>American Dilemma</u>.[5]

(Bold emphasis added.)

Rehnquist and some commentators have attempted to
attribute the memos to Rehnquist trying to memorialize
Jackson's thinking about the cases.[6] However, in *Terry v.
Adams*,[7] for example, the memo Rehnquist wrote states:

"It is about time the Court faced the fact that the white
people [in] the South don't like the colored people; the
Constitution restrains them from effecting this dislike
thr[ough] state action, but it most assuredly did not
appoint the Court as a sociological watchdog to rear up
every time private discrimination raises its admittedly
ugly head. To the extent that this decision advances
the frontier of state action and 'social gain,' it pushes

---

5. Rehnquist, available at https://www.gpo.gov/fdsys/pkg/GPO-CHRG-REHN
QUIST/pdf/GPO-CHRG-REHNQUIST-4-16-6.pdf.

6. *See, e.g.,* Brenner, p. 77 ("he tended to anticipate the views of his boss").

7. *Terry v. Adams*, 345 U.S. 461 (1953).

back the frontier of freedom of association and majority rule."[8]

In a second memo on the *Terry* case, Rehnquist wrote to Jackson:

> "[C]lerks began screaming as soon as they saw this that 'Now we can show those damn southerners, etc.' I take a dim view of this pathological search for discrimination . . . and as a result I now have something of a mental block against the case."[9]

Lest anyone doubt that Rehnquist was trying to channel the views of Justice Jackson for conference or otherwise, Rehnquist makes it clear in the first *Terry* memo that he is writing of his own thoughts and own advice to Jackson and not trying to write Jackson's thoughts, Rehnquist concluded the memo as follows:

> "This is a position that I am sure ought to be stated; but if stated by [Chief Justice Fred M.] Vinson, [Sherman] Minton, or [Stanley] Reed it just won't sound the same way as if you state it."[10]

Finally, Rehnquist wrote Associate Justice Felix Frankfurter a letter in 1955 that was critical of Justice Jackson

---

8. Lane, available at https://alumni.stanford.edu/get/page/magazine/article/?article_id=33966.

9. Yarbrough, p. 2.

10. *Id.* at 3.

but has disappeared. At least one article has cited the missing letter to be an expression of disappointment by Rehnquist in the *Brown* decision, based on other speeches and letters and conduct of Rehnquist in the late 1950s.[11] In addition, Adam Liptak, one of the great writers about the Supreme Court, in writing about the article referenced in the preceding sentence, asserted that "the new evidence only buttresses information available at the time that undermined the account offered by the future Chief Justice."[12] In any event, at his confirmation hearings, Rehnquist was able to address these issues to the Senate Judiciary Committee's satisfaction by attributing the memo in *Brown* to thoughts of Justice Jackson.[13]

Legal Career

After the clerkship, Rehnquist chose to establish his practice in Phoenix, Arizona, where he began work for a law firm, Evans, Kitchel & Jenckes. While many stories have been told about how Rehnquist came to choose Phoenix as

---

11. Snyder & Barrett, p. 631. Available at http://lawdigitalcommons.bc.edu/bclr/vol53/iss2/5.

12. Liptak, available at https://www.nytimes.com/2012/03/20/us/new-look-at-an-old-memo-casts-more-doubt-on-rehnquist.html.

13. Rehnquist in subsequent years, beginning in Phoenix in reaction to an ordinance proposed by the Phoenix City Council to address public accommodations in 1964, clearly expressed his views of such civil rights activities, arguing against the ordinance both at a public hearing and in a subsequent letter to a newspaper. *See* Jenkins, pgs. 69–71.

a place of practice, one thing often not told is that his future wife had grown up in Phoenix.[14] Rehnquist served in private practice from 1953 until 1969, and became involved in local politics, including with Barry Goldwater. His mentor at his initial law firm was Denison Kitchel, who helped Goldwater win a Senate seat and become a candidate for president of the United States.[15] The two lawyers eventually had a falling out, and Rehnquist would eventually form a firm, Powers & Rehnquist, with a liberal partner.[16] However, as part of his connections with Kitchel, he met another conservative operative, Richard Kleindienst.[17] Rehnquist's conservative views and his political involvement with Goldwater and other Arizona conservatives would pay off handsomely when Richard Nixon became president.

White House Work

In January 1969, just days after Richard Nixon was sworn in as president of the United States, Rehnquist was appointed the assistant attorney general for the Justice Department's Office of Legal Counsel. His mentor, Kleindienst, had been appointed to the number-two job at the Department of Justice, and Kleindienst recommended to Attorney General

---

14. Jenkins, p. 60.
15. *Id.* at 60–62.
16. *Id.* at 62.
17. *Id.* at 74.

John Mitchell that Rehnquist be hired.[18] Rehnquist's work in that role included the responsibility "to screen . . . candidates for potential Supreme Court positions."[19] Rehnquist saw Mitchell as a mentor and would display Mitchell's photograph as well as Nixon's in his Supreme Court chambers.[20] On September 17, 1971, Justice Hugo Black, who had checked into Bethesda Naval Hospital due to illness, notified Chief Justice Burger that he was retiring. Black would die on September 25, 1971. Burger called Mitchell on September 17, and disclosed that Black had submitted his resignation, but also more news- Justice John Marshall Harlan intended to retire as well because he was gravely ill. President Nixon was ready when he received this news of two additional vacancies- President Nixon had a list of candidates ready, folks that President Nixon was confident would "correctly" interpret the Constitution, would be conservative, and would be "law and order" justices.[21] The first two potential nominees that Nixon considered to

---

18. *Id.* at 76.

19. Cushman, p. 498. There is evidence that his work screening candidates was not done well. For example, Rehnquist was responsible for vetting Clement Haynsworth to replace Fortas. Haynsworth had a conflict of interest and was eventually rejected by the Senate, 55-45, "the first time since 1930 that the Senate had voted down outright a Supreme Court nominee, and only the second time in the twentieth century." Jenkins, p. 97. The next nominee, G. Harold Carswell, was a disastrous nominee who was a racist and who was discovered to be a homosexual. Carswell was not confirmed, garnering the same forty-five votes that Haynsworth had. Jenkins, pgs. 99–100.

20. Cushman, p. 498.

21. President Donald Trump was not the first president to have a list of pre-screened conservatives in the event a Supreme Court seat opened.

fill the vacancies of Justices Hugo Black and Harlan were found "unqualified" by the American Bar Association.[22] President Nixon eventually settled on Lewis Powell and Rehnquist to fill the vacancies. Attorney General John Mitchell notified Rehnquist "they had settled on some-one- Rehnquist himself."[23] Nixon was very pleased with his Supreme Court moves, gloating with Mitchell:

> "This means, John, that we will have appointed four good men. Everybody recognizes that Burger is a good man. Blackmun is a good man. Powell, of course, everyone will recognize it. And Rehnquist is the smart-est of the whole goddamn bunch. And he's on our side, isn't he?"[24]

Nixon a few years later would question those words and his confidence in his "four good men."

Associate Justice

On October 21, 1971, President Nixon formally nomi-nated both Rehnquist and Powell to the Supreme Court. Both were confirmed, but with Powell receiving a very easy, 89-1, Senate vote. Rehnquist did not fare as well, with some

---

22. The two were Mildred Lillie and Herschel Friday. They may have been red herrings submitted by President Nixon to divert attention from his actual selec-tion process. *See* Jenkins, p. 123.

23. Cushman, p. 498.

24. Jenkins, p. 129.

Senators raising issues that Rehnquist was opposed by numerous civil liberties groups and unions, including the ACLU, AFL-CIO, and the NAACP.[25] Late in the Rehnquist confirmation process, *Newsweek* disclosed it had obtained a memo from Rehnquist from 1952, his memo to Justice Jackson in the *Brown* case.[26] Rehnquist wrote a letter to Senator James Eastland that the memo reflected Jackson's, not Rehnquist's views, a claim that Jackson's secretary strongly refuted and attacked Rehnquist as smearing Jackson. In any event, after further debate, and a Senate wishing to adjourn and exhausted by the process, Rehnquist was confirmed on December 10, 1971, by a vote of 68-26.[27] Rehnquist would serve as an associate justice for a period of almost fifteen years. As an associate justice, Rehnquist did not necessarily rule by a set jurisprudential style (as did Antonin Scalia, for example), but rather was a justice who "is directed not so much by stare decisis (past judicial decisions) as by an inner compass that almost unfailingly evolved from a moral vision developed long ago."[28]

Rehnquist was often a dissenter in his early days on the Burger Court, earning the nickname "lone ranger"

---

25. Congressional Record—Senate, December 10, 1971, p. 46197, available at https://www.senate.gov/reference/resources/pdf/450_1971.pdf.

26. Jenkins, p. 134.

27. Congressional Record, p. 46197.

28. Jenkins, "The Partisan," available at https://www.nytimes.com/1985/03/03/magazine/the-partisan.html.

from his clerks.[29] For example, he dissented in *Roe v. Wade*, asserting:

> "To reach its result, the Court necessarily has had to find within the scope of the Fourteenth Amendment a right that was apparently completely unknown to the drafters of the Amendment."[30]

By 1975, Rehnquist had become "the leader of the ever-shifting conservative wing of the Court."[31] Some of his colleagues critiqued him for his willingness to ignore his stated vow to consistently interpret and apply the Constitution in order to achieve results:

> "Beneath Rehnquist's stated commitment to judicial consistency, the liberals saw his willingness to cut corners to reach a conservative result. Polished, articulate opinions seemed cleverly, sometimes deceptively, to gloss over inconsistencies of logic or fact. In one case (*Jefferson v. Hackney*), Douglas and Marshall objected that Rehnquist's majority opinion misrepresented the legislative history of the federal welfare program. Slow even to correct an outright misstatement, Rehnquist still insisted on publishing an opinion that twisted the facts."[32]

---

29. *See, e.g.,* "Biography: William Rehnquist," available at https://www.biography.com/people/william-rehnquist-9454479.

30. *Roe v. Wade*, 410 U.S. 113, 174 (1973) (Rehnquist, dissenting).

31. Cushman, p. 499.

32. Woodward & Armstrong, p. 222 (1979 edition).

Chief Justice

On June 17, 1986, Chief Justice Warren Burger announced his retirement, and, on the same day, President Ronald Reagan nominated Associate Justice Rehnquist to replace Burger.[33] Three days later, President Reagan nominated U.S. Court of Appeals for the District of Columbia Judge Antonin Scalia to take the seat that would be vacated by Rehnquist's elevation.[34] With the nomination and then confirmation, Rehnquist became only the third associate justice elevated from that position directly to the chief justice position.[35]

On September 17, 1986, the Senate approved Rehnquist as chief justice, 65-33,[36] and on September 26, 1986, Rehnquist and Scalia took their judicial oaths as chief justice and associate justice, respectively.[37] With the focus on Rehnquist and questions about his partisanship and scrutiny he faced in his hearings, Scalia was not subjected to much tough assessment by the Senate Judiciary Committee and received a unanimous vote from the Senate. Of all

---

33. Galub & Lankevich, p. 3.

34. *Id.*

35. The first two were White and Stone. The only other associate justices who eventually became chief justice were Rutledge and Hughes, but they had gaps in service and did other things between being associate justice and chief justice.

36. At the time, the large number of votes against Rehnquist as chief justice was the most negative votes for a confirmed justice. Yarbrough, p. 11. However, the current court has five justices with more than thirty-three negative votes who were confirmed (Associate Justices Alito, Thomas, Gorsuch, Kagan, and Kavanaugh).

37. Galub & Lankevich, p. 3.

the Nixon appointees, Rehnquist would be the truest adherent to the "law and order" type of justice that Nixon expected of his nominees.[38]

The Brennan Court

William J. Brennan Jr., served the seventh longest tenure on the Supreme Court of the United States, sitting as an associate justice from 1956 until his retirement in 1990. During that tenure, he served under three chief justices— Warren, Burger, and Rehnquist. Brennan is credited to a large extent with many of the decisions of the Supreme Court granting or finding rights for the individual, and the Supreme Court during his tenure has often been referred to as the "Brennan Court" because of his influence, despite not having been chief justice:

> "The Court on which Justice Brennan was a pivotal force for nearly 34 years was, in many respects, the Brennan Court, although he never served as Chief Justice. He was the author of numerous landmark opinions and, through his powers of persuasion and force of intellect, the prime mover behind many others. When he did not prevail, his voice in dissent was strong."[39]

---

38. *See infra* re Rehnquist and *habeas corpus*, for example.

39. Greenhouse, available at https://www.nytimes.com/1997/07/25/us/william-brennan-91-dies-gave-court-liberal-vision.html.

Brennan's legacy and impact on the Court cannot be overstated. The Brennan Center for Justice, in celebrating Brennan, posted:

> "Brennan's legacy was so powerful and far-reaching that even those who disagreed with his opinions still recognized his singular influence. According to the conservative National Review in 1984, 'there is no individual in this country, on or off the Court, who has had a more profound and sustained impact upon public policy in the United States.'"[40]

While Brennan only served a few years under Rehnquist as chief justice, the two were together on the Supreme Court for eighteen years, from 1972 to 1990, and during that time, "they headed the Court's liberal and conservative wings, and lobbied for the votes of moderate justices. . . . Each won major victories, but neither won a final triumph."[41] Despite that assessment, the Brennan Court:

> "[M]andated: pregnancy disability leaves for women; new trials for blacks who were convicted by all-white juries; a challenge under the Voting Rights Act to an Alabama town's annexing an all-white area; lawsuits by low-income public-house tenants who were angry

---

40. Brennan Center for Justice, available at https://www.brennancenter.org /celebrating-justice-brennan.

41. Irons, p. ix.

about utility rates; unemployment pay for a Seventh-Day Adventist fired for refusing to work on Saturdays; handicapped-worker protections for people with contagious diseases such as AIDS: half of future police promotions in Alabama for blacks, to overcome past egregious discrimination; relaxing asylum standards for aliens; and a hands-off policy against sexually explicit programming on cable television."[42]

Rehnquist dissented from each such decision. In Rehnquist's first term as chief justice, the Court decided more "than half of the decisions of the term" by 5-4 or 6-3 decisions.[43] A potential chance to turn the Supreme Court further right, to perhaps overturn *Roe*, came to President Reagan at the end of Rehnquist's first term as chief justice, when his fellow confirmee in 1971, Lewis Powell, announced his retirement. Powell had voted in the majority in *Roe*. President Reagan nominated Robert Bork, someone who had been on his shortlist along with Scalia when the chief justice vacancy occurred. Bork was an extreme conservative, and the Senate had flipped back to Democratic control. Bork was defeated, the first Supreme Court nominee to be rejected outright since 1970, and Reagan's next nominee, Douglas Ginsburg, withdrew his nomination. Anthony Kennedy was selected, and that third nominee was the

---

42. Jenkins, pgs. 229–30 (case citation notes omitted).
43. Jenkins, p. 231.

charm.[44] Kennedy won unanimous approval by the Senate, 97-0. In an early decision during Kennedy's tenure, the Court upheld a Missouri law regulating abortions by a 5-4 vote, with Rehnquist in the majority with Kennedy.[45] However, *Roe* was not overturned by the decision.

In a subsequent case, *Planned Parenthood v. Casey*,[46] conservatives felt good about their chances in finally overturning *Roe*. Thurgood Marshall, a very liberal justice who had voted in the *Roe* majority, had been replaced by Clarence Thomas, one of the most conservative justices in many years to sit on the Supreme Court. However, to the right's disappointment, the decision came out reaffirming *Roe*, with Kennedy and Justice Sandra Day O'Connor having switched their decisions from the previous case.

Legacy

Rehnquist led a Supreme Court during his tenure as chief justice that definitely became more conservative.[47] Rehnquist was "disrespectful of precedent and dismissive of social, economic, and political institutions that did not

---

44. Kennedy was a close friend of then-Attorney General Edwin Meese.

45. *Webster v. Reproductive Health Services*, 492 U.S. 490 (1989).

46. *Planned Parenthood v. Casey*, 505 U.S. 833 (1992).

47. One book written about Chief Justice Rehnquist in 2012 is titled, "The Partisan." Jenkins, "The Partisan: The Life of William Rehnquist." Rehnquist's original appointment to the Court is described as "a spur-of-the-moment selection, of a candidate bereft of judicial credentials. He is the last of a breed." *Id*. at xiv.

comport with his black-and-white view of the world."[48] According to at least one biographer, "Rehnquist made it respectable to be an expedient conservative on the Court,"[49] one with no real body of law that defines him or the Rehnquist Court in any manner. "His successor as Chief Justice, John Roberts, is his natural heir."[50] Rehnquist's long tenure on the Supreme Court was very right in ideology, someone who "was skeptical of government efforts to promote civil liberties and downright hostile to the Court's efforts to broaden individual rights."[51]

A good example of how far the Court shifted during this time can be seen by one of the associate justices appointed early in Rehnquist's Court tenure, John Paul Stevens. Stevens, appointed in 1975 by President Gerald Ford, was a Republican on the Court and considered a moderate conservative. By the time he retired in 2009, the Court included Republicans more conservative than he was and Stevens was labeled a liberal.

But while an affable, likeable person by all accounts, Rehnquist failed at making the Court a more coherent one:

> "Rehnquist has not been able to make the 'nine small law firms' perform in a more institutionally coherent fashion. Despite his human qualities, Rehnquist has

---

48. *Id.*
49. *Id.* at xv.
50. *Id.*
51. Toobin, The Oath, p. 38.

not marshalled the Court as effectively as some of his predecessors. He presides over but does not control an institution which gives the appearance of being disjointed and clumsy. Perhaps the Justices merely reflect the condition of a fragmented and deeply divided nation."[52]

Thus, Rehnquist failed to fulfill his vision for what a chief justice's role should be. In a 1976 speech, Rehnquist stated:

"Hughes believed that unanimity of decision contributed to public confidence in the Court. . . . Except in cases involving matters of high principle he willingly acquiesced in silence rather than expose his dissenting views. . . . Hughes was also willing to modify his own opinions to hold or increase his majority."[53]

Unfortunately, Rehnquist did not follow his own thoughts when he became chief justice. Unlike his predecessor, Burger, Rehnquist did not seem to change his views or opinions to increase a majority or try to convince his fellow justices to speak as one, but instead "made it respectable to be an expedient conservative on the Court."[54] One legacy left by the Rehnquist Court is the shrinkage of opinions

---

52. Galub & Lankevich, p. xi.
53. Cushman, p. 500.
54. Jenkins, p. xv.

generated by the Supreme Court. "In 1994 the Court issued only 84 decisions, the fewest since 1956."[55]

In the end, the Rehnquist Court, expected to chip away at precedents on abortion and other controversial issues that the Warren and Burger Courts decided, has been in the position "assuming an arbiter's role in preference to that of the activist" and thus "following the pattern of most Supreme Courts in American history."[56] Rehnquist also left the Supreme Court "as deeply divided politically as the executive and legislative branches of our government."[57]

One area in which the Rehnquist Court was very successful was in "the Court's withdrawal from the school desegregation effort as well as a retreat from affirmative action."[58] The Roberts Court would continue in that direction on those two issues, as we will see. The Rehnquist Court was "a generally conservative, yet essentially mixed" court on civil liberties, with race- and gender-conscious policies that "faced a heavy burden of justification."[59]

In a number of areas, Rehnquist as chief justice was very successful. One area that changed substantively as a result of the Rehnquist Court is *habeas corpus*.[60] Rehnquist had long decried the delays in executions of those convicted,

---

55. *Id.*

56. *Id.* at p. 12.

57. Jenkins, p. xv.

58. Coyle, p. 46.

59. Yarbrough, p. 267.

60. *Habeas corpus* writs derive their existence from the Magna Carta and permit a judge to assess the legality of a loss of personal liberty. The writs are

pointing to the myriad of *habeas* petitions that the Court reviewed and the length of delays they caused. In *Felker v. Turpin*,[61] a case that was held in a special term at the end of the Court's regular term, Rehnquist issued a unanimous opinion upholding the constitutionality of a new law, the Antiterrorism and Effective Death Penalty Act, which provided that "*habeas* petitions would be one and done, in order to speed up executions."[62] From the time of the *Felker* case, execution rates have increased.

Over his long career, "not one of Rehnquist's majority opinions stood out as distinguished."[63] That is surprising, given his longevity serving and that he had a large majority of Republican-appointed justices most of his service as Chief Justice.[64]

Rehnquist and his Court, especially post-Thomas, also significantly "diminished federal power" in a number of 5-4 decisions.[65] With the makeup of the Rehnquist Court consistent for the last eleven years of his chief justice tenure, federal statutes began to fall in earnest.[66] However, in the statistics of the Rehnquist Court, what emerges is a Court

---

common and have been used by affected parties from the beginning of our nation.

61. *Felker v. Turpin*, 518 U.S. 651 (1996).

62. Jenkins, p. 55.

63. *Id.* at 164.

64. *See* **Appendix A** for makeup of Supreme Court during Rehnquist's tenure as Chief Justice.

65. Jenkins, p. 238.

66. The Rehnquist Court remained the same for the last eleven years of Rehnquist's tenure, "the second-longest period of Supreme Court membership

that found O'Connor and Kennedy as swing votes.[67] Rehnquist refused to follow his predecessors, Vinson, Warren, and Burger, in being able to play the blocs in order "to gain the best result attainable."[68] In the end, his legacy may well be as summarized by Jenkins:

> "The politicization of the Court- a focus on finding nominees so reliably ideological that they could be considered an extension of the president's cabinetbegun with Rehnquist and continues unabated. Earlier choices among Rehnquist's contemporaries- Burger, Blackmun, and Powell- ultimately disappointed their conservative patrons, but Rehnquist fully delivered, as have his conservative successors on the current Court: John Roberts, Antonin Scalia, Clarence Thomas, and Samuel Alito."[69]

Politics and politicization have creeped into the Court on both sides of the ideological spectrum. Lest anyone think that the justices today are just "balls and strikes" umpires, neutral arbiters, apolitical, nonpartisan actors, not politicians in robes, they should research speeches and statements by some of the justices. For example, at the Inaugural

---

stability, and the longest for a nine-justice court." Jenkins, p. 239. The longest period was the Marshall Court.

67. Jenkins, pgs. 241–42.

68. Jenkins, p. 240.

69. *Id.* at 243. It is probably safe to add to that list the most recent additions to the Court, Gorsuch and Kavanaugh.

Gregory S. Coleman Memorial Lecture hosted by the Texas Chapters of by the Federalist Society on September 8, 2018, Justice Clarence Thomas was interviewed by the Society's Leonard Leo. Thomas told Leo that he and Justice Antonin Scalia had a ball together, noting, "I'll set the edge, and you'll run to the inside. My job was to make Scalia look moderate." There are many other examples.[70]

No case in the annals of the Supreme Court might more clearly demonstrate the politicization of the Court than its decision in *Bush v. Gore* in 2000.[71] In *Bush,* the Rehnquist Court's conservative faction, champions of federalism and the Court's refusal to interfere in state-specific issues, turned on its head the view that "state actions shouldn't be overruled or interfered with by the Court. Federalists would have left the state alone to do its job."[72] The majority opinion admonished that the decision was one-time, and was to have no precedential effect, stating in a sentence that has been subjected to enormous scrutiny, "Our consideration is limited to the present circumstances, for the problem of equal protection in election processes generally presents

---

70. During the Kavanaugh confirmation, the author was asked his opinions on the "Schoolhouse Rock" statements that Senator Ben Sasse made at the hearings, and whether it was agreeable that each nominee "should be evaluated by each Senator on whether that Senator believes that the nominee can put their political beliefs and their ideas on what the laws should be into a box marked 'irrelevant' and judge the cases that come before them based on the Constitution and the laws. In a perfect world and ideally, the author responded, that would be ideal, but has almost become impossible."

71. *Bush v. Gore,* 531 U.S. 98 (2000).

72. Jenkins, p. 249.

many complexities."[73] The sentence was "unprecedented" and was, according to at least one scholar, an "inappropriate application of equal protection doctrine in favor of a presidential candidate whose claim would have been dismissed under the rules that apply to everyone else."[74] Alan Dershowitz called attention to the Court for revealing the case's "true purpose."[75] Justice John Paul Stevens, in a strongly worded dissent, asserted:

> "One thing, however, is certain. Although we may never know with complete certainty the identity of the winner of this year's Presidential election, the identity of the loser is perfectly clear. It is the Nation's confidence in the judge as an impartial guardian of the rule of law."[76]

The *Bush* case "scarred Souter's belief in the Supreme Court as an institution."[77] He was not alone in his views that this case was nothing but political. At the end of the first term after President Barack Obama became president, Souter submitted his letter of retirement to Obama. Obama would have the first Democratic presidential opportunity

---

73. *Bush v. Gore*, 531 U.S. at 109.

74. Schwartz, p. 23. The right has referred to the Warren Court and to an extent the Burger Court as judicial activism, yet in many of the right's decisions, and more frequently with Roberts, he "was engaging in a consummate act of judicial activism. . . ." Toobin, The Oath, p. 259.

75. Jenkins, p. 250.

76. *Bush v. Gore*, 531 U.S. at 128–29.

77. Toobin, The Oath, p. 123.

in fifteen years to appoint a Supreme Court justice. Since *Bush* was decided, the Supreme Court has never again cited to the decision.[78]

Rehnquist had always spoken of not dying on the bench. However, after the death of his wife, Nan, the Court was what Rehnquist had and he remained for many years after her death in 1991. As he became extremely ill with thyroid cancer and after surgery on October 23, 2004, for cancer made him "an incurable invalid," Rehnquist struggled but with Associate Justice Sandra Day O'Connor planning to retire, Rehnquist remained on the bench.[79] On September 3, 2005,[80] Chief Justice William Rehnquist died, and his funeral at the Roman Catholic Cathedral of St. Matthew the Apostle was the largest since John F. Kennedy's funeral. Rehnquist died the fourth longest serving chief justice in history and the eighth longest serving justice in the Court's history. One final interesting tidbit about Rehnquist, in his long tenure on the Supreme Court, was that he only read a dissent from the bench once in his career.[81]

---

78. *Id.*

79. Obermayer, p. xxi.

80. *Id.* at ix.

81. Toobin, The Oath, p. 69. In recent years, it has become increasingly common for justices who do not agree with the majority opinion to summarize or, in some instances, read their dissents from the bench. Rehnquist is rather unique in the infrequency of doing so.

Chapter Nineteen

John Roberts: A Legacy in Formation

Nominated by President George W. Bush
Confirmed by Senate, 78-22, on September 29, 2005
Tenure: September 29, 2005 to Present
Presidents During Tenure
  W. Bush
  Obama
  Trump

Roberts had clerked for Rehnquist and was one of eight former clerks to serve as pallbearer at Rehnquist's funeral.[1] After Bush nominated Roberts for chief, he was confirmed on September 2005 by a 78-22 Senate vote.

---

1. The introduction to this chapter in italics is based on an article that originally appeared in the *Chicago Daily Law Bulletin* on May 7, 2015, Cotter, "Chief Justices Rehnquist, Roberts and a shift right."

After clerking for Judge Henry Friendly on the Second U.S. Circuit Court of Appeals and then for Rehnquist in 1980-81, Roberts became a special assistant U.S. attorney general and then an associate at the White House counsel's office.

Roberts then became an associate at a Washington, D.C., law firm, where he worked on litigation and a number of pro bono matters. He left in 1989 to become principal deputy solicitor general, a position he held until 1993, when he returned to his old law firm as a partner.

In the next ten years, he argued thirty-nine cases before the Supreme Court, winning twenty-five of those. This regular presence at the Supreme Court by an eventual justice is unprecedented, at least in modern times.

In 2003, Bush nominated Roberts to the U.S. Court of Appeals for the D.C. Circuit, which has been a rest stop for several judges on the way to the Supreme Court. He served for two years, until his nomination to be the seventeenth chief justice.

As of 2019, he has served fourteen full terms, and the current term will be his fifteenth. At sixty-five years old, Roberts could conceivably surpass Marshall for longest term as chief justice. His jurisprudence is conservative. He is a well-respected justice and chief.

Early Life and Career

John Roberts was born on January 27, 1955, in Buffalo, New York to John Glover "Jack" Roberts and Rosemary (nee Podrasky). Jack worked as a plant manager at Bethlehem Steel. When Roberts was five, his family moved to Indiana, where Roberts would attend private schools. Roberts attended Harvard University, entering as a sophomore based on his high school academic performance, and graduated with a B.A., *summa cum laude*, in History in 1976. He decided to pursue law, and enrolled at Harvard Law School, where he became managing editor of the *Harvard Law Review*. He graduated, *magna cum laude*.

Upon graduation, Roberts clerked for Judge Henry Friendly, a judge on the U.S. Court of Appeals for the Second Circuit, then clerked for Justice William Rehnquist.[2] From 1981 to 1982, Roberts served as Special Assistant to the then-U.S. Attorney General William French Smith. From 1982 to 1986, Roberts worked as Associate Counsel to President Ronald Reagan. In 1986, Roberts entered private practice at the law firm, Hogan & Hartson, where he practiced for three years before returning to public service.

In 1989, Roberts became the principal deputy solicitor general, a position he held for four years. In 1993, Roberts returned to Hogan, where he headed the appellate practice

---

2. This appears to be the first instance in the history of the Supreme Court where a former clerk to a justice of the Supreme Court became chief justice to replace the chief justice they had clerked for previously.

at the firm. He would spend the next decade as a partner at Hogan, where he argued numerous cases before the Supreme Court. Roberts argued a total of thirty-nine cases[3] before the Supreme Court in his career, winning twenty-five of those arguments.[4]

Nomination to D.C. Circuit

On May 10, 2001, President George W. Bush nominated Roberts to fill a vacancy on the U.S. Court of Appeals for the District of Columbia Circuit, but the Democratic-controlled Senate refused to hold hearings.[5] When Republicans came into the majority in 2003, President Bush resubmitted the Roberts' nomination on January 7, 2003. Roberts was confirmed on May 8, 2003 and took his judicial oath on June 2, 2003. Roberts authored forty-nine opinions in his short tenure on the D.C. Circuit.

Supreme Court Nomination

On July 19, 2005, President Bush announced the nomination of Roberts. However, it was not to become chief

---

3. For a list of the cases Roberts argued before the Supreme Court, *see* Washington University Law, available at https://law.wustl.edu/news/pages.aspx?id=5484.

4. The "wins" is a bit difficult to accurately count, given the nuances and multiple issues the Supreme Court decisions address. *See* Toobin, The Oath, p. 41.

5. George H.W. Bush had also nominated Roberts to the D.C. Circuit, but no hearings were held.

justice, but to fill the vacancy created by the retirement of Associate Justice Sandra Day O'Connor. When Chief Justice Rehnquist died on September 3, 2005, President Bush quickly pulled Roberts' pending nomination as associate justice and, on September 5, 2005, submitted Roberts' name to replace Rehnquist. At his confirmation hearings, Roberts discussed a number of Supreme Court precedents and his lack of a comprehensive judicial philosophy.[6] He compared his duty as a justice to that of an umpire, stating, "My job is to call balls and strikes, not pitch or bat."[7] History will judge whether Roberts adhered to that statement and his views on judicial restraint.[8]

Also, at his confirmation hearings, Roberts was questioned by Senator Arlen Specter, who was Chair of the Senate Judiciary Committee, about *stare decisis* in connection with *Roe v. Wade* and *Planned Parenthood of Southeastern Pennsylvania v. Casey*.[9] While refusing to answer questions about cases that might appear before the Supreme Court, Roberts did state:

"I do think that it is a jolt to the legal system when you overrule a precedent. Precedent plays an important

---

6. Roberts told the Senate Judiciary Committee, "I resist the labels." White, Judging Roberts.

7. *CNN*, "I come with 'no agenda,' Roberts tells hearing," available at http://www.cnn.com/2005/POLITICS/09/12/roberts.hearings.

8. Literature appears on various points of whether Roberts and the Roberts Court are activist or restrained.

9. *Planned Parenthood of Southeastern Pennsylvania v. Casey*, 505 U.S. 833 (1992).

role in promoting stability and evenhandedness. It is not enough—and the court has emphasized this on several occasions—it is not enough that you may think the prior decision was wrongly decided. That really doesn't answer the question, it just poses the question.

"And you do look at these other factors, like settled expectations, like the legitimacy of the court, like whether a particular precedent is workable or not, whether a precedent has been eroded by subsequent developments. All of those factors go into the determination of whether to revisit a precedent under the principles of stare decisis."[10]

Whether he has remained true to his views of *stare decisis* remains an open question, given the Roberts Court's track record to date.[11] What Roberts did make clear during the confirmation hearings was he had "two goals as Chief Justice- greater consensus on the Court and minimalism."[12]

---

10. *Washington Post*, "Transcript: Day Two of the Roberts Confirmation Hearings," available at http://www.washingtonpost.com/wp-dyn/content/article /2005/09/13/AR2005091300876.html. It is noteworthy that while Roberts was deputy solicitor general under President George H.W. Bush, "he had signed a brief urging the Supreme Court to overturn *Roe*."

11. A list of overturned precedents can be found at https://www.govinfo.gov /conent/pksg/GPO-CONAN-2017/PDF/GPO-CONAN-2017.13.pdf. During the 2017 Term, the Roberts Court overturned several additional precedents, including a soft one for *Korematsu*. Jonathan Adler wrote a very good piece on the Roberts Court and its frequency of ignoring *stare decisis* compared to Roberts' three predecessor Courts. *See* Adler.

12. Coyle, p. 24.

Roberts was confirmed by the Senate on September 29, 2005, by a vote of 78-22. Roberts took his judicial oath on October 3, 2005, the first day of the new term, and has been chief justice since that day.

Legacy

It is extremely difficult, perhaps impossible, to assess a justice while he is active, and doubly so for a chief justice. The jurisprudence of the Roberts Court is still a work in progress and depending on how long Roberts serves and how many more justices are appointed during his tenure, the Roberts Court is one that may evolve and change. Currently, the Supreme Court is about as conservative as it has been in several generations, with a solidly right outlook and philosophy. Gone are the days where a Brennan or Warren might be appointed by Eisenhower, justices whom from all assessments decided based on what they saw as the right answer, and not tethered to politics or the party of the president who appointed them.[13] The Court bloc today of

---

13. This is not to suggest everything is politically biased on the Court, but the Court is seen more and more today as a third political branch. This was not always the case. As this book hopefully has demonstrated, the Supreme Court, like society and like our nation, has had a kind of pendulum effect, with for example civil liberties being seen as expansive, then contracted, then expanded further. Another area where the interpretation of the Constitution has undergone a major pendulum effect is in the area of the Second Amendment. For most of its history, the Second Amendment was read to be a right for the militia and supporting the "common defense." That view has changed and now the reading is that the Second Amendment gives the individual the right to "keep and bear arms."

Roberts, Alito, Thomas, Gorsuch, and Kavanaugh[14] seldom, if ever, decide against their political party and ideology.[15] It is in many ways the result of justice by design, with those who appointed these justices[16] knowing what they were getting. President Donald J. Trump announced before his inauguration a list of twenty-one potential Supreme Court nominees[17] that primarily was compiled

---

14. In fairness, Gorsuch has been on the Court less than two full terms and Kavanaugh is in his first term when the book went to press, so it is too premature to conclusively assess how Kavanaugh and Gorsuch will rule. However, given the vetting process that has taken place, and the dark money spent, the likelihood is they will be reliable conservative votes.

15. An interesting timeline comparison of the Court's more politicized and conservative bent is to look to the creation and existence of the Federalist Society for Law and Public Policy Studies (the "Federalist Society") (https://fedsoc.org). Established in 1982 by law students at Yale Law School, Harvard Law School, and the University of Chicago Law School, the Federalist Society has as its principles:

> "It is founded on the principles that the state exists to preserve freedom, that the separation of governmental powers is central to our Constitution, and that it is emphatically the province and duty of the judiciary to say what the law is, not what it should be. The Society seeks both to promote an awareness of these principles and to further their application through its activities." https://fedsoc.org.

The influence of the Federalist Society cannot be understated—many at all levels of government are members, and during President George W. Bush's presidency, all appointees to federal judgeships were members. Current Supreme Court members include Roberts, Alito, Thomas, and Gorsuch. Scalia was a Federalist Society member and one of the initial faculty advisers (along with Robert Bork). Newest Supreme Court member, Brett Kavanaugh, is also a Federalist Society member. In fact, of the twenty-five potential Supreme Court nominees on Trump's list, all are Federalist Society members—not surprising, given the Federalist Society helped draft the list.

16. Rehnquist and Scalia were also in this categorization.

17. In November 2017, four additional potential candidates, including Kavanaugh, were added.

by the Federalist Society and the Heritage Foundation and included very conservative candidates. Trump added four names, including Brett Kavanaugh, to the list in November 2017.

With those caveats, the Roberts Court has issued some rulings that have raised concerns about just how conservative Roberts is. The best example of this is Roberts' opinion in *National Federation of Independent Business v. Sebelius*,[18] in which the Court upheld Congress's power to enact most provisions of the Patient Protection and Affordable Care Act, aka Affordable Care Act aka Obamacare. Conservatives decried the decision. According to some media reports, including an article by Jan Crawford,[19] Roberts originally sided with the dissent to overturn the mandate, but changed his mind. Crawford noted:

> "Chief Justice John Roberts initially sided with the Supreme Court's four conservative justices to strike down the heart of President Obama's health care reform law, the Affordable Care Act, but later changed his position and formed an alliance with liberals to uphold the bulk of the law, according to two sources with specific knowledge of the deliberations."[20]

---

18. *National Federation of Independent Business v. Sebelius*, 567 U.S. 519 (2012).

19. Crawford, available at https://www.cbsnews.com/news/roberts-switched -views-to-uphold-health-care-law.

20. *Id.*

Roberts followed the *Sebelius* decision with his opinion in *King v. Burwell*,[21] which upheld the Affordable Care Act's tax credits and thus the Affordable Care Act in general. Conservatives were once again disappointed in the decision and decried Roberts as not being loyal to the party. However, Roberts may have been acting in his "umpire" role:

> "Roberts has remained steadfast in deferring to the existing power structure and interpreting, not creating, law- even in the face of angering his usual political party."[22]

Notwithstanding the Affordable Care Act cases, it remains clear where Roberts is ideologically and where his court is likely to go:

> "Even after the health care case, it is easy to say what John Roberts stands for. He remains a skilled and powerful advocate for the full Republican agenda; he is still the candidate (in robes) of change. Roberts did refrain from embracing the unprecedented extremism of his conservative colleagues in the health care case; on that occasion, the Chief Justice acted like a true conservative and deferred . . . to the elected branches of government. . . ."[23]

---

21. *King v. Burwell*, 576 U.S. ____ (2015).

22. *Oyez*, "John G. Roberts, Jr.," available at https://www.oyez.org/justices /john_g_roberts_jr.

23. Toobin, The Oath, p. 298. Occasionally, Roberts has sided with the more liberal justices in denying *cert* or in a decision. The most recent example of a

In an interview five years into his tenure as chief justice, and after the *Citizens United v. Federal Election Commission*,[24] Roberts reasserted this "balls and strikes" role of the Supreme Court, telling C-SPAN:

> "I think the most important thing for the public to understand is that we are not a political branch of the government. They don't elect us. If they don't like what we're doing, it's more or less just too bad- other than impeachment, which has never happened, or a conviction on impeachment. . . . So they need to understand that when we reach a decision, it's based on the law and not on a policy preference. . . . We're just exercising our responsibility to say what the law is; we're not ruling in favor of one side or in favor of another."[25]

Justice Stevens issued the longest dissent of his career in *Citizens United*, writing a fiery opinion that attacked Chief Justice Roberts and the broadness of the decision, quoting Roberts from his D.C. Circuit days: "If it is not necessary to decide more, it is necessary not to decide more."[26]

---

decision where Roberts joined the liberal justices was *June Medical Services v. Gee*, 586 U.S. ___ (2019), available at https://www.supremecourt.gov/opinions/18pdf/18a774_3ebh.pdf, which stayed enforcement of a Louisiana abortion law that was identical to a Texas statute that the Court found unconstitutional just two years previously. In the previous decision, Roberts was in the dissent.

24. *Citizens United v. Federal Election Commission*, 558 U.S. 310 (2010).

25. Lamb, p. 6.

26. Toobin, p. 189 (quoting Stevens).

As has been discussed, chief justices are equals, but they also are most attuned to the public pulse. Perhaps Roberts saw that the Affordable Care Act was working and the public wanted it to continue.[27] In the last sixty-five years, we have seen chief justices act in a similar fashion. For example, the efforts of Chief Justice Warren in the *Brown* case to obtain a unanimous decision. In each case, the chief had to know that the decision would be derided by large segments of the public, but that the approach and result was right and justified. We will perhaps not know the full deliberations of Roberts until after his retirement or death, if ever.

Another decision that many have attacked and could face reversal if the Supreme Court in its current configuration were to accept another case in the area is the 2015 decision, *Obergefell v. Hodges*,[28] which upheld the right of same-sex couples to marry. Justice Anthony Kennedy, whose libertarian principles and philosophy led to some decisions in which he voted with the more liberal bloc, wrote the majority opinion in the case. Roberts dissented. Kennedy has retired, with the much more conservative Kavanaugh replacing him. Whether we see anything like *Obergfell* again is open to question.

The Roberts Court has also been aggressive in limiting the effectiveness of the Voting Rights Act, and in particular

---

27. Perhaps what Roberts was doing was following his views where he "praised justices who were willing to put the good of the Court above their own ideological agendas." Rosen, p. 224.

28. *Obergefell v. Hodges*, 576 U.S. ___ (2015).

the "coverage provision" in Section 4(b).[29] In *Shelby County v. Holder*,[30] Chief Justice Roberts, in a 5-4 decision, held that the coverage formula contained in Section 4(b) of the Voting Rights Act of 1965 was unconstitutional, because it relied on old data and that it was not justified to treat some states differently than others.[31] While the Section 5 language was left alone, without the Section 4(b) language, there is no effective way to enforce the Voting Rights Act of 1965.[32] The impact of the decision has been seen in subsequent elections, with many polling places in the South having been closed.

One interesting demographic detail about the current Supreme Court is that there are five justices who are Roman Catholic,[33] three are Jewish,[34] and one (Gorsuch) was raised Roman Catholic but since his marriage has attended an

---

29. The Voting Rights Act of 1965 prohibits racial discrimination in voting. The Voting Rights Act has been amended several times, but the original law passed is available at http://avalon.law.yale.edu/20th_century/voting_rights_1965.asp. For a history of voting rights laws, including the amendments, *see* https://www.justice.gov/crt/history-federal-voting-rights-laws. Section 4(b) contains a coverage formula.

30. *Shelby County v. Holder*, 133 S.Ct. 2612 (2013).

31. *Id.* at 2629.

32. Section 2 of the Voting Rights Act, which prohibits every state and local government from imposing any voting law that results in discrimination against racial or language minorities, remains in effect and is a very important part of the Voting Rights Act. The impact of the *Shelby County* decision was seen in full display during the last few election cycles, with obstacles and voting changes imposed with the apparent intent of denying people of color the right to exercise their rights to vote.

33. Alito, Roberts, Thomas, Kavanaugh, Sotomayor.

34. Ginsburg, Breyer, Kagan.

Episcopal Church. What influence their religions have had on their decision making is not fully known, but likely has had some influence.[35]

With the retirement of Kennedy, who as noted was a swing vote in some areas, especially in personal rights and liberties, and replacement by a much more conservative justice, Kavanaugh, we are likely to see the Roberts Court become more conservative, and the counter-revolution that the right has been hoping for since Warren was replaced by Burger may finally become reality. Time will tell, and the Roberts Court legacy will continue to be closely watched. If the reports of Roberts strong interest in seeing the integrity of the judicial process maintained and the prestige upheld are true, watchers on both sides of the aisle might be disappointed by how Roberts and the Court decide matters.

One should make no mistake that the Roberts Court is a conservative court and one with "a willingness to act aggressively and in distinctly unconservative ways by: Boldly raising questions not asked or not necessary to resolve. . . . Refusing to defer to decisions by elected and accountable local or national officials. . . . And overruling precedent, both old and recent. . . ."[36] As has been noted, it is Roberts

---

35. For an interesting discussion of the justices and how various factors and influences might impact their jurisprudence and how justices decide cases, *see* Zirin.

36. Coyle, Marcia, p. 3.

"who was determined to use his position as Chief Justice as an apostle of change."[37]

Marcia Coyle examines four areas in her excellent book that the Roberts Court has explored and how it has acted aggressively as quoted in the previous paragraph—(1) Race,[38]

---

37. Toobin, The Oath, p. 16.

38. An interesting discussion by Coyle in connection with race and educational settings might suggest why many of President Donald J. Trump's nominees to the federal bench refuse to affirmatively state that *Brown v. Board of Education* is settled law. *See, e.g.,* de Vogue, available at https://www.cnn.com/2018/05/17 /politics/judicial-nominees-senate-committee-brown-v-board-of-education /index.html. In a 2006 decision, *League of United Latin American Citizens v. Perry*, 548 U.S. 399 (2006), the plurality decision by Justice Anthony Kennedy held that one district in Texas violated the Voting Rights Act. Chief Justice Roberts concurred and dissented in part. Roberts' dissent addressed issues with the part of the opinion that the one district violated the Voting Rights Act, and wrote a few sentences that put the public on notice that civil rights issues might be treated differently by the new chief justice: "I do not believe it is our role to make judgments about which *mixes* of minority voters should count for purposes of forming a majority in an electoral district, in the face of factual findings that the district is an effective majority-minority district. It is a sordid business, this divvying us up by race." *Perry*, 548 U.S. (Roberts, Concurring in part and dissenting in part); *see also*, Coyle, p. 29 (quoting "sordid business sentence"). In the case, *Parents*, Roberts concluded his decision that efforts to achieve racial mixtures in Louisville and Seattle were unconstitutional with the statement that "the way 'to achieve a system of determining admission to the public schools on a nonracial basis,' *Brown II*, 349 U. S., at 300–01, is to stop assigning students on a racial basis. The way to stop discrimination on the basis of race is to stop discriminating on the basis of race." Breyer ended his fiery dissent summary from the bench with words not found in the dissent: "It is not often in the law that so few have so quickly changed so much." Coyle, p. 112 (quoting Breyer from the bench). Stevens in another dissent attacked Roberts' use of *Brown* to support the outcome. Coyle, p. 114. Stevens' dissent included the following language: "The Chief Justice fails to note that it was only black schoolchildren who were so ordered; indeed, the history books do not tell stories of white children struggling to attend black schools. In this and other ways, The Chief Justice rewrites the history of one of this Court's most important decisions." Shortly after the decision, three lawyers advocating in the *Brown* case were interviewed and "they accused

(2) Guns, (3) Money, and (4) Health Care.[39]

A recent instance of the Roberts Court overturning precedent is in its decision in *Janus v. American Federation of State, County, And Municipal Employees, Council 31, et al.,*[40] in which the Court held by a 5-4 majority that public unions cannot compel any government employee who does not belong to that union to pay a fee to cover the union's costs to negotiate a contract that applies to all employees. The 5-4 decision overturned a unanimous 1977 SCOTUS decision, *Abood v. Detroit Bd. of Ed.,*[41] that permitted "fair share" or "agency" fees to be used for nonpolitical purposes. Many hailed *Janus* as a major victory for the First Amendment. Justice Elena Kagan issued a fiery dissent, warning that the ruling could disrupt "thousands of ongoing contracts involving millions of employees."[42] Alito concluded his opinion by overturning *Abood*, stating, "*Abood* was wrongly decided and is now overruled."[43]

Roberts of misinterpreting their arguments and the meaning of *Brown*." Coyle, p. 115. Perhaps it is this line of thinking by the four conservative justices that "the Constitution is color-blind and prohibits almost all use of racial classifications" that is behind this refusal to answer or confirm that *Brown* is settled law. *Id.* What is interesting is that Kavanaugh likely will not change the outcomes, as Kennedy "has never voted to uphold an affirmative action plan." Coyle, p. 116. As noted, Breyer, in a fiery dissent, stated, "It is not often in the law that so few have so quickly changed so much." Toobin, p. 93.

39. Coyle.

40. *Janus v. American Federation of State, County, and Municipal Employees, Council 31, et al.,* 585 U.S. ___ (2018).

41. *Abood v. Detroit Bd. of Ed.,* 431 U.S. 209 (1977).

42. *Janus,* 585 U.S. ___ at ___.

43. *Id.*

The Roberts Court has also been described as being pro-business. While any generalization tends to fail because of the nature of Supreme Court decisions, in which the Supreme Court is considering the facts of the one case and deciding based on the particular case, an interesting comparison of the Roberts Court against his predecessor court, the Rehnquist Court, would suggest that the basic attribution to this current court is true:

> "Comparing the last five years of the Rehnquist Court, which ended in 2005, to the first five years of the Roberts Court, the study found that the Roberts Court ruled for business 61 percent of the time to 46 percent for the Rehnquist Court, and to 42 percent for all Supreme Court since 1953—a 'statistically significant' difference. The study also found that of the top five most pro-business terms since 1953, two were in the Roberts Court."[44]

When this current court, the seventeenth chief justice's court, ends in the future, a final reconciliation of the Roberts Court legacy will be written. One expects (but hopes to be proven wrong) that it will be a court that increasingly turned political, that increasingly was partisan, and that overturned precedent in a wide variety of areas.

One way to determine a court's skew along party lines or generally is by the number of close decisions. By that

---

44. Coyle, p. 315.

assessment, some have asserted that the Roberts Court is not as partisan as many would argue[45] but instead has done as he said he would do during his confirmation hearings—be a chief justice of consensus. However, others argued that the Roberts Court is indeed more partisan, citing the increase in 5-4 decisions in the last two courts (Roberts and Rehnquist).[46] In one article, the increased partisanship on the Supreme Court was summed up:

> If we consider the number of cases decided by single vote majorities to be a fair proxy for a Court's polarization, it becomes easy to see that our current Court is by and large the most partisan in years. In the period between 1801 and 1940, less than 2 percent of

---

45. *See, e.g.,* Turberville & Marcum, available at https://www.washingtonpost .com/news/posteverything/wp/2018/06/28/those-5-4-decisions-on-the-supreme -court-9-0-is-far-more-common/?utm_term=.53629277f355 (arguing that the 9-0 decisions are the biggest percentage of decisions in the Roberts Court, and that the 5-4 decisions are approximately 19%). The article also discusses a few other cases that were 7-2 and so did not fit the partisan mode. However, those statistics should be taken with a grain of salt, because in the cases that matter, the Constitutional ones of major import, the number of close decisions remains high. In addition, as was raised by Senator Richard Durbin in Samuel Alito's confirmation hearings, when he made it clear that Alito replacing Justice Sandra Day O'Connor had been crucial to protecting a number of rights. He referred to the "statistics of 193 5-4 decisions, where Sandra Day O'Connor was the deciding vote in 148 of those instances. She was a critical vote in issues of civil rights, human rights, workers' rights, women's rights, restraining the power of an overreaching President. If you look at the record, the enviable record which Sandra Day O'Connor has written, you find she was the fifth and decisive vote to safeguard Americans' right to privacy. . . ." Coyle, p. 66 (quoting Richard Durbin in the hearings on the nomination of Samuel Alito, Jr.)

46. *See, e.g.,* Rodriguez, available at https://stanfordpolitics.org/2016/01/07 /troubling-partisanship-supreme-court.

all the Supreme Court's decisions were decided by a 5–4 vote. By contrast, the Rehnquist and Roberts Courts have seen just over 20 percent of their cases be decided by this small margin. This shift provides a clear indication that polarization has indeed spread to the judiciary.

"Modern justices seem to often vote in ideological alignment with the party of the President that appointed them. This phenomenon is relatively new. In the past, the party of the appointing President did not predict a justice's votes. Twentieth century justices Earl Warren, William Brennan, and Harry Blackmun all leaned liberal despite being appointed by Republican Presidents. Now, these types of justices have become extinct. In the 2014–2015 term, virtually every 5–4 decision the Court gave out was split perfectly along party lines. This, combined with the increase in 5–4 decisions, is an indicator of just how partisan the Supreme Court has become."[47]

During Roberts' second year as chief justice, unanimous decisions decreased to 25% and approximately one-third of the decisions were 5-4, "the highest percentage in more than a decade."[48] Of those, only a quarter found the liberal

---

47. *Id.*
48. Toobin, The Oath, p. 82.

justices (Stevens, Souter, Ginsburg, and Breyer) in the majority position.[49]

Perhaps when we look back and assess the Roberts Court, we will conclude that it is indeed the legacy of the Rehnquist Court:

> "The Roberts Court is Rehnquist's true legacy, and Roberts himself—once a Rehnquist clerk—is Rehnquist's natural heir."[50]

It appears that "Roberts's mission [is] to lead the counterrevolution that his mentor had begun."[51]

One thing appears to be true—the five conservative justices on the current Court (Roberts, Thomas, Alito, Gorsuch, and Kavanaugh) may be the most reliably conservative ideology group on the Supreme Court in its long history, and many areas of law likely will be different in the coming years as this group revisits *stare decisis* in its case-by-case jurisprudence.[52] Roberts is someone "who wanted to usher in a new understanding of the Constitution, with dramatic implications for both the law and the larger society."[53]

---

49. *Id.*

50. Jenkins, p. 243.

51. Toobin, The Oath, p. 39.

52. Prior to being nominated to the Supreme Court, Alito sat on the U.S. Court of Appeals for the Third Circuit, where "his record on the bench offered no promise of moderation." Toobin, The Oath, p. 37. Alito "made a particular name for himself as an opponent of abortion rights." *Id.*

53. Toobin, The Oath, p. 16.

Chapter Twenty

Conclusion

Seventeen men have occupied the chief justice position in the court's 230 plus-year history. Each has contributed something to the legacy of the court. Rehnquist and Roberts are no exceptions.

One must note that while the chief justice has other duties, his vote is one of nine, and the eight associate justices at any given time work on opinions, limiting some language, suggesting other language, and voting according to his or her own interpretation of the case before the court. As a result, the chief can guide but not mandate how the court rules. And yet, of the seventeen, several have clearly shown that they are of a different cloth, of a different character, of a pure leadership quality. They are able to politick not in the nature of true politics, but in their ability to sense the times and do what they believe is the right thing at the right time regardless of the pushback, outcry, or negative attacks they may suffer. One need not look back well into our history to find examples. The most recent example might well be Chief Justice Roberts and the Affordable Care Act decisions.

As we stated at the beginning, politics is involved in rising to the Supreme Court of the United States and no more so than to sit in the center seat. To date, we have had the following backgrounds (can be more than one category):

- Two presidents (Jay (Second Continental Congress), Taft);
- Four involved in ratification of the Constitution (Jay, Rutledge, Ellsworth, and Marshall);
- Several judges at the state level (Jay, Rutledge, Ellsworth, White, Taft);
- Prior experience on federal courts (Taft, Vinson, Burger, Roberts, Hughes);
- Former governors (Rutledge, Chase, Hughes, Warren);
- Former Cabinet members (Jay, Marshall, Taney, Chase, Hughes, Taft, Stone, Vinson, Rehnquist, Roberts) (in the last two instances, assistants or deputies);
- Former Senators or Representatives (Ellsworth, Marshall, White, Vinson);
- Former Supreme Court clerks (Rehnquist and Roberts);
- Past military experience (Marshall, White, Vinson, Warren, Rehnquist);
- Five previously served as associate justices, three immediately preceding elevation (Rutledge, White, Hughes, Stone, Rehnquist);

- Most experience in state and local politics or national politics at some level; and
- At least one extremely experienced Supreme Court advocate (Roberts).

Supreme Court seats do not come about often (in the Court's history, there have been only 119 seats filled, including the five who served as associate justice first) in the nation's 230 years, so just over half a justice per year is seated in the Court's history. With few exceptions, the justices had been involved in local or national politics for many years.[1]

As we were finalizing this book and getting it ready for submission to eventually get published, a battle over the latest President Donald J. Trump nominee for the vacancy created by the retirement of Associate Justice Anthony Kennedy ensued. Many fear the confirmation will result in a 5-4 majority of Republican-nominated jurists who will,

---

1. The only exceptions that would be considered outliers are:

- Roberts (but he clerked and worked for the White House and was the principal deputy solicitor general);
- Rehnquist (but like Roberts, he clerked and worked as an assistant U.S. attorney general and legal counsel);
- Stone;
- Fuller; and
- Waite.

Reportedly, when Rehnquist's name was first brought up to President Nixon, who was having difficulties with his nominees, he did not care for Rehnquist and asked whom he was. For President Nixon, Rehnquist may have turned out to be the only one of his nominees who remained loyal to the expectations that Nixon had when he set out to reshape the Supreme Court and erase the activism of the Warren Court and the failure of the Burger Court to reverse various decisions in civil rights and criminal defendants' rights.

despite vows of faithfully and without partisanship interpreting the U.S. Constitution, eviscerate certain rights and holdings of past Courts, whether it is in the area of abortion rights (*Roe v. Wade*) or other areas. In *June Medical Services*, LLC v. Gee, 586 U.S. ___ (2019), Justice Kavanaugh dissented from the stay that Chief Justice Roberts and the four liberal justices granted. Kavanaugh wrote a dissent to it. While Chief Justice Roberts sided with the stay temporarily, many noted the nature of the dissent by Kavanaugh and fears remained. As has been set forth time and again in this book, prior concerns or hopes that a new Court would overturn substantive law in a variety of areas have not been justified in the end. While some areas of law have been rolled back in some subsequent Courts, the Court has been a measured body, slow to effectuate great changes. The Chief Justices are the ones that pace the Court and strive to maintain the Court's prestige in the eyes of we, the people. Time will tell if the Court is now different.[2]

---

2. The Court has ebbed and flowed in its importance and in its game changing nature, as has been noted throughout the book. Some periods have been referred to as "a trough." *See* Fuller chapter, footnote 21, *supra*. On occasion, a chief is "at most mediocre." *See* Vinson chapter, footnote 17, *supra*. Some justices, including the Court's Chief, have been referred to as arriving at the center seat due to "the rule of chance in the selection of American judges." *See* Fuller chapter, footnote 6, *supra*.

We do not have a mediocre chief in Roberts, who by all accounts is very interested in the Court's history and continued stature. Perhaps like Vinson, he thinks "change should be evolutionary rather than revolutionary." *See* Vinson chapter, footnote 38, *supra*. Other chiefs have pointed to precedents and *stare decisis*, including Burger, who stated that "we are bound in this Court by our precedents, even those with which we disagree strongly." *See* Burger chapter, footnote 46,

One need go back just over one hundred years ago to find a time when political party of appointment did not have anything to do with decisions, although the modern courts as outlined in this book appear to be more political.[3] When Chief Justice Fuller died and President Taft, a Republican, had to choose a replacement, he selected a Democratic

---

supra. Chief Justice Hughes, who then-Associate Justice Rehnquist quoted (but alas, did not follow when he became chief), also was willing to acquiesce "in silence" and "modify his own opinions." *See* Rehnquist chapter, footnote 53, *supra.*

Roberts has expressed his preference for slow movement as well and so we will learn over time if he practices restraint. In the Affordable Care Act and some other instances, especially during the first term with Kavanaugh, Roberts did appear to be more worried about the long-term prestige and reputation of the Court than quickly tearing prior precedents asunder. On the other hand, Roberts did say to C-SPAN that if the public doesn't "like what we're doing, it's more or less just too bad. . . ." *See* Roberts chapter, footnote 25, *supra.* Time will tell if the Roberts Court is revolutionary and delivers on what Rehnquist and Burger failed at, or merely the evolutionary Court it has been for most chiefs in the Court's history.

3. One additional reason for the makeup of the Court (but not necessarily the strong ideological bents) is the times during history when there was hegemony of one party in the White House and Congress. According to Lamb and Halpern, the following pattern emerges when placed in historical context:

- 1861 to 1893—Republican presidents made eighteen of twenty appointments to the Court, Congress controlled by Republicans for most part.
- 1897 to 1932—Republican hegemony reasserted, Republican presidents made seventeen of twenty appointments.
- 1932 to 1968—Democratic presidents made sixteen of twenty-one appointments, Democrats typically controlled.
- 1969 to 1988—Republican president 80% of time, Republicans never controlled both houses.

Halpern & Lamb, p. 10.

From 1988 to 2008, there was unified party only five years (Clinton's first, Bush four years from 2003 to 2006). Obama's first two years were unified, then divided his last six years. During Trump's first two years, he enjoyed a Republican majority in both houses of Congress, but that changed in 2018.

Justice, Edward Douglass White, to replace him. But party designations were of little importance. Quoting a 1911 law review article by Robert P. Reeder, author Charles Warren wrote:

> In view of the number of vacancies which will be filled by President Taft and the Senate, and the many statements which have been made concerning the political importance of these appointments, in more than eighteen years since the decision in *Field v. Clark*, in 1892, there has been but one case which involved a question of constitutional law and in which all the Republican members of the Court took one position and all the Democratic members took a contrary position; that case (*Snyder v. Bettman*, 190 U.S. 249, in 1903) was whether a Federal inheritance tax, which was collected while the property was in the hands of an executor, could constitutionally be applied to a bequest to a municipality for public purposes; the Court upheld the tax, against the dissents of the Chief Justice and Justices White and Peckham; this decision will not be of much practical importance, until the people of the United States have become far more eager to make bequests to municipalities than they are today.[4]

---

4. Warren, Vol. 2, p. 721.

It was not that long ago that the Supreme Court's decisions were not so divided. As noted in Chapter 14, until the Stone Court, which was from 1941 to 1946, the Supreme Court did not have any chief justice with a majority of the Court's decisions "with divided opinions."[5]

Joe Biden, at the time the Senate Judiciary Committee Chair, gave a long, rambling speech on June 25, 1992, discussing the Supreme Court and judicial nominees and how the process and the Supreme Court have become overly politicized and partisan.[6] Biden described how the nomination process had become increasingly bitter and partisan, referencing the Clarence Thomas nomination, but also giving a history of nominations in an election year during the election cycle. Part of this speech became known as the "Biden Rule,"[7] and was used by Senators Mitch McConnell and Chuck Grassley to refuse to hold any hearings on President Barack Obama's 2016 Supreme Court nominee, Merrick Garland. Biden noted, after discussing what he felt a better process, stating in part how ideological picks had become:

---

5. *See* Chapter 14, *supra*, p. 281.

6. Biden, available at https://www.grassley.senate.gov/sites/default/files/judiciary/upload/SCOTUS%2C%2003-24-16%2C%201992%20Biden%20Speech.pdf.

7. For more on the "Biden Rule" and how it was actually presented in context, *see* Cotter, "Biden Rule debunked," available at https://www.chicagolawbulletin.com/biden-rule-debunked-20180924.

"With this in mind, let me start with the nomination process and how that process might be changed in the next administration, whether it is a Democrat or a Republican. It seems clear to me that within the Bush administration, the process of selecting Supreme Court nominees has become dominated by the right intent on using the Court to implement an ultraconservative social agenda that the Congress and the public have rejected."[8]

Will we get to a place where politics are cast aside and the justices rule on issues rather than alignment politically again during the Roberts Court? What has changed to raise questions about the partiality of the chosen nine who at any given point in history, guided by the person in the middle, the chief justice, have the last chance, the ultimate say, to determine what the law is?

We will see if the fears and worries about a truly conservative, very right ideology with five justices on the Court are justified or if the Court, as it has done in prior times, will adjust to the expectations and mores of the nation as a whole. We do know that the process has changed in the last decade or so, with the Republicans having seen what happens when justices are appointed who are not hard conservatives. The Burger Court and to a lesser degree the Rehnquist Court disappointed many in the party, because

8. *Id.*

those Courts did not achieve the reversal of much of the Warren and Vinson Courts' jurisprudence in the areas such as criminal defendants' rights and civil rights. The Republicans have had better success in their views being faithfully affirmed during the first thirteen years of the Roberts Court.

What also is different with this Court is that the five Republican appointed justices (Roberts, Thomas, Alito, Gorsuch, and Kavanaugh) have all been seriously vetted and were known quantities, all are committed to their views on a variety of issues. Other than Thomas, who was not (except for the Anita Hill part of it) seriously vetted for his views on various matters (but was a staunch conservative known for his views on a variety of substantive issues) and had been an appellate judge for just over a year with few opinions, the other four had track records and views generally that aligned with various groups that supported their nominations. Gorsuch was on a list of potential nominees that President Donald J. Trump published in 2016 and then updated in 2017, each person named on that list vetted for views by the Heritage Foundation and Federalist Society. Brett Kavanaugh's name was added to the same list in 2017 and was selected by President Trump in 2018. While one never knows how a justice will rule on particular matters that come before the Court, evidence strongly suggests that the Supreme Court has become much more partisan and that the justices consistently apply their views to their votes, effectively nullifying any chance that they will surprise with their votes.[9]

But in the past, there have been "swing votes" on the Courts and justices who had decided various cases inconsistently with how the nominating president's party would have expected them to. In the last sixty-five years, any number come to mind, but would include: Chief Justice Earl Warren and William Brennan (Eisenhowser); Chief Justice Warren Burger and Harry Blackmun (Nixon); John Paul Stevens (Ford); Sandra Day O'Connor and Anthony Kennedy (Reagan); and David Souter (H.W. Bush). Roberts is identified as the potential swing vote on his Court, but there

---

9. The Editorial Board of the Portland Press-Herald discussed the politicization and views in an editorial on Sunday, September 29, 2018, stating about Brett Kavanaugh's nomination in part:

"Kavanaugh also showed himself to be impermissibly political for a job that is supposed to be above politics. We're not naive. We understand that federal judges are nominated by presidents and confirmed by senators, and that electoral politics influences their decisions about who gets to serve.

"But we have never had a Supreme Court nominee who ripped off the nonpartisan mask the way Kavanaugh did Thursday and identified himself as an enemy of a political party that represents the policy preferences of millions of Americans. He blamed his predicament on bizarre conspiracy theories, claiming that his troubles stemmed from 'pent-up anger about President Trump' and opponents seeking 'revenge on behalf of the Clintons' and were not the result of allegations that emerged while he was being evaluated for an important job. After his partisan rant, Kavanaugh will never be able to judge a case without the animus he expressed being considered a factor in his decision. This is not the road we want to take."

Editorial Board, "Our View: Brett Kavanaugh has shown he doesn't belong on the Supreme Court," September 28, 2018, as updated September 29, 2018, available at https://www.pressherald.com/2018/09/28/our-view-brett-kavanaugh-has -shown-he-doesnt-belong-on-the-supreme-court.

is little evidence that he will be a swing vote in many areas to side with the four Democratically appointed justices.[10] The last of the potential swing voters on the current court, Associate Justice Anthony Kennedy, retired in 2018. And Kennedy was at times a swing vote siding with the liberal bloc, but as has been discussed, that has not been in too wide an array of topics. His replacement, Brett Kavanaugh, is not expected to fill any swing vote role on the Court.

Some look to the recent decision of the Supreme Court in *Crossroads v. Crew, et al.*,[11] which denied an application for stay and vacated Chief Justice Robert's order, as a signal that the Court is reassessing and tampering some of its decisions. In *Crossroads*, the district court judge had ordered politically active nonprofit groups to disclose the identity of any donor giving more than $200 when those groups advertise for or against political candidates, and the D.C. Circuit Court of Appeals rejected an emergency stay. Some see this decision as a narrowing or limiting of *Citizens United*, but given the Supreme Court merely rejected the emergency stay appeal, it is too early to see what *Crossroads* really means, and the underlying case remains on appeal.

In late 2018, in response to comments President Trump made about decisions from the ninth Circuit and references

---

10. As discussed, his decisions in the Affordable Care Act cases appear to be one instance in which he did so.

11. *Crossroads v. Crew, et al.*, 585 U.S. ___ (2018), available at https://assets .documentcloud.org/documents/4901417/scotus1.pdf.

by Trump to an "Obama judge," Chief Justice Roberts issued an unusual official statement, noting:

"We do not have Obama judges or Trump judges, Bush judges or Clinton judges. What we have is an extraordinary group of dedicated judges doing their level best to do equal right to those appearing before them. That independent judiciary is something we should all be thankful for."[12]

The exchange between the president and the chief justice suggests that as has been noted, the courts have become more politicized and the chief justice felt the need to specifically address the attacks on the judiciary. Whether it means anything for the Court's decisions is yet to be determined.

Seventeen chief justices have served. Like any institution, the Court has ebbed and flowed in its quality and public approval over the years. The Supreme Court has seen times of being in a holding pattern or transition period more or less, and times of great judicial activism. That restraint or activism is not necessarily the direct result of who serves as chief justice, but more so on the other justices who make up his Court. However, we have seen in the Court's history chief justices who by persuasiveness and personality have kept a Court aligned to be more unanimous and to find

---

12. Williams, available at https://www.nbcnews.com/politics/supreme-court /rare-rebuke-chief-justice-roberts-slams-trump-comment-about-obama-n93 9016.

justice in its results. (Marshall and Warren come to mind.) Over time, the Supreme Court has gotten decisions mightily wrong but also has helped guide us through the challenges and often came out as the leader in setting the expectations and norms for our nation. Let us hope it continues to do so, that it retains its respect, and that partisan politics can be put aside in the branch that was given lifetime tenure to ensure its independence and ability to decide what is right and true for its citizens without fear of political retribution at the polls. If that does not happen, we must agree with retired Justice Kennedy, who recently stated to students during a Constitution Day exercise, "the country is seeing the 'death and decline of democracy.'"[13]

One final thought—both sides of the aisle agree on one thing—elections matter. As **Appendix A**[14] demonstrates, the Democrats have not had a majority of Democratically appointed justices on the Supreme Court since 1971 and have been as low as one Democrat sitting on the Court during that time frame (Byron White who had been appointed by President Kennedy in 1962 was the only Democrat on the Court in 1991). After Chief Justice John Roberts was confirmed by the Senate, then-Senator Barack Obama, who

---

13. Hutzler, available at https://www.newsweek.com/former-justice-anthony-kennedy-warns-democracy-danger-1145017?utm_medium=Social&utm_campaign=NewsweekTwitter&utm_source=Twitter.

14. *See* **Appendix A** *infra.*

voted no, posted on the DailyKos website echoing the importance of elections:

> "There is one way, over the long haul, to guarantee the appointment of judges that are sensitive to issues of social justice, and that is to win the right to appoint them by recapturing the presidency and the Senate. And I don't believe we get there by vilifying good allies . . . over one vote or position."[15]

Obama's statement was prescient, for it noted not only winning the White House back (which he did) but the crucial additional step of winning back the U.S. Senate, whose duty to provide "advice and consent"[16] is crucial to the process. As the nation witnessed during President Obama's last year in office, when Associate Justice Antonin Scalia died, President Obama nominated D.C. Circuit Court Judge Merrick Garland as Scalia's replacement. Garland, a centrist

---

15. Toobin, The Oath, p. 37 (quoting Obama's posting on DailyKos.com).

16. The role of the Senate to provide advice and consent for Supreme Court justices (and other positions) derives from Article II, Section 2, Paragraph 2 of the U.S. Constitution, which provides:

> [The President] shall have Power, by and with the Advice and Consent of the Senate, to make Treaties, provided two thirds of the Senators present concur; and he shall nominate, and by and with the Advice and Consent of the Senate, shall appoint Ambassadors, other public Ministers and Consuls, Judges of the Supreme Court, and all other Officers of the United States, whose Appointments are not herein otherwise provided for, and which shall be established by Law: but the Congress may by Law vest the Appointment of such inferior Officers, as they think proper, in the President alone, in the Courts of Law, or in the Heads of Departments.

who had garnered support and compliments from Senate Republicans when he was confirmed to the D.C. Circuit and when his name was announced, was never given a hearing before the Senate Judiciary Committee. Senate Republicans, who had regained control in the 2014 mid-terms, asserted the "Biden Rule" and that the nation must vote for a president. This posturing by Senators Chuck Grassley, chair of the Senate Judiciary Committee, and Senator Mitch McConnell, Senate Majority Leader, ran counter to their insistence previously that the Senate's "advice and consent" duty was to vote on nominees for the judicial bench.[17]

In addition, on November 21, 2013, the Senate, on the motion of Senate Majority Leader Harry Reid (Democrat), voted 52-48 to change cloture rules[18] pursuant to the "nuclear option" so "the vote on under Rule XXII for all nominations other than for the Supreme Court of the United States is by majority vote."[19] The reason given was that it was necessary based on what were purported frustrations with his Republican counterparts' lack of movement on President Obama's judicial nominees, and in

---

17. *See* "90 Times Senators on the Judiciary Committee Demanded a Vote on Judicial Nominees," Media Cap Action, March 3, 2016, available at https://medium.com/@CAPAction/27-times-chuck-grassley-demanded-the-senate-vote-on-judicial-nominees-8717e2a7762c.

18. Cloture rules are rules set by the Senate to be a more deliberative body by requiring sixty Senators to bring cloture to a pending action. When the nuclear option or constitution option is invoked as a parliamentarian procedure, the rule can be overruled and a simple majority vote brings cloture.

19. "Congressional Record: Senate." November 21, 2013, available at https://www.congress.gov/crec/2013/11/21/CREC-2013-11-21-pt1-PgS8413-5.pdf.

particular three nominees to the U.S. Circuit Court for the District of Columbia Circuit. The Republicans had allegedly expanded the use of filibuster to prevent consideration of President Obama's nominees. The sixty-vote cloture rules remained in effect for nominees to the U.S. Supreme Court. In a version of bad facts and circumstances making for bad laws and rules, Reid's short-term "win" on the "nuclear option" would lead to the exception being erased in 2017. Whatever short-term advantage the Democrats enjoyed as a result of this exercise by Reid led to the current environment.

On April 6, 2017, Senate Republicans invoked the nuclear option to remove the Supreme Court exception created in 2013 and, with that, the means to get a Supreme Court justice confirmed became easier. The Republican action was in response to Senate Democrats filibustering Neil Gorsuch's nomination, after the Senate Republicans had previously refused to take up Merrick Garland's 2016 nomination by President Obama.

Then Senator Barack Obama was correct—elections matter. With the current Supreme Court, it is likely that the Republican hold on the Supreme Court will remain for decades. The two oldest Supreme Court justices, Justice Ruth Bader Ginsburg and Justice Stephen Breyer, are 85 and 80, respectively. (Both Ginsburg and Breyer were Democratic appointments.) If either left the bench, President Trump likely would replace them from his list of potential nominees, many of whom are in their 40s or 50s, and the conservative makeup of the Court might well remain intact for decades to come.

As **Appendix A** shows, Democrats have not held a majority on the Supreme Court for almost 50 years, with October 1970 Term being the last such time. In October 1991, the Court became an 8-1 Republican majority. However, that Court had Stevens, O'Connor, Souter, and Kennedy on it, four more moderate justices and the last three often seen as swing voters. This current Court has five very conservative justices on it and, should President Trump have the opportunity to add one or two more justices during his presidency, we will have a much different Court than we have seen in the last fifty years. Let us hope that the words of Chief Justice Earl Warren to President Nixon on Warren's last day as Chief Justice never come to fruition: "If it ever comes to such a pass [that nine justices agree always on the most important and controversial things of life], I would say that the Court will have lost its strength and will no longer be a real force in the affairs of our country."[20] A reminder to Chief Justice Roberts and to President Trump and future presidents from 1969 and from a wise former Chief Justice.

20. Cray, p. 513.

Appendix A

Makeup of Supreme Court from 1900 to Present by Party Appointing the Justices[1]

TERM*	CHIEF JUSTICE	REPUBLICAN APPOINTEES	DEMOCRATIC APPOINTEES
OCTOBER 1900	FULLER (D)	6	3
OCTOBER 1910	WHITE (D)	5	4
OCTOBER 1916	WHITE (D)	4	5
OCTOBER 1921	TAFT (R)	5	4
OCTOBER 1922	TAFT (R)	6	3
OCTOBER 1923	TAFT (R)	5	4
OCTOBER 1932	HUGHES (R)	4	5
OCTOBER 1937	HUGHES (R)	3	6
OCTOBER 1938	HUGHES (R)	2	7[2]
OCTOBER 1941	STONE (R)	2	7
OCTOBER 1946	VINSON (D)	1	8

1. Source: "Justices of the United States Supreme Court (by Term of Court)," TheGreenPapers.com, available at https://www.thegreenpapers.com/Hx/Justices USSC.html.

2. Felix Frankfurter was an Independent, but for this chart/table, is categorized as a Democrat, given his politics pre-court and support of FDR.

TERM*	CHIEF JUSTICE	REPUBLICAN APPOINTEES	DEMOCRATIC APPOINTEES
OCTOBER 1953	WARREN (R)	2	7
OCTOBER 1954	WARREN (R)	3	6
OCTOBER 1957	WARREN (R)	4	5
OCTOBER 1962	WARREN (R)	3	6
OCTOBER 1964	BURGER (R)	3	5[3]
OCTOBER 1970	BURGER (R)	4	5
OCTOBER 1971	BURGER (R)	5	4
OCTOBER 1976	BURGER (R)	6	3
OCTOBER 1990	REHNQUIST (R)	7	2
OCTOBER 1991	REHNQUIST (R)	8	1
OCTOBER 1994	REHNQUIST (R)	7	2
OCTOBER 2009	ROBERTS (R)	6	3
OCTOBER 2010	ROBERTS (R)	5	4
OCTOBER 2015	ROBERTS (R)	4[4]	4
OCTOBER 2016	ROBERTS (R)	5[5]	4
OCTOBER 2017	ROBERTS (R)	4[6]	4
OCTOBER 2018	ROBERTS (R)	5	4

*Terms are listed only when a justice was replaced by one of different party. Several times a justice was replaced by one of the same party.

3. Abe Fortas resigned and so at the beginning of the term, his seat was vacant.

4. Justice Antonin Scalia died in February 2016, and his seat remained vacant for more than a year.

5. Neil Gorsuch was sworn in on April 7, 2017. When Justice Anthony Kennedy retired in 2018, he was replaced by Brett Kavanaugh, so the makeup of the Court did not change.

6. Anthony Kennedy retired effective August 1, 2018.

Appendix B

Number of Justices Confirmed by President

PRESIDENT	NUMBER	CHIEFS
1. George Washington	11[1]	3 (Jay/Rutledge/Ellsworth)
2. John Adams	3	1 (Marshall)
3. Thomas Jefferson	3	
4. James Madison	2	
5. James Monroe	1	
6. John Quincy Adams	1	
7. Andrew Jackson	6	1 (Taney)
8. Martin Van Buren	2	
9. William Henry Harrison	0	
10. John Tyler	1	
11. James Polk	2	
12. Zachary Taylor	0	

1. At the time of the creation of the Supreme Court, pursuant to the Judiciary Act of 1789, the Supreme Court of the United States had six justices, including the chief justice. That number was changed to seven in 1807, pursuant to the Seventh Circuit Act of 1807; nine in 1837, pursuant to the Eighth and Ninth Circuit Act of 1837; ten in 1863, pursuant to the Tenth Circuit Act of 1863; back to seven in 1866, through eventual attrition, pursuant to the Judicial Circuits Act of 1866; and, then, back to nine where it has remained, pursuant to the Judiciary Act of 1869.

PRESIDENT	NUMBER	CHIEFS
13. Millard Fillmore	1	
14. Franklin Pierce	1	
15. James Buchanan	1	
16. Abraham Lincoln	5	1 (Chase)
17. Andrew Johnson	0	
18. Ulysses S. Grant	4	1 (Waite)
19. Rutherford B. Hayes	2	
20. James A. Garfield	1	
21. Chester A. Arthur	2	
22. Grover Cleveland	2	1 (Fuller)
23. Benjamin Harrison	4	
24. Grover Cleveland	2	
25. William McKinley	1	
26. Theodore Roosevelt	4	
27. William Howard Taft	6	1 (White)
28. Woodrow Wilson	3	
29. Warren G. Harding	4	1 (Taft)
30. Calvin Coolidge	1	
31. Herbert Hoover	3	1 (Hughes)
32. Franklin D. Roosevelt	9	1 (Stone)
33. Harry S. Truman	4	1 (Vinson)
34. Dwight D. Eisenhower	5	1 (Warren)
35. John F. Kennedy	2	
36. Lyndon B. Johnson	2	
37. Richard Nixon	4	1 (Burger)
38. Gerald Ford	1	
39. Jimmy Carter	0	
40. Ronald Reagan	4	1 (Rehnquist)
41. George H.W. Bush	2	
42. William J. Clinton	2	
43. George W. Bush	2	1 (Roberts)

PRESIDENT	NUMBER	CHIEFS
44. Barack Obama	2	
45. Donald J. Trump[2]	2	

---

2. Current president. It is possible that he will have additional vacancies to fill during his term.

Appendix C

Ranking the Justices

The task of ranking the justices literally is an impossible one. So many factors go into the exercise, including the times the chief justice faced, the makeup of his court and collegiality, and many other factors. But what would be the fun of ducking the exercise? I do not include Roberts, as he is presiding currently, but if had to rank him, he would likely find himself in the top five or six, based on his handling of the Court and his administrative talents. For the first three, I used the rankings or listings at History.net.

1. John Marshall—put the Court on the map.
2. Charles Evans Hughes—saved the Court.
3. Earl Warren—landmarks on many fronts.
4. William Rehnquist—intellectual leadership, longevity.
5. Oliver Ellsworth—move away from seriatim opinions, other administrative.
6. Fred Vinson—beginning of desegregation and civil rights, continued and enhanced by Warren.

7. Warren Burger—more on administrative side of Courts and efficiencies.

8. Harlan Stone—Carolene Products footnote 4 as an associate justice.

9. John Jay—*Chisholm v. Georgia* main result. First chief justice, set out how the Court should administer its business.

10. William Howard Taft—achieved his dream, but by all accounts, not a great chief justice. Did oversee building of Supreme Court Building.

11. Salmon Chase—presided over first presidential impeachment hearing.

12. Edward White—sat on a very conservative court and his main contribution or way he is remembered may well be his approach to antitrust cases.

13. Melville Fuller—narrowly interpreted Reconstruction Amendments.

14. Morrison Waite—same.

15. John Rutledge—recess only, not confirmed.

16. Roger Taney—perhaps unfair, but *Plessy* decision looms large.

Works Cited and Referenced

A

Adler, Jonathan, "The Stare Decisis Court," The Volokh Conspiracy, July 8, 2018, available at https://reason.com/volokh/2018/07/08/the-stare-decisis-court.

Allen, Arthur M., The Opinions of Mr. Justice Hughes, 16 Colum. L. Rev. 566 (1916). Available online at https://books.google.com/books?id=U4FMAAAAYAAJ&pg=PR3&lpg=PR3&dq=columbia+law+review+xvi+arthur+m.+allen&source=bl&ots=cAsXJLjvhK&sig=ssgyRsopbKncAWUqlAEl_t4rqMI&hl=en&sa=X&ved=0ahUKEwia5P642KfcAhWo7IMKHZO3AwkQ6AEIKjAB#v=onepage&q=able%20pronouncements&f=false.

Allen, Austin. *Origins of the Dred Scott Case: Jacksonian Jurisprudence and the Supreme Court, 1837–1857.* Athens, Georgia: The University of Georgia Press. 2006. Print.

B

Baker, Leonard. *John Marshall: A Life in Law.* New York: Macmillan. 1974. Print.

Barry, Peter J., "*Ex Parte Milligan,*" *Indiana Magazine of History,* 109 (December 2013), available at file:///C:/Users

/DCott/Downloads/20475-Article%20Text-45436-1-10
-20151201.pdf.

Belknap, Michal R. *The Vinson Court: Justices, Rulings, and Legacy.* Santa Barbara, CA: ABC-CLIO. 2004. Print.

Beveridge, Albert J. *The Life of John Marshall: In Four Volumes, Volume I Frontiersman, Soldier Lawmaker.* Boston: The Riverside Press Cambridge, Houghton Mifflin Company. 1919. Print.

Beveridge, Albert J. *The Life of John Marshall: In Four Volumes, Volume II Politician, Diplomatist, Statesman 1789–1801.* Boston: The Riverside Press Cambridge, Houghton Mifflin Company. 1919. Print.

Beveridge, Albert J. *The Life of John Marshall: In Four Volumes, Volume III Conflict and Construction 1800–1815.* Boston: The Riverside Press Cambridge, Houghton Mifflin Company. 1919. Print.

Beveridge, Albert J. *The Life of John Marshall: In Four Volumes, Volume IV the Building of the Nation 1815–1835.* Boston: The Riverside Press Cambridge, Houghton Mifflin Company. 1919. Print.

Biden, Joe, Reform of the confirmation process (Senate—June 25, 1992). Available at https://www.grassley.senate.gov/sites/default/files/judiciary/upload/SCOTUS%2C%2003-24-16%2C%201992%20Biden%20Speech.pdf.

Bindler, Norman. *The United States Supreme Court Volume 6: The Conservative Court 1910–1930.* Danbury, CT: Grolier Educational Corporation. 1995. Print.

Blasi, Vincent. *The Burger Court: The Counter-Revolution That Wasn't*. New Haven, CT: Yale University. 1983. Print.

Bradley, Curtis A., The Story of Ex parte Milligan: Military Trials, Enemy Combatants, and Congressional Authorization," Draft- 11/13/07, available at https://www.law.virginia.edu/pdf/workshops/0708/bradley.pdf.

Brandwein, Pamela. *Reconstructing Reconstruction: The Supreme Court and the Production of Historical Truth*. Durham and London: Duke University Press. 1999. Print.

Brennan Center for Justice, Celebrating Justice Brennan. Available at https://www.brennancenter.org/celebrating-justice-brennan.

Brenner, Saul, The Memos of Supreme Court Law Clerk William Rehnquist: Conservative Tracts, or Mirrors of His Justice's Mind, 76 Judicature 77 (1992–1993).

Brookhiser, Richard. John Marshall: The Man Who Made the Supreme Court. New York: Basic Books. 2018. Print.

Butler, Charles Henry. *A Century at the Bar of the Supreme Court of the United States*. New York: G.P. Putnam's Sons. 1942. Print.

C

Casto, William R. *Oliver Ellsworth and the Creation of the Federal Republic*. New York: Second Circuit Committee on History and Commemorative Events. 1997. Print.

Casto, William R. *The Supreme Court in the Early Republic: The Chief Justiceships of John Jay and Oliver Ellsworth*.

Columbia, South Carolina: University of South Carolina Press. 1995. Print.

Choper, Jesse H. *The Supreme Court and Its Justices: A Treasury of Insights by William Rehnquist, Earl Warren, Robert Jackson, Felix Frankfurter, Charles Evan Hughes, Laurence Tribe, Alpheus Mason, Barry Goldwater and Others.* Chicago: ABA. 1987. Print.

Clemetson, Lynette, Meene's Influence Looms in Today's Judicial Wars. *The New York Times.* August 17, 2005. Available at https://www.nytimes.com/2005/08/17/poli tics/meeses-influence-looms-in-todays-judicial-wars .html.

CNN, "I come with 'no agenda,' Roberts tells hearing." September 13, 2005. Available at http://www.cnn.com/2005 /POLITICS/09/12/roberts.hearings.

Cotter, Daniel. Chief Justice Roger B. Taney (1777–1864). *Constituting America.* 2017. Article.

Cotter, Daniel. Justice Joseph Story (1779–1845). *Constituting America.* 2017. Article.

Cotter, Daniel. Justice George Sutherland (1802–1942). *Constituting America.* 2017. Article.

Cotter, Daniel. Marbury v. Madison (1803). *Constituting America.* 2017. Article.

Cotter, Daniel. *Dred Scott v. Sandford (1857). Constituting America.* 2017. Article.

Cotter, Daniel. The president and the governor who later became chief justices. *Chicago Daily Law Bulletin, Cotter's Corner.* 2015. Article.

Cotter, Daniel. Although rebels, some Founding Fathers had ties to London legal community. *Chicago Daily Law Bulletin, Cotter's Corner.* 2017. Article.

Cotter, Daniel. Biden rule debunked. *Chicago Daily Law Bulletin, Cotter's Corner.* 2018. Article.

Cotter, Daniel. California governor and 14th chief justice. *Chicago Daily Law Bulletin, Cotter's Corner.* 2015. Article.

Cotter, Daniel. Chief Justices Rehnquist, Roberts and a shift right. *Chicago Daily Law Bulletin, Cotter's Corner.* 2015. Article.

Cotter, Daniel. How a school teacher and a semi-pro baseball player became chief justices. *Chicago Daily Law Bulletin, Cotter's Corner.* 2015. Article.

Cotter, Daniel. Hight Court's 'Four Horsemen' Laid Waste to Much of FDR's New Deal. *Chicago Daily Law Bulletin, Cotter's Corner.* 2016. Article.

Cotter, Daniel. Japanese-American internment and U.S. loyalty. *Chicago Daily Law Bulletin, Cotter's Corner.* 2015. Article.

Cotter, Daniel. Kennedy retirement gives pause for reflection and some trepidation. *Chicago Daily Law Bulletin, Cotter's Corner.* 2018. Article.

Cotter, Daniel. Meet the Lawyers who Argued more than 100 Cases before High Court. *Chicago Daily Law Bulletin, Cotter's Corner.* 2017, Article.

Cotter, Daniel. Four chief justices spanned nearly six decades on court. *Chicago Daily Law Bulletin, Cotter's Corner.* 2015. Article.

Cotter, Daniel. Melville Fuller: The first Supreme Court justice from Chicago. *Chicago Daily Law Bulletin, Cotter's Corner.* 2015. Article.

Cotter, Daniel. Minnesotan rises to become chief justice. *Chicago Daily Law Bulletin, Cotter's Corner.* 2015. Article.

Cotter, Daniel. Supreme Court Makes Seismic Shift 58 Years after Plessy v. Ferguson. *Chicago Daily Law Bulletin,* Cotter's Corner. 2016. Article.

Cotter, Daniel. Supreme Court, at times, became a more-than-close family affair. *Chicago Daily Law Bulletin, Cotter's Corner.* 2016. Article.

Cotter, Daniel. Taney: The first Catholic U.S. Supreme Court justice. *Chicago Daily Law Bulletin, Cotter's Corner.* 2015. Article.

Cotter, Daniel. Yes, there were chief justices before Marshall. *Chicago Daily Law Bulletin, Cotter's Corner.* 2014. Article.

Cotter, Daniel. The cleanup hitter, Supreme Court Justice John Marshall. *Chicago Daily Law Bulletin, Cotter's Corner.* 2014. Article.

Cotter, Daniel. The three shortest Supreme Court tenures. *Chicago Daily Law Bulletin, Cotter's Corner.* 2016. Article.

Cotter, Danial. Trustees of Dartmouth College v. Woodward (1819). *Constituting America.* 2017. Article.

Cotter, Danial. Two Stories a Century Apart: Dark Money and Bench; 6th Circuit Court Feeder. *Chicago Daily Law Bulletin,* Cotter's Corner, 2017, Article.

Cox, Archibald. *The Court and the Constitution*. Boston: Houghton Mifflin Company. 1987. Print.

Coyle, Marcia. *The Roberts Court: The Struggle for the Constitution*. New York: Simon & Schuster. 2013. Print.

Crawford, Jan, Roberts Switched Views to Uphold Health Care Law. *CBS News*. July 1, 2012. Available at https://www .cbsnews.com/news/roberts-switched-views-to-uphold -health-care-law.

Cray, Ed. *Chief Justice: A Biography of Earl Warren*. New York: Simon & Schuster. 1997. Print.

Cullen, Charles T. & Johnson, Herbert A. *The Papers of John Marshall: Volume I Correspondence and Papers, November 1775–June 1788, Account Book, September 1783–June 1788*. Chapel Hill: The University of North Carolina Press. 1977. Print.

Cullen, Charles T. & Johnson, Herbert A. *The Papers of John Marshall: Volume II Correspondence and Papers, July 1788–December 1795, Account Book, July 1788–December 1795*. Chapel Hill: The University of North Carolina Press. 1977. Print.

Cullen, Charles T. *The Papers of John Marshall: Volume III Correspondence and Papers, January 1796–December 1798*. Chapel Hill: The University of North Carolina Press. 1979. Print.

Cullen, Charles T. *The Papers of John Marshall: Volume IV, Correspondence and Papers, January 1799–October 1800*. Chapel Hill: The University of North Carolina Press. 1984. Print.

Cushman, Clare. *The Supreme Court Justices: Illustrated Biographies 1789–1995*. Second Edition. Washington, D.C.: Congressional Quarterly. 1995. Print.

D

De Tocqueville, Alexis, *Democracy in America, Chapter VIII: The Federal Constitution, Part 1*, available at https://www.marxists.org/reference/archive/de-tocqueville/democracy-america/ch08.htm.

de Vogue, Ariane, Brown v. Board takes center stage at hearing for Trump's judicial nominees. *CNN*. May 17, 2018. Available at https://www.cnn.com/2018/05/17/politics/judicial-nominees-senate-committee-brown-v-board-of-education/index.html.

E

Eisman, Dale, Anonymous donor footed most of the bill for Gorsuch confirmation. *Common Cause*. November 22, 2017. Available at https://www.commoncause.org/democracy-wire/anonymous-donor-footed-most-costs-in-gorsuch-fight/#.

Elliot, Jonathan, ed. The Debates in the Several State Conventions on the Adoption of the Federal Constitution as Recommended by the General Convention at Philadelphia in 1787: Volume 2. 1827. *Online Library of Liberty*.

Ellis, Charles M. Roger B. Taney and the Leviathan of Slavery. *The Atlantic*. February 1865. Article.

Ellis, Joseph J. *The Quartet: Orchestrating the Second American Revolution, 1783–1789*. New York: Vintage Books. 2015. Print.

Ely, James W. Jr. *The Chief Justiceship of Melville W. Fuller 1888–1910*. Columbia, South Carolina: University of South Carolina Press. 1995. Print.

F

Fabrikant, Robert, Remembering Warren E. Burger, 40 J. Sup. Ct. Hist. 203 (2015).

Farrand, Max. *The Records of the Federal Convention of 1787: Volume II*. New Haven: Yale University Press. 1966. Print.

Feldman, Noah. *Scorpions: The Battles and Triumphs of FDR's Great Supreme Court Justices*. New York and Boston: Twelve. 2010. Print.

Fisher, Louis, CRS Report for Congress: Recess Appointments of Federal Judges. September 5, 2001, p. CRS-15. Available at https://www.senate.gov/reference/resources/pdf/RL31112.pdf.

Fridlington, Robert. *The United States Supreme Court, Volume 4: The Reconstruction Court 1864–1888*. Danbury, CT: Grolier Educational Corporation 1995. Print.

Furer, Howard B. *The United States Supreme Court, Volume 5: The Fuller Court 1888–1910*. Danbury, CT: Grolier Educational Corporation. 1995. Print.

G

Galub, Arthur L. *The United States Supreme Court, Volume 9: The Burger Court 1969–1986*. Danbury, CT: Grolier Educational Corporation. 1995. Print.

Galub, Arthur L. & Lankevich, George J. *The United States Supreme Court, Volume 10: The Rehnquist Court 1986–1994*. Danbury, CT: Grolier Educational Corporation. 1995. Print.

Glass, Andrew, House votes to impeach Andrew Johnson, February 24, 1868. *Politico.com*. February 24, 2015. Available at https://www.politico.com/story/2015/02/this-day-in-politics-115420.

Glover, Samuel T. (Samuel Taylor), 1813–1884. *Slavery in the United States, Emancipation in Missouri. Speech of Samuel T. Glover, at the Ratification Meeting in St. Louis, Held at the Court House, July 22, 1863*. 1863. Speech.

Gould, Lewis L. *Chief Executive to Chief Justice: Taft Betwixt the White House and Supreme Court*. Lawrence: University Press of Kansas. 2014. Print.

Graetz, Michael J. & Greenhouse, Linda. *The Burger Court and the Rise of the Judicial Right*. New York: Simon & Schuster. 2016. Print.

Greenberg, Jan Crawford. *Supreme Conflict: The Inside Story of the Struggle for Control of the United States Supreme Court*. New York: The Penguin Press. 2007. Print.

Greene, Bob, On Main Street, Signs of the Times Tell Two Stories. *Chicago Tribune*. July 12, 2000. Available at http://articles.chicagotribune.com/2000-07-12/fea tures/0007120319_1_main-street-billboard-impeach-earl -warren.

Greenhouse, Linda, William Brennan, 91, Dies; Gave Court Liberal Vision. *The New York Times.* July 25, 1997. Available at https://www.nytimes.com/1997/07/25/us/william -brennan-91-dies-gave-court-liberal-vision.html.

Greenhouse, Linda, Roberts's Files from 80's Recall Big Debates of Era. *The New York Times.* August 16, 2005. Available at https://www.nytimes.com/2005/08/16/poli tics/politicsspecial1/robertss-files-from-80srecall-big -debates-of-era.html?mtrref=undefined&gwh=A87B29 FB01B938B7FB7748FCB85340E8&gwt=pay.

H

Halpern, Stephen C. & Lamb, Charles M. *The Burger Court: Political and Judicial Profiles.* Urbana and Chicago: University of Illinois Press. 1991. Print.

Harrington, Matthew P. *Jay and Ellsworth, the First Courts: Justices, Rulings, and Legacy.* Santa Barbara: ABC-CLIO. 2008. Print.

Hendel, Samuel. *Charles Evan Hughes and the Supreme Court.* New York: King's Crown Press, Columbia University. 1951. Print.

Highsaw, Robert B. *Edward Douglass White: Defender of the Conservative Faith.* Baton Rouge: Louisiana State University Press. 1981. Print.

Hobson, Charles F. *The Papers of John Marshall: Volume V Selected Law Cases, 1784–1800.* Chapel Hill: The University of North Carolina Press. 1987. Print.

Hobson, Charles F. *The Papers of John Marshall: Volume VI Correspondence, Papers, and Selected Judicial Opinions November 1800–March 1807.* Chapel Hill: The University of North Carolina Press. 1990. Print.

Hobson, Charles F. *John Marshall: Writings.* New York: The Library of America. 2010. Print.

Horwitz, Morton J. *The Transformation of American Law 1780–1860.* New York and Oxford: Oxford University Press. 1992. Print.

Hutzler, Alexandra, Kavanaugh Confirmation: Former Supreme Court Justice Anthony Kennedy Says We're Seeing the "Death And Decline Of Democracy." *Newsweek.* September 29, 2018. Available at https://www.newsweek.com/former-justice-anthony-kennedy-warns-democracy-danger-1145017?utm_medium=Social&utm_campaign=NewsweekTwitter&utm_source=Twitter.

I

Irons, Peter. *Brennan vs. Rehnquist: The Battle for the Constitution.* New York: Alfred A. Knopf. 1994. Print.

J

Jenkins, John A. The Partisan: The Life of William Rehnquist. *PublicAffairs.* 2012. Print.

Jensen, Merrill. *The Documentary History of the Ratification of the Constitution, Volume III: Ratification of the Constitution by the States Delaware, New Jersey, Georgia, Connecticut.* Madison: State Historical Society of Wisconsin. 1978. Print.

Johnson, Eliana, PR firm helped Whelan stoke half-baked Kavanaugh alibi. *Politco.com.* September 21, 2018. Available at https://www.politico.com/story/2018/09/21/ed-whelan-kavanaugh-tweets-pr-firm-836405.

Johnson, Herbert A. *The Papers of John Marshall, Volume I: Correspondence and Papers, November 10, 1775–June 23, 1788, Account Book, September 1783–June 1788.* Chapel Hill: The University of North Carolina Press. 1974. Print.

K

Kalman, Laura. *The Long Reach of the Sixties: LBJ, Nixon, and the Making of the Contemporary Supreme Court.* New York: Oxford University Press. 2017. Print.

Kens, Paul. *The Supreme Court under Morrison R. Waite 1874–1888.* Columbia, South Carolina: University of South Carolina Press. 2010. Print.

King, Willard L. *Melville Weston Fuller: Chief Justice of the United States 1888–1910.* Chicago: The University of Chicago Press, Phoenix Books. 1967. Print.

Kroll, Andy, Will dark money rescue Brett Kavanaugh's confirmation? *RollingStone.* September 21, 2018. Available at https://www.rollingstone.com/politics/politics-news/brett-kavanaugh-supreme-court-dark-money-727706.

Kurland, Philip B. Judicial Biography: History, Myth, Literature, Fiction, Potpourri Judicial Biography Symposium: Keynote, 70 N.Y.U. L. Rev. 489, 497 (1995).

L

Lamb, Brian & Halpen, Stephen. *The Burger Court: Political and Judicial Profiles.* Urbana and Chicago: University of Illinois Press. 1991. Print.

Lamb, Brian, Swain, Susan & Farkas, Mark. *The Supreme Court: A C-Span Book Featuring the Justices in Their Own Words.* New York: Public Affairs. 2010. Print.

Lane, Charles, Head of the Class. July/August 2005. Available at https://alumni.stanford.edu/get/page/magazine /article/?article_id=33966.

Lankevich, George J. *The United States Supreme Court, Volume I: The Federal Court 1787–1801.* Danbury, CT: Grolier Educational Corporation. 1995. Print.

Lazarus, Edward. *Closed Chambers: The First Eyewitness Account of the Epic Struggles inside the Supreme Court.* New York: Times Books, Random House. 1998. Print.

Leeds, Jeffrey T., A Life on the Court. *The New York Times Magazine.* October 5, 1986. Available at https://www.nyti mes.com/1986/10/05/magazine/a-life-on-the-court.html.

Lerner, Max. *The Mind and Faith of Justice Holmes: His Speeches, Essays, Letters and Judicial Opinions.* Boston: Little, Brown & Company. April 1951. Print.

Leuchtenburg, William E. *The Supreme Court Reborn: The Constitutional Revolution in the Age of Roosevelt.* New York and Oxford: Oxford University Press. 1995. Print.

Liptak, Adam, New Look at an Old Memo Casts More Doubt on Rehnquist. *The New York Times.* March 19, 2012. Available at https://www.nytimes.com/2012/03/20 /us/new-look-at-an-old-memo-casts-more-doubt-on -rehnquist.html.

M

Magrath, C. Peter. *Morrison R. Waite: The Triumph of Character.* New York: Macmillan. 1963. Print.

Maltz, Earl M. *The Chief Justiceship of Warren Burger 1969– 1986.* Columbia, South Carolina: University of South Carolina. 2000. Print.

Maltz, Earl M. *Slavery and the Supreme Court, 1825–1861.* Lawrence: University Press of Kansas. 2009. Print.

Mason, Alpheus Thomas. *Harlan Fiske Stone: Pillar of the Law.* New York: The Viking Press. 1956. Print.

Mayer, Robert. *The United States Supreme Court, Volume 7: The Court and the American Crises 1930–1953.* Danbury, CT: Grolier Educational Corporation. 1995. Print.

McMillion, Barry J. & Rutkus, Denis Steven, Supreme Court Nominations, 1789 to 2017: Actions by the Senate, the Judiciary Committee, and the President. Congressional

Research Service. July 6, 2018. Available at https://fas.org /sgp/crs/misc/RL33225.pdf.

N

Newmyer, R. Kent. *John Marshall and the Heroic Age of the Supreme Court.* Baton Rouge: Louisiana State University Press. 2001. Print.

Newton, Jim. *Justice for All: Earl Warren and the Nation He Made.* New York: Riverhead Books. 2007. Print.

Niven, John. *Salmon P. Chase: A Biography.* New York: Oxford University Press. 1995. Print.

O

Obermayer, Herman J. *Rehnquist: A Personal Portrait of the Distinguished Chief Justice of the United States.* New York: Threshold Editions. 2009. Print.

Olken, Samuel R. Chief Justice John Marshall and the Course of American Constitutional History, 33 J. Marshall L. Rev. 743, 745 (2000).

Oyez, "John G. Roberts, Jr." Available at https://www.oyez .org/justices/john_g_roberts_jr.

P

Paul, Joel Richard. *Without Precedent: Chief Justice John Marshall and His Times.* New York: Riverhead Books. 2018. Print.

Pearson, Drew & Allen, Robert S. *The Nine Old Men.* Garden City, NY: Doubleday Doran & Company. 1937. Print.

Perkins, Dexter. *Charles Evan Hughes and American Democratic Statesmanship.* Boston: Little, Brown & Company. 1956. Print

Powell, H. Jefferson. Attorney General Taney and the South Carolina Police Bill. *Green Bag.* Autumn 2001. Article.

Pringle, Henry F. *The Life And Times of William Howard Taft: A Biography. Volume One.* Norwalk: The Easton Press. 1967. Print.

Pringle, Henry F. *The Life And Times of Willam Howard Taft: A Biography. Volume 2.* Norwalk: The Easton Press. 1967. Print.

Pusey, Merlo J. *Charles Evan Hughes: In Two Volumes: Volume I.* New York: Macmillan. 1951. Print.

Pusey, Merlo J. *Charles Evan Hughes: In Two Volumes: Volume II.* New York: Macmillan. 1951. Print.

Q

R

Rehnquist, William H. *The Supreme Court.* New York: Alfred A. Knopf. 1987. Print.

Rehnquist, William, 1952. A Random Thought on the Segregation Cases, memo to Associate Justice Robert Jackson,

available at https://www.gpo.gov/fdsys/pkg/GPO-CHRG
-REHNQUIST/pdf/GPO-CHRG-REHNQUIST-4-16-6.pdf.

Renstrom, Peter G. *The Stone Court: Justices, Rulings, and Legacy.* Santa Barbara, CA: ABC-CLIO. 2001. Print.

Rice, Arnold S. *The United States Supreme Court, Volume 8: The Warren Court 1954–1969.* Danbury, CT: Grolier Educational Corporation. 1995. Print.

Rodriguez, Lucas, The Troubling Partisanship of the Supreme Court. *Stanford Politics.* January 7, 2016. Available at https://stanfordpolitics.org/2016/01/07/troubling
-partisanship-supreme-court.

Rosen, Jeffrey. *The Supreme Court: The Personalities and Rivalries That Defined America.* New York: Times Books, Henry Holt and Company. 2006. Print.

Rosenberg, Paul, Can the Supreme Court be saved? Kavanaugh hearings could be a turning point. *Salon.* September 30, 2018. Available at https://www.salon.com/2018/09/30
/can-the-supreme-court-be-saved-kavanaugh-hearings
-could-be-a-turning-point.

Ross, William G. *The Chief Justiceship of Charles Evan Hughes 1930–1941.* Columbia, Souther Carolina: The University of South Carolina Press. 2007. Print.

S

Schermerhorn, Calvin, On the Supreme Court, Difficult Nominations Have Led to Historical Injustices. *CNBC.com.* September 28, 2018. Available at https://www.cnbc

.com/2018/09/28/supreme-court-difficult-nominations
-have-led-to-historical-injustices.html?__source=shareb
ar%7Cemail&par=sharebar.

Schwartz, Bernard. *Super Chief: Earl Warren and His Supreme Court—A Judicial Biography*. New York and London: New York University Press. 1983. Print.

Schwartz, Herman. *The Rehnquist Court: Judicial Activism on the Right*. New York: Hill and Wang. 2002. Print.

Segall, Eric J. Invisible Justices: How Our Highest Court Hides from the American People, 32 Ga. St. U. L. Rev. Article 1. Available at http://readingroom.law.gsu.edu /gsulr/vol32/iss4/1.

Segall, Eric J. *Originalism as Faith*. Cambridge: Cambridge University Press. 2018. Print.

Sessa-Hawkins, Margaret & Perez, Andrew, Dark money group received massive donation in fight against Obama's Supreme Court nominee. *MapLight.org.* October 24, 2017. Available at https://maplight.org/story/dark-money-group -received-massive-donation-in-fight-against-obamas -supreme-court-nominee.

Sexton, John, Chief Justice Warren E. Burger, the Court, and the Nation, 43, Issue 2, J. Sup. Ct. Hist. 174. 2018.

Siegel, Adrienne. *The United States Supreme Court, Volume 2: The Marshall Court 1801–1835*. Danbury, CT: Grolier Educational Corporation. 1995. Print.

Siegel, Martin. *The United States Supreme Court, Volume 3: The Taney Court 1836–1864*. Danbury, Connecticut: Grolier Education Corporation. 1995. Print.

Simon, James F. *Lincoln and Chief Justice Taney: Slavery Secession and the President's War Powers.* New York: Simon & Schuster. 2006. Print.

Simon, James F. *FDR and Chief Justice Hughes: The President, the Supreme Court, and the Epic Battle over the New Deal.* New York: Simon & Schuster. 2012. Print.

Smith, Edward Jean. *John Marshall: Definer of a Nation.* New York: Henry Holt and Company. 1996. Print.

Snyder, Brad & Barrett, John Q., Rehnquist's Missing Letter: A Former Law Clerk's 1955 Thoughts on Justice Jackson and Brown, 53 B.C.L. Rev. 631 (2012). Available at http://lawdigitalcommons.bc.edu/bclr/vol53/iss2/5.

Stahr, Walter. *John Jay: Founding Father.* New York and London: Hambledon Continuum. 2006. Print.

Stevens, John Paul. *Five Chiefs: A Supreme Court Memoir.* New York: Little, Brown & Company. 2011. Print.

Stewart, David O. *The Men Who Invented the Constitution.* New York: Simon & Schuster. 2007. Print.

Story, Joseph, *Commentaries on the Constitution of the United States.* Boston: Hillard, Gray, and Company. 1833.

Supreme Court Historical Society, The Marshall Court, 1801–1835. Available at http://supremecourthistory.org/timeline_court_marshall.html.

Swindler, William F. *The Constitution and Chief Justice Marshall.* New York: Dodd, Mead & Company. 1978. Print.

Swisher, Carl Brent. *Roger B. Taney: Attorney General of the United States, Secretary of the Treasury of the United States, Chief Justice of the United States*. New York: Macmillan. 1935. Print.

T

Taheny, Josephine C. *Chief Justice Roger Brooke Taney's Attitude toward Slavery*. Loyola University Chicago. 1942. Master's Thesis.

Tartakovsky, Joseph. *The Lives of the Constitution: Ten Exceptional Minds That Shaped America's Supreme Law*. New York: Encounter Books. 2018. Print.

Tewell, Jeremy J. Roger B. Taney Was as Bad as You Think. *Columbian College of Arts & Sciences: History of News Network*. 2013. Article.

Toobin, Jeffrey. *The Nine: Inside the Secret World of the Supreme Court*. New York: Anchor Books. 2008. Print.

Toobin, Jeffrey. *The Oath: The Obama White House and the Supreme Court*. New York: Anchor Books. 2012. Print.

Toth, Michael C. *Founding Federalist: The Life of Oliver Ellsworth*. Wilmington, Delaware: ISI Books. 2011. Print.

Turberville, Sarah & Marcum, Anthony, Those 5-to-4 decisions on the Supreme Court? 9 to 0 is far more common." *The Washington Post*. June 28, 2018. Available at https://

www.washingtonpost.com/news/posteverything/wp/2018/06/28/those-5-4-decisions-on-the-supreme-court-9-0-is-far-more-common/?utm_term=.53629277f355.

U

United States. 91st Congress, 2nd Session. *Tributes to the Honorable Earl Warren Chief Justice of the United States: To Commemorate the Occasion of His Retirement from the Supreme Court June 23, 1969.* Washington: United States Government Printing Office. 1970. Print.

Urofsky, Melvin I. *Dissent and the Supreme Court: Its Role in the Court's History and the Nation's Constitutional Dialogue.* New York: Pantheon Books. 2015. Print.

Urofsky, Melvin I. *Division and Discord: The Supreme Court under Stone and Vinson, 1941–1953.* Columbia, South Carolina: University of South Carolina Press. 1997. Print.

V

W

Waite, Morrison Remick, Rawle, William Henry, & Philadelphia Bar Association, *Exercises at the ceremony of unveiling the statute of John Marshall by Morrison Remick Waite, William Henry Rawle, Philadelphia Bar Association.*

Available at https://books.google.com/books?id=vc8E AAAAYAAJ&dq=John+Marshall+statue+United+States +Bar+Association&printsec=frontcover&hl=en #v=onepage&q&f=true.

Warden, Robert W. *An Account of the Private Life and Public Services of Salmon Portland Chase V1.* Cincinnati: Kessinger Legacy Reprints. 1872. Print.

Warden, Robert W. *An Account of the Private Life and Public Services of Salmon Portland Chase V2.* Cincinnati: Kessinger Legacy Reprints. 1872. Print.

Warren, Charles. *The Supreme Court in United States History: Volume One 1789–1835.* New York: The Legal Classics Library. 1992. Print.

Warren, Charles. *The Supreme Court in United States History: Volume Two 1836–1918.* New York: The Legal Classics Library. 1992. Print.

Washington University Law, Chief Justice John G. Roberts Cases before the Supreme Court. Available at https://law .wustl.edu/news/pages.aspx?id=5484.

Washington Post, "Transcript: Day Two of the Roberts Confirmation Hearings." September 13, 2005. Available at http://www.washingtonpost.com/wp-dyn/content/arti cle/2005/09/13/AR2005091300876.html.

Weaver, John D. *Warren: The Man, the Court, the Era.* Canada: Little, Brown & Company. 1967. Print.

White, Adam J. Judging Roberts the Chief Justice of the United States, Ten Years in. *The Weekly Standard.* November 23, 2015. Magazine Article.

White, G. Edward. *Earl Warren: A Public Life*. New York and Oxford: Oxford University Press. 1982. Print.

White, G. Edward. *The Marshall Court and Cultural Change 1815–1835. Abridged Edition*. New York: Oxford University Press. 1991. Print.

Whitman, Alden, Earl Warren, 83, Who Led High Court in Time of Vast Social Change, Is Dead. *New York Times*. July 10, 1974. Available at https://archive.nytimes.com/www.nytimes.com/learning/general/onthisday/bday/0319.html?mod=article_inline.

Williams, Pete, In Rare Rebuke, Chief Justice Roberts Slams Trump for Comment about "Obama judge," *NBC News*. November 21, 2018. Available at https://www.nbcnews.com/politics/supreme-court/rare-rebuke-chief-justice-roberts-slams-trump-comment-about-obama-n939016.

Winkler, Adam, *We the Corporations: How American Businesses Won Their Civil Rights*. New York: Liverright. 2018.

Woodward, Bob & Armstrong, Scott. *The Brethren inside the Supreme Court*. New York: Simon & Schuster. 1979. Print.

X

Y

Yarbrough, Tinsley E. *The Rehnquist Court and the Constitution*. New York: Oxford University Press. 2000. Print.

Z

Zirin, James D. *Supremely Partisan: How Raw Politics Tips the Scales in the United States Supreme Court*. Maryland: Rowman & Littlefield. 2016. Print.

Index

Note: Page numbers followed by "n" indicate footnotes.